To Keith

CORONATION
❉ VILLAGE ❉

North Muskham in the 1950s

Best wishes
Trevor Brecknell

CORONATION ✼ VILLAGE ✼

North Muskham in the 1950s

Trevor Frecknall

HiP
HISTORY INTO PRINT

First published by
History into Print, 56 Alcester Road,
Studley, Warwickshire B80 7LG in 2009
www.history-into-print.com

© Trevor Frecknall 2009

All rights reserved.

ISBN: 978-1-85858-327-3

The moral right of the author has been asserted.

A Cataloguing in Publication Record
for this title is available from the British Library.

Typeset in Plantin
Printed in Great Britain by
Hobbs the Printers Ltd.

CONTENTS

DEDICATION	vi
INTRODUCTION	vii
ABOUT THE AUTHOR	viii
PREFACE	xi
1. THE MAIN STREET	1
2. CRAB LANE TO FERRY	87
3. THE LANES TO BATHLEY	125
4. THE OLD NORTH ROAD	158

DEDICATION

Coronation Village, North Muskham in the 1950s is dedicated to: all of the people who lived in the village, especially those who have shared their memories and photographs for this publication; staff at Newark Library and the Nottinghamshire County Archive for their patience, expertise and help; Harry and Ivy Annie Frecknall, my late parents who brought me up so well that I was in my middle teens before I began to realise how poor we had been; Gill Frecknall, who has been my wife since 1966 and my inspiration for longer, and has now financed this labour of love.

INTRODUCTION

Veteran journalist Trevor Frecknall set out to trace the folk who lived around him at the time of the Coronation of Queen Elizabeth II in 1953 – and emerged seven years later with a fascinating perspective on rural life in middle England during the decade when Prime Minister Harold Macmillan came up with his bold electioneering slogan: "You've never had it so good!"

North Muskham, four miles north of Newark in Nottinghamshire, sits in a triangle formed by the river Trent, the Great Northern Railway and the Great North Road. The Trent flooded the village's marshlands most winters and found its own height through the sandy soil so regularly that some housewives had to stand on duckboards to go about their chores in their pantries. The railway throbbed to the sights and sounds of steam engines powering people and products between London and Scotland, their chimneys spewing enough smoke into the damp atmosphere to create fogs as thick as pea soup for days on end. The more popular the main road became, the more spectacular the accidents – including one that catapulted a coach driver off a railway bridge and onto the line.

So the recollections of how the village adapted to the most intensive period of modernisation in the history of Great Britain amount to an immensely readable contribution to the country's living heritage.

ABOUT THE AUTHOR

Trevor Frecknall, born on 11 February 1945, was brought up in Bathley by his dad, Harry, a railway platelayer, and his mum, Ivy, who would rush from Chapel on a Sunday night to do a pot-washing shift in the village pub to pay for the boy's Newark Magnus Grammar School uniform. The picture (right) was taken in 1953 when Trevor was at South Muskham Church of England Primary School.

The family moved a mile or so east to North Muskham when Trevor was in his early teens. He learned to love the place by delivering daily newspapers before going to school, working in one of the village shops at weekends to fund his love of football and cricket and, most proudly of all, helping the village men's team win a cricket trophy when he was only 15.

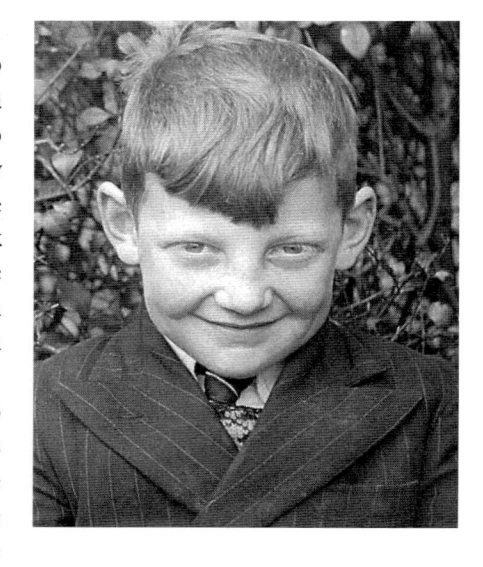

Leaving school aged 16, he began a lifetime in journalism by working at the Nottingham News Service. Catching the 8.20am bus into Newark before taking the train to Nottingham stopped being such a chore after a few months when he spotted the love of his life, Gill Weaver, on her way to work at Boots in Newark. They wed in 1966 and Trevor moved to the Nottingham Evening Post in search of shorter working hours. Some hope! After a variety of roles in news, promotions and features departments, he was handed his dream job at Christmas 1978 – Sports Editor. He had the privilege of reporting on Nottingham Forest's two European Cup triumphs in 1979 and 1980, as well

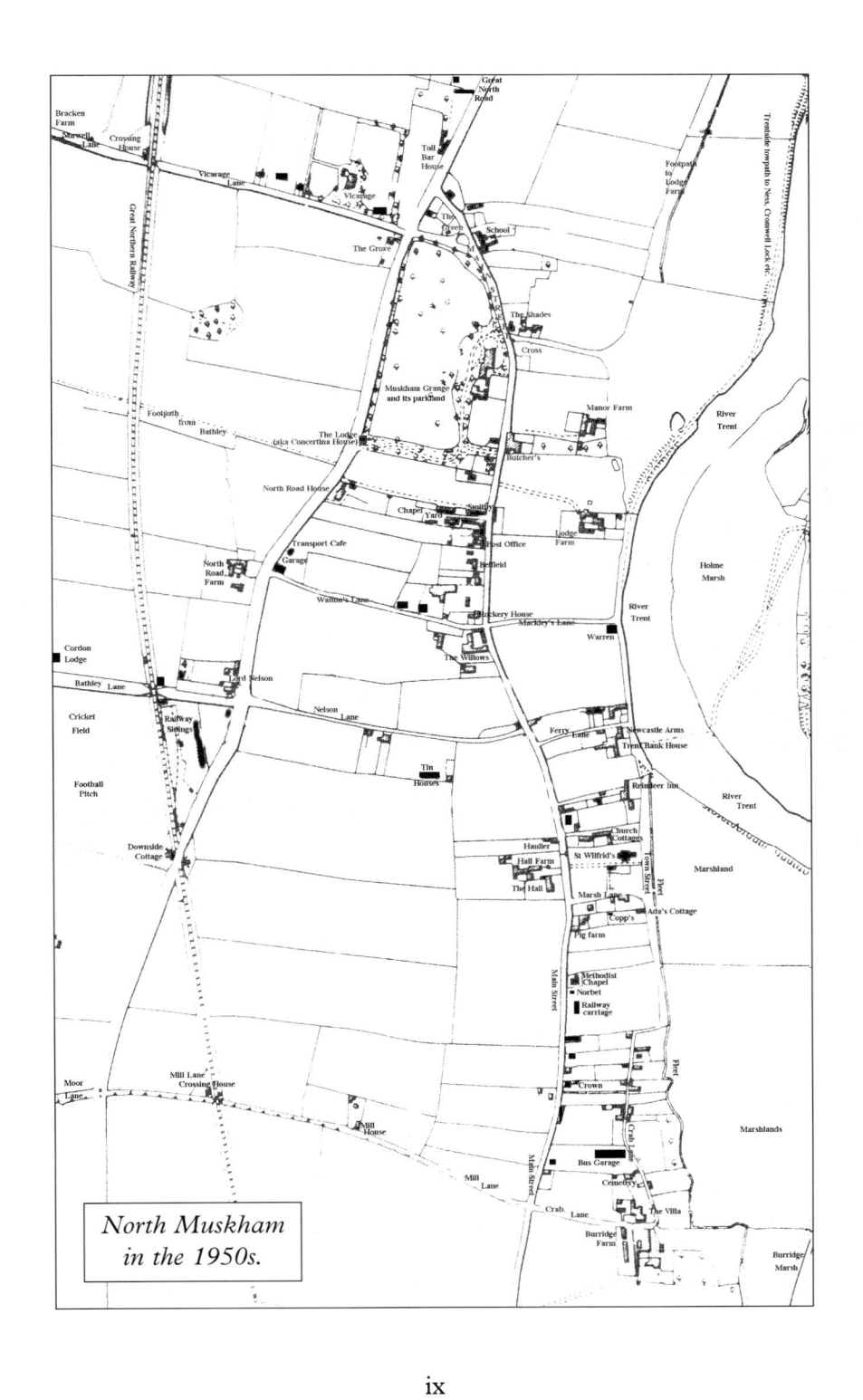

North Muskham in the 1950s.

The proudest night of my North Muskham life, Friday, August 12 1960 – and here I am sitting on the floor of the Lounge in the Lord Nelson beside Cyril Marriott and Ian Phillips, celebrating North Muskham and Bathley Cricket Club's victory over Dunham in the Subsidiary Cup Final at Elm Avenue. The rest of the team, secretary Fred Blore and scorer Joan Bass are behind us (though Hugh Kent is almost hidden by Joan back right). I'd taken 6 wickets for 30 runs, special reason for a 15-year old to be in the pub "just this once".

as many of the milestones achieved by Notts County in reaching the old First Division of the Football League and cricket trophy wins by Nottinghamshire under Clive Rice. Moving into athletics in the early 1990s, he reported on the 1996 Olympic Games in Atlanta and acted as Media Officer for Great Britain teams at several World and European Championships.

But he remained based in North Muskham – where his heart is, as you will quickly gather by reading on…

PREFACE

Welcome to Coronation Village – North Muskham circa 2 June 1953, the rainy day when Queen Elizabeth II was crowned 130 miles away in London…

An era when the village had more shops than pubs (but very few televisions)…

When men had returned from the Second World War to their jobs on Civvy Street and were utterly embarrassed to be called 'Hero'…

When Mums stayed at home to look after the children and do the housework without the aid of washing machines, electric cookers or electrically-driven floor sweepers – meaning they spent hours ponching the dirty clothes in out-houses, producing hearty meals from coal-fired ovens and crawling on their knees to scrub bare-brick floors…

When Dads came home from a full day's work and diligently spent as long as it took in the garden to grow all the vegetables the family would eat in the foreseeable future…

When you could judge a tenant's size by the height of his garden hedge; no man could effectively wield a plasher at above shoulder height but woe betide anyone tempted to lower the standards of tidiness…

When parents had the choice of sending their 5- to 10-year-olds to a village school at North Muskham or South Muskham (or Norwell or Sutton-on-Trent) and were mighty suspicious of a plan to introduce an 11-Plus exam from which successes would go to Newark, to the Magnus Grammar School (for boys) or the Lilley and Stone High School (for girls), and the failures would go to the newly built Sconce Hills Secondary Modern School…

When central 'eating meant the family gathering round the table for a square meal each day and the kids who turned their noses up at the greens were sternly told they'd eat up before they had anything else…

When folk who could not afford a coal fire scavenged for drift wood on the Trentside marshes…

When coal and/or wood fires burned in every home, meaning we could almost eat the air we had to breathe and were guaranteed fogs every day in winter when the wind didn't blow...

When tenant farmers instinctively tended the land, often sharing tractors that were smaller than the 4x4s that were to become family run-abouts 50 years later, and never dreamt of a day when their land would be sold for housing...

When farmers and their workers habitually toiled from dawn till dusk, and knew and cared enough about conservation to plash hedges and dig ditches each year, clear the rubbish away, and maintain field gates that actually opened and closed...

When the parish was self-sufficient for milk and meat, and the village stores faced increasing competition from mobile shops selling everything from soap to bread to meat to paraffin for the oil lamps...

When the railway was kept safe by a dedicated gang of local workers who risked – and occasionally lost – their lives to keep the steam trains running on time, unfailingly turning out at all hours in spells of fog, ice and/or snow to lay detonators or spread salt to ensure passengers, goods and mail were not delayed...

When the early morning service buses were packed with workmen raking in the dosh from Newark's successful engineering works, confident that Ransome & Marles would be famous for ever for making the ball bearings on which the Allies' victorious war machine over-ran Nazi Germany; Worthington Simpsons were bent on similar world domination in the manufacture of industrial pumps; Coopers up past the old Fire Station towards Farndon were foremost among the town's contributors to the rag trade; Nicholson's beside Trent Bridge employed yet more engineers – all thriving reasons why brewers James Hole & Son and Warwicks & Richardson's had massive thirsts to quench...

When the local builders were happy to be called "midnight cowboys", moving into cottages after the occupants had gone to bed, removing their crumbling old fire grates and inserting new fireplaces before the man of the house arose at 5.30–6am to go to work...

When private transport was a bike (usually secondhand) and only the rich or the brash had a car of their own...

When death crashes on the increasingly busy Great North Road were frighteningly frequent – though one inebriated bull of a villager somehow survived being hit by a London to Edinburgh express coach one chill Saturday night...

When village pride for men meant a place in the cricket or football teams, which moved from a field off Nelson Lane over the North Road to the Bathley Lane side of the railway line and thrived to such an extent that volunteers built a brick pavilion...

When a break from drudgery for the wives and mothers meant membership of the Women's Institute at the Church Hall down Chapel Yard or the Mothers' Union at the chilly old Church or the Bright Hour at the Chapel...

When the children were spoilt for choice of orchards to scrump yet scrubbed-up angelically to go to Sunday School at the Chapel or the Church – or else...

When the menfolk battled for places in the darts or dominoes or skittles teams at the Crown, Newcastle Arms or Nelson...

When a family night out was a whist drive at the Church Hall, a jumble sale at any of the schools, or a dance at either the Transport Café or the barn above the Nelson's stables...

When for the kiddies a bar of chocolate was a special treat and school outings on Thomas's buses to the seaside were the annual highlights...

When a Sunday trip was a walk along the towpath to Cromwell Lock and back or an outing in one of Thomas's buses...

When no front door had to be locked to keep out thieves and through virtually every window you'd glimpse a character – including...

- The football hero whose poorly Mum lived in a shed in the garden...
- The former debutante who froze to death in abject poverty...
- The royalist who had a road accident in his bed...
- The compassionate nurse who emerged out of Africa...
- The village's very own version of *On The Buses*...
- The tyrannical teachers who divided the village...
- The kindly teacher who battled against multiple sclerosis...
- The post mistress who was secretly a bookie's runner...
- The olde worlde gent who genially grew tomatoes while the big house crumbled...
- The widow's son who lied about his age to go to War...
- The brassy women who helped win the War...
- The little princess who broke the village's heart...
- The builder brothers who were too forgetful – or compassionate – to send out bills...
- The *Good Life* farmer who baked exceedingly good cakes...

- The tragedies on the North Road and the railway…
- The farmer who became the flood-beater called Mr. Trent…
- And the village pub that, in another era of trendy bars, might have been called Leno's…

This recollection sets out to chart who lived where – and who did what – in North Muskham in the 1950s, before the A1 dual carriageway arrived to change the quality of life in more ways than the obvious.

The geographical effect was considerable. A sweeping bridge replaced the winding lane that led to South Muskham. Half of Nelson Lane, a twisting and narrow link between Main Street (the original North Road) and the old A1 (the Great North Road), disappeared and the other half was widened and straightened. A third of Walton's Lane was similarly swallowed, including the village garage; and, just round the corner along the A1 north towards what later became known as Muskham Castle, the death knell finally tolled for a transport café that had also been a dance hall for the village. Round the left-hand curve to the junction with Vicarage Lane, the north end of the village was decimated: nine or more homes disappeared, along with the local building firm's base, and several more became virtually uninhabitable. In short, it was probably the first bypass to scythe through, rather than go round, a community's lifeblood.

Such a swifter, safer road had two effects. Many of Muskham's "Coronation children" took flight in search of a less rustic life. They were replaced, probably four-fold, by folk from far away who flocked to what became a builder's paradise as the farmers tired of battling floods on largely infertile land. The village became more of a dormitory than a largely self-contained community.

But those evolutions were far from the minds of the Coronation Villagers of 1953. Read on and savour life in Middle England a few years before Prime Minister Harold Macmillan won a General Election by reminding us all: "You've never had it so good!" Life gets even better in the pages of *Coronation Village* than it was on actual Coronation Day. For it rained on the day Queen Elizabeth II was crowned, so persistently that North Muskham's celebratory procession had to be cancelled. This book recreates the route that would have been taken – and takes you into each cottage, bungalow and fine house along the way. And that's only Chapter one.

Here's what village life entailed in North Muskham's Dark Ages, i.e. before the Parish Council decided we could afford street lights…

1. THE MAIN STREET

The organizers of North Muskham's Coronation celebrations were a down-to-earth bunch. They devised two timetables for 2 June 1953: one a kind of wish-list, the other an alternative in the event of rain…

ITINERARY
2.00pm: FANCY DRESS PARADE commences at the Crown Inn, moving up Main Street to THE PARK.
Music will be provided for the procession.
2.30pm: JUDGING of FANCY DRESS
3.00pm: CHILDREN'S SPORTS
4.00pm: CHILDREN'S TEAS, The School.
5.00pm: * OLD FOLKS' TEAS, The School.
BUFFET TEA for all other residents
6.30pm: ADULTS' SPORTS.
Ladies ankle competition.
8.30pm: DANCE… spot waltz, musical chairs.
SIDESHOWS – Bowling for Pig, Darts, etc. – will be in progress during the afternoon and evening. Ices and minerals will be available.
* NOTE: Will old folks wishing to be provided with transport please hand in their names to Sycamore Cottage before 2 June to enable the necessary arrangements to be made.

ALTERNATIVE IF WET
2.00pm: FANCY DRESS PARADE. Assemble at the Church Hall.
2.30pm: JUDGING of FANCY DRESS
3.00pm: INDOOR GAMES with music.

4.00pm: CHILDREN'S TEAS, The School. Transport will be provided as far as possible.
5.00pm: OLD FOLKS' TEAS, The School. Transport will be provided as far as possible.
BUFFET TEA for all other residents.
After tea the children will return to Church Hall for further games.
8.00pm: DANCE, The School.
NOTE: Sports will be held later. Date to be announced as soon as weather permits.

So now let's get on with our procession…

CROWN INN: SO NEARLY LENO'S!
The legalistic sign above the front door of the smallest of the village's three pubs proudly proclaimed in the early years of the 1950s: "Walter Lenoard Barratt, licensed to retail beer to be consumed on the premises. Dealer in tobacco."

Len Barratt never tired of quietly denying that his sign-writer had excessively tested the contents of the ale house (note he was not licensed to sell wines or spirits) before inscribing his second Christian name. But, so far ahead of the days when a Continental-style bistro might have appeared trendy, it never occurred to him to rename the establishment Leno's.

Len took over as landlord when his in-laws, the Goodwins, decided to retire – a kind of happy return to the part of the village in which he had grown up. For the Barratts had lived in half of Salt 'n' Pepper Cottages, just up the Main Street towards South Muskham, before moving to one of the terraced cottages down Chapel Yard. Now Len was back with his bride, Kath Goodwin, keeping a kind of family business running in a traditional way.

They had wed on 8 April 1939 just down Main Street in St. Wilfrid's. At a time when everyone worried what the future held, Walter Leonard (that's how it is spelt on his marriage certificate) Barratt, aged 23, and 20-year-old Kathleen Violet Goodwin swore to remain together till death did them part.

To further help the regulars consider the Crown a home from home, its public rooms were laid out like the average house – apart from having a bar that had you feeling you were seeing double as soon as you walked down the passageway from the front door and acclimatized your eyes to the smoky surroundings. The reason: half the bar opened up to the front room to the left; the other half faced the back room to the right. All three of its rooms were reached through the front door. Only one of them was really big enough to swing a cat – the one reached via a sharp left-hand U-turn at the end of the

1. The Main Street

short entrance passage. It possessed the dartboard and, except on the hottest of evenings, a roaring fire. The back room kept the table skittles fraternity happy. The right-hand front room, reached by a sharp right-hand U-turn at the end of the entrance passage, was the smallest, darkest of the trio despite having a window open on to the Main Street – testing the eyesight of the dominoes players to the utmost – and seemed, to young invaders, to be the smoky sanctum of the elderly regulars.

Outside, in a further concession to the sporting aspirations of the villagers, there was the chance to play long alley skittles. But above all, a pub was a home from home in the '50s – a place where friends met and put the world to rights in an age before it was all done for them by experts on television.

HOLLY HOUSE: HOME OF RAILWAY FOLK

The Marshalls gave way to the Thornleys as occupants of the cottage behind the holly hedge and immediately to the north of The Crown in the mid-1950s. So the cottage, with its huge vegetable garden at the rear, remained in the hands of railway folk.

Christopher Marshall moved into Holly House after he retired as gatekeeper at Norwell Lane crossing and had to vacate the little tied cottage that went with it. The place was so close to the downside (north) of the line that pottery rattled along its mantelpiece every time a train approached. He married Lizzie late in life; but they seemed no less happy for that... probably considering a home next to a beer house to be quieter than the railway cottage.

Of the family that followed the Marshalls into the green-painted cottage in the early 1950s, 'Young Frank' Thornley was a platelayer in the railway gang on the local length of track – and an ardent football supporter of Mansfield Town, the poor relations of the three professional Football League clubs in the county. Frank's loyalty stemmed from the fact that his family came from the Mansfield area; and he not only owned a season ticket in the Main Stand at Field Mill, he was also happy to take along anyone else interested in cheering on 'The Stags'. Such adventures were a rush in the days when platelayers worked six-and-a-half days a week to maintain the lines so well that they frequently boasted you could set your watch by the time the trains sped past. The regular working week was 7.30am to 5pm Monday to Friday and 7.30am to 12 noon on Saturdays. Every Sunday brought welcome overtime – they were paid "time-and-a-half" for minimum 12-hour shifts of relentless heavy work, usually involving up-rooting aged rails and sleepers and man-handling fresh replacements into position. One such major job involved the bridge over the Trent (known officially as Muskham Viaduct since it had been laid in 1852, but 'Tubular Bridge' to the locals) being closed for three weekends in the summer of 1957 for extensive repair work. Passengers were bussed between Newark and Retford (from where trains diverted via Lincoln to Grantham) while the men wrestled with new track and hundreds of tons of supporting ironwork and rocks from 1.30pm Saturdays to 1.30pm Mondays, then resumed their normal work Tuesday morning.

Of Frank's parents who pretty much enjoyed their retirement in North Muskham, chatting over their front gate to any pedestrian with the time and inclination, his mum Mary Ann died aged 87 on 1 March 1969 and his dad, also Frank, passed away aged 82 on 16 October 1971. 'Young Frank', already into middle age, married and moved out of the village.

LYNTON COTTAGE: A 'GREEN' MAN IN A GREEN BUNGALOW

Raymond Rippin and his wife Esther lived in a green painted, wooden Walton's bungalow sandwiched between Holly House and the 'jitty' down to Crab Lane. The pair had wed at St. Wilfrid's on 30 July 1927, when both were 22. Esther was one of the Ridge family from one of the little cottages squeezed in between the Crown Inn at Bathley and the junction of Muskham Lane with Main Street. Ray was a joiner by trade and worked his way up to become a British Waterways inspector in an era when gangs worked endlessly to dredge the River Trent (a) to reduce the risk of flooding; (b) to ensure the barges were not hampered as they carried their loads of oil and other cargoes between Hull and Nottingham; (c) to yield gravel for building projects years before farmers were persuaded to surrender their grassland to gravel pits that became lakes.

Conservation was never far away from Ray's mind as he rode from work on his motorcycle. He always saved a farthing's worth of fuel by switching off his engine as he passed a big tree in the hedge just past the Old Hall and cruised the last couple of hundred yards to his front gate. Nobody ridiculed him. Money was tight in every household. Good luck to him!

One day in May 1963, 59-year-old Ray came home unusually early – not long after dinner time. Said he had chest pains. Few houses had phones in those days; and North Muskham's public phone box was half a mile or more down the Main Street, outside the Post Office run by the Story family. By the time Esther managed to get a doctor to Ray, he was dead. A post mortem examination cited natural causes, but that did not diminish the shock.

Esther survived him by five-and-a-half years. She was 63 when she also died suddenly, on 22 November 1968. The difference was that they'd managed to get her to Newark Hospital before she passed away.

1. The Main Street

HOLLY TREE COTTAGE: HOME TO AN EXTENDED FAMILY

The Jackson family ran a carpentry and joiner's business from the side-on cottage that faced the jitty from the north end of Crab Lane to the Main Street. It had been a row of two-up, two-down cottages; but became a single property as the family extended naturally in an age when it was accepted that aged parents would be tended by their offspring.

Frank Jackson had been a parish councillor until his death early in 1950. As a matter of course, the woodworking business was continued by his son, William, whose wife also carried on something of a family tradition. William's grandmother, Nellie Jackson (as the villagers knew Mrs. Elizabeth Jackson) ran a sweet shop in the 1920s (when another occupant of the row, John Kemp, the village mole-catcher, used to hang the furs of his captures in a cupboard on the stairs)... and in November 1953, his wife made the sweets that were raffled as prizes at the monthly meeting of North Muskham Women's Institute. The winners, for the record, were Mrs. Josephine Crawley, of Little Carlton, whose elder son Douglas would be looking forward to his eighth birthday on that Christmas Day and Mrs. Parsons, who lived in South Muskham.

Another invaluable member of the family in the 1950s was the Jacksons' son-in-law, Horace Kemm, a balding but usually beaming man who stood 6 foot 5 or 6 inches tall and was an eager member of the North Muskham and Bathley cricket team whenever he was selected.

Mrs. Jackson was an energetic committee member of the Mothers' Union as well as the WI. Husband William was also happy to lend a hand to good causes: he ran the skittles stall for a North Muskham Church garden fete in 1957. There was family sadness the following year: William's Aunt Ellen (Frank's sister) died at the age of 74 "after a long illness patiently borne" – a description usually reserved for cancer, which was considered an insidious and untreatable illness in those days.

NORBET: NEW BUNGALOW AND OLD RAILWAY CARRIAGE

There were extra-special reasons for the bunting flying from the new bungalow in the field just south of the Chapel on Coronation Day. Norman and Betty Pollard were celebrating more than the crowning of Queen Elizabeth II. It was also a kind of home-warming because Norman had finally completed building their new bungalow.

His Dad had given him the plot when Norman Leslie Pollard married Miss Betty May Marsh at Newark Parish Church on Saturday 24 June 1950. The bride, who hailed from Hardwick Avenue, Newark, wore a gown of silk organdie and silver lame. It was entirely predictable that sprays of carnations should be draped from her hips: her father-in-law, Cec (short for Cecil), who lived in a cottage overlooking the Trent Marsh, was renowned for growing carnations in two great big greenhouses that stretched behind the Chapel. Cec was far from landed gentry, but he had clubbed together with a market gardener called Mrs. Goldson to buy the three and a half acre Chapel Field from Ada Smalley.

The women were a couple of unlikely landowners. Mrs. Smalley lived in the most frequently flooded cottage on the Marsh. Mrs. Goldson lived in a converted railway carriage close to the Garage up beside the North Road. And when Mrs. Goldson was widowed and elderly, it seemed natural for her and her home to be moved to Chapel Field; and the newly-wed Norman and Betty proved to be considerate neighbours. The problem was that Norman also had a living to earn as a self-employed builder, so the newly-weds' bungalow was very much a labour of love. It took two years to be made habitable.

They had two sons: John and Tim. After Mrs. Goldson passed away, Norman eventually moved his growing family into a larger bungalow built almost exactly where the old railway carriage had stood – hence its long, narrow shape. John became a motor engineer, working for many years for Milnes before launching his own business and working out of Smalley's Garage at Bathley while still living in North Muskham with his own family. Tim made a career with Travis Perkins.

Much of Chapel Field became the Meadow Close housing development. After Betty died, aged 69, on 13 April 1997, Norman made history as the only Muskhamite ever to live in three different homes without leaving the same field; he moved to a newly-built house at the far end of his garden, overlooking the Trent Valley.

METHODIST CHAPEL: FUN, GAMES AND A WARM WELCOME

Virtually every youngster in the village spent every Sunday morning (10.30am) and afternoon (2.30pm) at Sunday School. "If you didn't and your Dad found out, you got a clout", says Barry Talbot with a smile. He remembers the lay teachers being two dads, Tom Baxter from Nelson Lane and later Jack Needham from Ferry Lane, plus June and Tom Elliott, who were not much more than kids themselves. "We used to have a laugh", Barry says.

And he cherishes memories of fun Saturday afternoon tours of the village every Anniversary on drays hauled by cart horses that belonged to Taylors, a

1. The Main Street

farming family at Cromwell. An organ was loaded on to the lead dray, and Mrs. Elliott sat there, playing all the appropriate hymns with not a sign of fear that she might be tipped off her precarious perch at the next pothole. "If the horses galloped a bit, it used to get a bit scary but otherwise it was all right", recalls Barry. "We used to go all the way round the village, turning round at the level crossings.

"The anniversary services were a bit daunting. I remember standing in the pulpit when I was 15 and getting my recitation all wrong. Mr. Baxter was very understanding and said: 'You'll perhaps do better after tea'. I didn't because I never went back".

There were also fun and games once a year when the children from North Muskham Sunday School were taken to a spectacular in town. It was called the Newark and District Sunday School Festival, and more than 1,200 children took part in the 1953 edition. They all gathered in the London Road Car Park and marched to Sconce Hills, where they took part in a great exhibition of country dancing. Except some of the lads have closed their memories to their *Billy Elliott* moments. "We used to go off and play football", insists Barry. See? The game was already pretty much a religion all those years ago!

But there was another reason for celebration at North Muskham Chapel in 1953: one of its Sunday School teachers, Harry Nutt, was married on Saturday 17 October. The service actually took place at North End Methodist Church in Newark where his bride, Miss Beryl Horton, was a Sunday School teacher. Harry worked as a turner at Worthington-Simpson,

Ladies of North Muskham Bright Hour, and Sunday School teacher Tom Baxter, on a day-out.

the Newark area's second-biggest employer. He was the only son of Mr. and Mrs. Fred Nutt who lived in Hollywood – a house opposite the garage on North Road, South Muskham.

So far as the serious business of adults' worship went, there were services at North Muskham Chapel at 6pm every Sunday... lively hymns, brief but to-the-point sermons from a variety of lay preachers who did 'ordinary' jobs in the week... and it was all the cosier from the mid-50s when heating was installed. Extra efforts were made to pay for it – and after a bring and buy sale brought in "the useful sum of £3" in January 1958, the debt was down to £5 and "it is hoped to pay this off without touching the normal church accounts". There was no shortage of volunteers to run stalls at the money-raisers. Among those who made that £3 were Mrs. Lucy Newbold, Mrs. Doris Needham (Jack's wife) and her teenage daughter Marjorie, Mrs. Adie Talbot and her teenage daughter Mavis, Mrs. Tom Baxter, Mrs. Ron Phillips-Moul, Mrs. Mary Key, Mrs. Ada Thurston and Tony Suter from North Muskham; and Mrs. Nutt, the mother of the Coronation groom from South Muskham.

WESTHOLME: A LITTLE OF OLD DONCASTER
One of the village's coalmen, Jim Nickerson, lived in Westholme, a Walton's bungalow a few yards north of the Chapel, along with his wife Mary, who was the Chapel organist for more than 20 years. Alas, Mary died on 7 June 1952 and Jim followed her on 11 February 1953. His demise left the village as a battleground for coal merchants, who were charging anything between £2 4s 2d (£2.21) and £2 1s 3d (£2.06) for half-a-ton for 'group 5' (which was the most popular) depending on the time of year and, therefore, demand.

Westholme was put on the market and described in the *Newark Advertiser* of 16 May 1953 as: "a timber and asbestos lined bungalow". It was sold by estate agents B. G. Selby & Sons for £800. The purchasers were Norman Burch, a retired butcher from Doncaster, and his wife who added to the historical tone of the village by renaming the bungalow Danum, the Roman name for their former home city in South Yorkshire. Illustrating how quickly the transaction was completed, Mrs. Burch was welcomed as a new member of North Muskham Women's Institute on 20 June 1953 – a night when the monthly meeting was to have been in the grounds of The Grange but had to be moved into the Church Hall because of bad weather.

Resuming the Walton tradition of building where a building needed to be built, Norman was one of the first modern in-fillers of the village in that he had a bungalow built for his sister-in-law behind Westholme/Danum, and

1. The Main Street

created access to it via a lane beside the Chapel. When Mr. and Mrs. Burch moved on to their own newly-built bungalow in Ferry Lane, they took the property name Danum with them. Norman was 73 when he died on 25 February 1967.

SIDE COTTAGE: HARRY HAPPY WITH HIS PIGS
One of the smallest cottages in the village was occupied by Harry Houghton, a joiner whose most memorable work was involved in the building of the original Staythorpe Power Station. The cottage, long since demolished, was not as wide as a football goal (and not much higher, either). Its back gave a courtyard effect to the entrance to a couple of cottages that were occupied in the '50s by the Guys and the Thurstons and, 50 years and more later were occupied by John Pollard and his family.

Harry's little home faced south (which was the good news) but was much smaller than the sties in which he tended his pigs after he retired from his joinery work. One of the next door neighbours, Mick Thurston remembers helping Harry fetch the roofs for the sties from Sibcy and helping to put them on. He says: "The tongue and groove boards slid together like a jigsaw puzzle. And long after the cottage was pulled down, the sties were still there... and the roofs were still on!" By 2008, they had been replaced by the rather grander-looking estate called Glebelands.

Harry – who had inherited the cottage from his parents Charles Henry and Ada Houghton – never wed and died, aged 64, on 30 June 1974.

SEMI-DETACHED COTTAGES: TALES OF TWO SETS OF SONS
Two families were being raised in the 1950s in a couple of smart looking cottages that were thoughtfully set back from the Main Street (and eventually became home to John Pollard and his family).

In the bigger of the two were the Guys: Tom and his wife Dorothy (daughter of the Ranyards who lived on Bathley Lane after they retired from running first the Crown Inn and then the Lord Nelson). There could have been few more emotional wedding ceremonies than theirs, at St. Wilfrid's Church on Easter Monday of 1926. For Tom was the third son of Mr. and Mrs. Henry Guy; and the first two had been victims of the Great War. The first, John had died aged 23 of wounds suffered in 1917. The second was even more harrowing: Richard Henry (Dick) Guy had fought through France and Belgium for two years with the Machine Gun Corps before being badly gassed in 'the great push' of 1918. He was shipped back across the Channel and sent to a convalescent home near Eastbourne that did nothing to improve his health. He finally died, at home among his family, at Christmas time seven years later aged only 29, and his coffin was borne into St. Wilfrid's by four of his Army mates for his funeral on 31 December 1925.

Four months later, the Guys massed again at St. Wilfrid's for an immeasurably happier occasion: the marriage of Thomas to Dorothy May Ranyard. Afterwards, 50 guests were entertained at the reception at the bride's home, which just happened to be the Crown Inn. Quite how they fitted in so many has been lost in the mists of time, but it was clearly a happy union. They had two children, Mavis and Dennis. Tom died aged 63, on 17 January 1961. Dorothy was 72 when she passed away on 30 July 1975.

Mavis moved away from Muskham on her marriage but never lost touch with her childhood neighbours, the Thurstons – Norman, his wife Ada and their four lads, Mick, Pat, Pete and David.

Norman Thurston drove a lorry for Whitney's haulage firm (based just down Main Street, past the Old Hall) and later worked as a mechanic, first for Guy Weatherhead at his garage beside the North Road at Cromwell (also finding time to tend his hunting horses until the bypass took the traffic away from the business) and then with Lincolnshire Road Car based in Newark. Ada played an increasingly influential role in village life as the lads grew up, and eventually served for many years on the Parish Council.

And the lads turned out to be a bright bunch. All four passed exams to reach the Thomas Magnus Grammar School. The family watched the Coronation on a 9-inch Bush television bought from Southwell Television Services.

Mick spent Coronation Year as a 13-year-old, mixing his studies with a nightly job as paperboy, collecting his bundle of *Nottingham Evening Posts* off the Lincolnshire Road Car bus in the middle of the village at the Blacksmith's Shop and delivering them around both North and South Muskham. On leaving the Magnus, he served an apprenticeship as a motor mechanic at Brooks on Farndon Road, Newark. His pay was 10 old pence and three farthings an hour (about 4½p) and he worked from 8am to 5pm Monday to Friday and 8am to noon Saturday. He saved the official certificate that records during his first year of work, he paid in tax the princely sum of 2 shillings (10p) to the Exchequer. It will surprise nobody to learn that when Hoveringham Gravel appeared in Nottinghamshire, the 21-year-old Mick decided to move for the simple reason that "there was more money in quarrying".

Pat followed his Magnus education by going on to the Nottinghamshire School of Agriculture at Brackenhurst, Southwell, and then becoming a farmer at Collingham. He was one of those kids who just knew what he

1. The Main Street

wanted to do with his life at an early age – and went out and did it. By 1957, when he was at the Magnus, he was starring in the Caunton team of three in the annual public speaking competition for Nottinghamshire Young Farmers' Clubs. His team-mates were Brian Maskell, who lived up Debdale Hill on the road from Little Carlton to Caunton, and Mick Saxby, whose parents' farm was down the lane opposite the Kelham Sugar Factory. In 1961, Pat won a national award as the best junior in the pig judging competition at the Royal Dairy Show at Olympia, London. At Brackenhurst, he was so highly rated that he was put in charge of the pig herd. Greater glory came his way within months of his move to work at Don Kirk's farm at Collingham in the autumn of 1966. He won the senior dairy cattle judging competition at the Royal Dairy Show, defeating young farmers from every county in England and Wales to earn the Harold Jackson Trophy. He also brought home medals presented by the Ayrshire Cattle Society and the English Guernsey Cattle Society for the highest marks in the mixed breed ring – all of which was a source of enormous pride at the time. It goes without saying that Pat won many prizes at local and county shows.

Pete's achievements are special. He was born with deformed feet and spent many months of his childhood in Harlow Wood Orthopaedic Hospital near Mansfield undergoing painful remedial operations – pioneering surgery at the time. One can imagine the pride in the family when in May of 1955 he became one of only two pupils from North Muskham Primary School to pass the selection examination (universally known as the dreaded 11-plus) for admission to grammar schools. How ironic that, 50 years on, Pete was working shifts at the Sugar Factory for a company called Silver Spoon. Here was one determined little boy who grew up in the Fifties without a silver spoon in his mouth!

So the pressure was on David, born on 18 April 1956, as he grew up in the wake of his big brothers. His response? To earn seven GCE O levels at the Magnus. As an adult, he brought much more satisfaction to villagers by working from time to time as a barman at The Ferry, as the pub at the bottom of Ferry Lane was unimaginatively renamed when new owners deemed 'Newcastle Arms' to be too old fashioned. Alas he died aged only 47 on 23 February 2004.

OLD POLICE HOUSE: IRONY AS RON REPLACES THE LAW
Ron Newbold was larger than life – the perfect mischief-maker to live in the last house to have been vacated by the law in the village. He survived an horrific collision with an express coach on the North Road to play a

greater role than could be expected of any man in keeping the village's three public houses viable, become the self-appointed cheerleader at village cricket and football matches with his uncannily stirring imitation of a huntsman's horn, and generally defy most lifestyle rules to live to within a week of his 78th birthday.

Ron, born on 27 November 1918, was the son of George and Lucy Newbold. The trio moved in 1952 to the house on the corner of Marsh Lane and Main Street after the Nottinghamshire Constabulary decided North Muskham was far too lawful to require the presence of a full-time officer. The last lawman to live full-time in North Muskham was Constable Frank Needham, whose daughter Shirley was a promising piano player towards the end of the Second World War, and who retired to a cottage in the grounds of Hexgrave Hall and became a gamekeeper. At least one family was not sorry to see him go: The Walters from Bathley – Frank, Eileen and daughter Lois – were fined 15 shillings each (£2.25, a good slice of a week's wage) by Newark County Magistrates on Wednesday 16 April 1950 for riding their cycles without lights on Nelson Lane at 10.45pm on 1 March.

While PC Reg Hollingsworth patrolled South and North Muskham, Little Carlton and Bathley by cycle from the new purpose-built police house at South Muskham (where Crow Lane meets the North Road), Ron proved himself to be the life and soul of any party. He was in his mid-30s – going on 13, reckoned his friends – when Queen Elizabeth II came to the throne.

They arrived five years after his dad retired from farming in Kneesall, doubtless worn-out as much by the relentless demands of the Second World War as by his land. For while farmers and farm workers were exempt from being called for National Service even in times of hostilities, they still had responsibilities. George had been a special constable during the First World War, and they elevated him to sergeant in the special constabulary from 1939 to 1945. Which meant that, after a day labouring on the land, he could be called out at all hours of the night whenever there were problems in the parish. And as Kneesall was in the flight path for take-off from Ossington airfield, there were an uncomfortable number of alarms and dramas to keep him and his colleagues occupied. As if that wasn't enough, while young Ron helped his Dad on the farm, the Newbolds lost their other son, Harold. He was killed while serving as a lieutenant in the Fleet Air Arm during the War.

George William Newbold died on 18 February 1968 at home at the age of 85. Lucy, who was a regular at the Chapel, followed on 12 February four years later. Confounding all those who reckoned that he would sink without

1. The Main Street

them, Ronald William Newbold muddled on with the help of his friends and neighbours (and the occasional light ale) – spending only his last few years in a nursing home at Winthorpe – before passing away on 19 November 1996. But his memory lives on: there are still many villagers who shudder at the thought of being awakened in the middle of the night by Ron imitating a hunting horn as he wandered home.

MARSH LANE
CHURCH COTTAGE: GERTIE THE DUTIFUL DAUGHTER

Dutiful daughter that she was, Gertie Gibson spent pretty much all her life looking after one aspect of the village or another – and made sure that she finally got right away from the place when she passed on.

For many years, she was the village postwoman. Her father George had become postmaster in May 1905, taking over from the Baxter family (see Nelson Lane). Eight years later, Church Cottage was sold by the Duke of Newcastle to the Southwell Diocesan Finance Association; and George was quick to fire off a letter to them which can be found these days in the *Nottinghamshire County Archives*: "I hope you will furnish me with a copper and fireplace in the wash-house. The east wall of the house requires attention as when the rain comes from the east it makes the two bedrooms practically useless and consequently means moving the furniture". Presumably, he got his way: the cottage never looked less than snug and warm in the 1950s. South-facing and with a large garden stretching to Marsh Lane, it was always an extremely picturesque little place from the outside.

When George died aged 64 on 27 January 1920 – only 14 months after the family had suffered the shock of Gertie's brother, George, dying at the age of 28 – Gertie took over running the Post Office from the small cottage and looking after her grieving mother, Elizabeth, who reached the age of 70 before passing away on 20 January 1937.

It also acted as a registry office when the area registrar ventured from his office in Ollerton to record any new births that had occurred since his last visit. Being house-proud as any lady at the time, Gertie toiled tirelessly to make the best of the cosy cottage, inside and out. And after she retired from stamp duties (and the Post Office was taken over by the Story family), Gertie laboured for years to make sure the interior of the Church remained a picture. When ill-health forced her to decide in 1967 that it was time she gave up the Church cleaning job, Mrs. Syd Thomas volunteered "a band of Women's Institute members" to replace her, on a rota system. And a Ladies' Committee was formed to arrange the floral decorations on a weekly basis.

After Miss Gertrude Gibson passed away in Hawtonville Hospital, Newark, aged 76 in November 1968, the popularity of the cottage led to it being considerably extended, though she would doubtless have been surprised that her garden disappeared, partially to make way for yet another Vicarage. Gertie had made sure she would not be anywhere near these modernisations. Rather than being buried in the Churchyard she had seen on virtually every day of her life, with her parents and brother, she insisted on being cremated at Wilford Hill, Nottingham.

FOXGLOVE COTTAGE: BRICKS AND MORTARS

On the opposite side of Marsh Lane to the Churchyard, Herbert Clipsham, second oldest of the brothers who ran a building firm from the north end of the village, lived in Foxglove Cottage, facing the back of the Old Police House, with his wife, Violet, and their children, Edna and Ron.

For many years, Herbert was a member of North Muskham Parish Council. He also served as a manager of North Muskham County School, over-looking the Green at the north end of the village.

His wife Violet was a memorable character who never lost her Cockney accent or sense of irony. She had worked during the First World War in an ordnance factory at High Wycombe – and always said that she did not realise she had angina until she stopped filling shells to fire at the Germans. Today, sufferers get their doses of nitrate less spectacularly via tablets or, in times of emergency, a pump spray.

Herbert Clipsham died at the family home, aged 76, on 19 September 1966. Violet Emily Clipsham was 74 when she died on 24 March 1969. Both of their children married – Edna became Mrs. L. Wright – and each had a son.

THE NOOK: DULCIE THE DEVOTED WIDOW

Dulcie Charles was a widow for 54 years – a blue-rinsed, strong-minded fore-runner of genuine emancipation in the days when a woman's peacetime place was normally in the home. Her husband, Clement Richmond Charles, a son of the family that farmed at the Old Hall, died aged only 47 on 18 November 1942. He had been ill for a long time but had obviously made many friends during his 25 years' service at Worthington-Simpson (where he rose to be chief wages clerk) and 20 years as a Church Warden at St. Wilfrid's. Virtually every department of the factory insisted on sending its own wreath. There was one from "the employees". Another from "the directors". And others from "the drawing office", "the sales department", "the general office staff",

1. The Main Street

"the foundry and laboratory staffs", "the canteen" and "from Mr. R. Smithson at the Gatehouse".Yet it was the inscription on another wreath that best summed him up: "Think what a man should be, and he was that".

Dulcie Muriel Irene Charles lived to be 95 before she passed away in 1996. She spent her working life at Bainbridge's, a treasure trove for women's clothes, household furnishings and a host of other fabrics, in Newark Market Place, and for years caught the 8.30am bus among the schoolchildren. Back home in the evening, usually on the 5.45pm from the Newark Bus Station that was situated in the yard of the Robin Hood Hotel, she spent years endeavouring to foster community spirit, rarely missing a chance to offer an incoming housewife a warm welcome rapidly followed by an invitation to join the Women's Institute. Indeed, it was at Dulcie's suggestion that North Muskham WI was formed in the late 1940s. She continued to play an active role, too, as one of the branch's most active and innovative committee members. For example, when fog prevented ladies from North Muskham travelling to a group meeting at East Stoke in November 1953, Dulcie gave a talk, in that matter-of-fact yet moving way of hers, on a visit to Spalford Hall, described as "a home for problem mothers and their children". She took the opportunity to launch an appeal for clothing that the mothers would be able to take home with them, and fostered quite an industry in knitted squares which she made up into blankets for the residents at the hall. Earlier in the year, in her capacity as the WI branch's Outings Secretary, she had organised for a bus party to visit the Little Theatre in Nottingham on 26 March.

All of which was a thoughtful world away from the drama that had driven out of the village the man who had built The Nook in 1914 – a symbol of future hope and solidity amid the despair of the Great War.

George Welch and his wife lived in the wash-house in the garden while they built the house. It was a fine place, as out-houses went at the time, with a fine old black-leaded fireplace providing a welcome glow on a cold night as exhaustion set in. He was 61 at the time and, as he had spent his lifetime working as a builder, brick-laying was truly a labour of love. His wife Bianca acted as his labourer. They could never have dreamed that in January 2002, their creation would go on the market for £135,000 complete with entrance hall, sitting room with feature fireplace, kitchen big enough to double as a breakfast room, study, rear lobby, utility room, master bedroom, study or second bedroom, bathroom, extensive gardens, the obligatory space for extension. It goes without saying that the modern estate agent did not have to mention the water pump outside or the toilet down the bottom of the big garden, all overlooking the marshlands that looked out between Holme and

Langford. They built their dream home with its back to Marsh Lane so that the sun would shine brightly on them as they basked in their retirement; and, for their last innovation, they turned the wash-house into a pig sty so they would never go short of meat.

They were even joined by their daughter, Mrs. Rebecca Fernley, and her children, May and Walter, after Rebecca's husband was killed towards the end of the Great War. May, looking forward to her 88th birthday in May of 2002, vividly remembered the journey on the back of a lorry from the smoky, bustling city of Manchester to the sanctity of a cottage near the butcher's shop in North Muskham… "My toes still bear the scars from the chilblains I caught on that journey". But, allowing for the devastation of losing her Daddy before she was five, she became a pretty contented child; and her poorly toes did not stop her trotting all the way to the Mill at the South Muskham end of the village to fetch yeast with which her Mum and Grandma made bread. While her Mum became particularly friendly with Alice Clipsham of the building family (probably because of George Welch's connection with the trade), young May became an eager little pupil at North Muskham School, though she recalls her first sweetheart got her into no end of trouble with Mr. King. The mischievous little lad was Syd Thomas, and while they were playing one day before school, he popped one of the pennies she'd brought for her bank account down a drain in the schoolyard. Mr. King was not amused; but May recalls a nice teacher called Lois Marsh coming to her aid. "I enjoyed my childhood", she says – but with a hint of sadness in her voice because the listener knows that there just has to be a 'but' to ruin the idyllic happy family.

And sure enough, shame forced Mr. and Mrs. Welch out of their dream home, out of the village. Their world blew up on 17 February 1926. Mr. Welch was 73. Around mid-morning, he went down on to the Marshes to scavenge for driftwood for the 'feature fireplace' that would so impress estate agents 76 years later. He obviously did a bit of drifting himself, past the Church, beyond the Ferry, because the occupiers of Manor Farm and Trent Farm, Harry Broadberry and Robert Dye, espied him near a fence about 200 yards away. Mr. Broadberry accused him of tearing wood out of one of his fences and chopping it up with his slasher (a long handled implement with a sharp blade basically used for plashing hedges). Quite what happened subsequently was to be contested, but Mr. Broadberry spent two weeks abed with quite horrific head injuries and Mr. Welch was eventually found guilty of unlawful and malicious wounding. Despite his great age, he was sentenced at the Nottinghamshire Quarter Sessions at Retford to six months' hard labour.

1. The Main Street

By the time he was released, Mrs. Welch had found somewhere else for them to live. That was no big deal. "My grandma had 36 flits in her life", says May. Harry Broadberry left the village, too. As for The Nook… after changing hands in 2002, it was demolished and replaced by an even grander house.

RIVERSIDE COTTAGE: CHARLIE THE BELL RINGERS' DARLING

Friday night was music night on the wireless. Except in North Muskham, Charlie Copp made sure Friday night was bell ringing night. That's when he assembled his forces for tireless (non-admirers within earshot reckoned 'tiresome') rehearsals of bing-bang-bong or, for a change, ching-chang-chong. Strangers who tired of the din would, however, have struggled to find Charlie in the lair he shared with his wife Mary. For they lived in a little wooden bungalow that was totally hidden from view by the Old Police House and the Dye/Thurston cottages from Main Street; by The Nook from Marsh Lane and by old Mrs. Smalley's cottage and garden hedge from the footpath formerly known as Town Street beside the Fleet.

By day, Charlie took the workmen's bus to Newark, where he toiled at Farrar's, the boiler-makers, in Northgate. But his heart never strayed far from the Church, where he was also a devoted Warden for many years. And few could doubt that the bell ringers put their hearts and souls into their pastime. They claimed a slice of local history on Saturday 7 January 1950 when Miss Kathy Streeton became the first Muskham person to ring a peal of bells in St. Wilfrid's Church. They claimed first peal, first attempt by treble and tenor, first attempt on an "inside bell" by fourth, and first peal of Grandsire as conductor. And then they went on (and on!) to claim a peal of Grandsire Doubles (5,040 was rung) in 3 hours 9 minutes. The ringers were Kathy Streeton (treble), Freddie Hooper (2, conductor), C.F. Briggs (3), Bill Midwinter (4), H.J. Claxton (5) and Charlie Copp (tenor).

Little did they realise that their next moment in the news would occur on the death of King George VI in February 1952. They spent two hours 50 minutes playing the fully muffled bells in "a tribute of loyal affection to his late majesty". Again, as on the record-breaking day, it consisted of 5,040 changes by ringers Simon Barley, Bill Midwinter, Anthony Barley, Freddie Hooper, C.F. Briggs and Charlie Copp. On the Sunday evening after the funeral of the King, a quarter peal was rung half-muffled, prior to a memorial service, by Kathy Streeton, the Barley boys, Alan Muddell, Bill Midwinter and, inevitably, Charlie Copp.

Reginald Charles John Copp died on 12 February 1971 aged 75. His wife, Mary Elizabeth, had been 73 when she passed away on 6 October

1969 in Hawtonville, the hospital in Newark that tended for elderly folk too ill to be safely looked after at home. When they had departed, their little home was demolished. As the 21st century began, their little plot became part of Glebelands.

BACK ON MAIN STREET...
OLD HALL: LECTURER AND WIFE DO GOOD

Maurice W. Barley's post-war search for a family home ended unexpectedly one night when he took an extra-mural class in local history at North Muskham Church Hall. In hope rather than expectation, as an aside, he asked if anyone knew of a house that might be available to him, his wife Diana (a cousin of the Rowntree family that made delightful chocolates in York), two sons (Anthony and Simon) and baby daughter (Harriet). Dulcie Charles chuckled: "You'd better take a look at the Old Hall". He looked at it by moonlight and the next morning agreed to rent it for £72 a year... "a string of large and lofty rooms linked by a passage", he recalled later. "It seemed to Diana and me that it could not have been a pleasanter place in which to bring up a family young enough to stand the cold in winter and the distance from board to bed". That was in 1946, when the sons were aged 10 and eight, and Harriet was a babe in arms. Six years on, the boys were at the Magnus Grammar School, Harriet was at South Muskham Church of England School, Diana was settling into most aspects of the social life of the village and Maurice was marvelling at the profusion of blue stalks (a kind of mushroom) to be found in the village's soggy fields. Among the garden's well-established fruit trees were some that were "now rare or unobtainable, such as a first-rate baking apple, Warner's King".

Maurice Barley's book, *The Chiefest Grain* (published in 1993), included this insight into what may be termed responsible parenthood in the post-war years:

"Superficially, it was an idyllic life for the children. The boys were always welcomed in the farmyard by Tom and Fred Charles, either as watchers or as helpers. Harriet's school at South Muskham gave her a ready supply of friends for tea parties, exchanges of visits and the like. For me, family life was for much of the year a matter of family breakfasts and rather hurried teas before I set off for classes, and home only long after the children were in bed. Lacking experience, we were quite strict parents, attaching what may now seem undue importance to table manners, for instance, and expecting all three to share in washing-up, shoe-cleaning and mowing a large lawn. As Harriet was so much younger, less was expected of her, and failure to discuss this led to resentment by Anthony and Simon. It was easier for Diana to relate to Harriet,

1. The Main Street

partly because of the feminine things they said and did together, but mostly because with the boys there was the unbridgeable gap of the War years. We were all so busy and absorbed in day to day affairs that we made no opportunity to talk about feelings... The boys were, I think, afraid to question decisions. With Harriet, the relationship was easy and she was very open and uninhibited. When she was in her teens, she once asked Diana whether we would have turned her out of the home if she became pregnant and that led to a constructive discussion".

Life became less sweet when the Charles brothers decided to become pig farmers: the Barleys had to put muslin over the bedroom windows in the heat of summer to keep the flies out and, in the absence of yet-to-be-invented double glazing, failed to shut out the endless clunks of the lids on the automatic feeders. Such setbacks did not reduce their zeal for village life, and they began a weekly vegetable stall in their coach-house, inviting the village's more productive gardeners to sell their surplus produce.

And Diana's zeal took another turn with the outbreak of the Korean War in 1950. As president of North Muskham Women's Institute and a member of the Nottinghamshire WI Public Relations Committee, she persuaded the village members to adopt a resolution appealing to the Government to come to an understanding with the USA and Soviet Union over the control of the use of the hydrogen and atom bomb. Despite her undoubted eloquence, the motion was left to lie on the table by the county committee; and, in truth, nobody else in the village shared the Barleys' views... until the Vicar who succeeded Arthur Rigden, the Rev. Hilary Dunn, supported Simon Barley in 1957 when he decided he had a conscientious objection to National Service. Simon won exemption, went to St. Thomas' Hospital Medical School and in 1963 at the age of 24 wed a fellow student doctor, 20-year-old Keren Johnson, who was the younger daughter of the Dean of Canterbury.

The Barleys had, however, departed North Muskham late in 1957 and Maurice went on to make a reputation as an archeological lecturer at Nottingham University while Diana became equally well respected as a magistrate – though initially she was alternately patronised and disregarded by the admiral, colonel and major who were the senior members of the Newark County Bench – and as a member of the Nottinghamshire County Council's newly-formed Children's Committee, which was the forerunner of the Social Services Department. It came as no surprise to the friends she left behind in North Muskham that Diana should do so much good work before 'do-gooding' became either fashionable or well-funded. As early as the summer of 1953, she had been the North Muskham WI delegate to a Child Neglect Conference; and her report back to the village ladies "opened the minds of many to a world they had not dreamed existed", said a contemporary report in the *Newark Advertiser*.

ST. WILFRID'S CHURCH: TRANSFORMING DUTY TO ENJOYMENT

Worship during the 1950s was still considered by many grown-ups to be something of a duty rather than a matter of conscience in an old church that still looked remarkably like it did when it was originally built. Much of the old roofing timbers were still there. The original plaster remained, though an audit in the mid-50s reported it had been "made good". Piers, arches, walls, windows and part of the screen were all old. But the altars, choir stalls, chancel roof, chairs, flooring, organ and west gallery were all "modern".

And the Vicar of North Muskham (and South Muskham) at the start of the second Elizabethan reign, the Reverend Edward Arthur Rigden, did his best to make worship more of a pleasure than a duty. Among his innovations was a Sunday School, similar to the one that had proved popular for years up at the Chapel. It proved to be Peggy Granger's first opportunity to become a teacher. She recalls: "I think I was getting to be a young lady – 14 or 15 – when it started, and I was landed with teaching at it by the time I was 16! I was involved from 1953 to '69. We started off with about a dozen children... I remember Ronnie Milnes from the Garage, the Swannacks, and a little later the Kent girls and children out of the new bungalows. While I was away at college, Mum taught at the Sunday School while my big brother Jock played the organ". Jock was still playing half a century later, at the age of 84, at St. Albans Church in Mansfield!

As for the Rev. Rigden, he was so quietly spoken that one would never have guessed he was a veteran of both World Wars. Educated at Bedford School and Cambridge University, he had spent the Great War in the Army. After the Armistice was signed, he returned to Cambridge to complete his MA degree then became a curate at Plymouth before embarking on a career as a man of the cloth in the Royal Navy. One of his more intriguing postings was to China in the Cruiser Squadron. Back in England, he served in a couple of English churches. When the Second World War began, he was called into the Royal Naval Volunteer Reserve and posted to Falmouth. On his arrival at South Muskham Vicarage in 1946 – with his sister as his housekeeper – he maintained his links with the sailing fraternity by acting as chaplain of Newark Sea Scouts. He was also a keen bell ringer and was a member of the Southwell Diocesan Guild of Change Ringers.

For much of his time at the Muskhams, however, he did not enjoy the best of health; and there was genuine sadness when, after six weeks in Nottingham

General Hospital, he died aged 59 on Thursday 18 August 1955. While his funeral took place at South Muskham, a three-hour muffled peal was rung at North Muskham Church. In a further illustration of unity between the two parishes, the Rev. Rigden's coffin was borne by North Muskham Churchwardens Charlie Copp and John Gascoigne and their South Muskham counterparts John Beckett and Bill Cooper. The funeral service was conducted by Father William Dolman, who was the Vicar of Cromwell; the committal was by the Rev. Robert Keal, Vicar of Sutton-on-Trent; and the blessing was pronounced by Bishop A. M. Gelsthorpe of Bingham. The organist was Jock Granger. And there was touching recognition of the Rev. Rigden's efforts to welcome the younger generation into the ways of the church when the children of North Muskham Sunday School placed bunches of flowers at his graveside, beside the path in South Muskham Churchyard.

The Rev. Rigden was succeeded by the Rev. William Snow, a quietly-spoken, naturally friendly gent who effortlessly continued the process of making the Church more appealing and less daunting without driving away the core worshippers. Mind you, modernisation kicked-in apace at the Parochial Church Council meeting of 1967 when a decision was taken to insure the Church roof against lead thieves for the first time. In a totally unrelated appointment, Colin Granger was welcomed as the new clock-winder (and also volunteered to try and keep the Church path clear of moss). Colin thus became the fourth member of his family to work in a voluntary capacity for the Church.

THE COTTAGE: HOME FOR A HAULAGE COMPANY
Henry Whitney ran a haulage business, complete with his own petrol pumps outside the kitchen door, in the cottage – he named it "The Cottage" – just across Main Street from the Churchyard and Church Lane. The place was originally built centuries earlier as a changing room for clerics travelling from Southwell to preach at St. Wilfrid's. Mr. Whitney had three lorries; and his drivers included Norman Thurston; Les Avis, who went on to live a long retirement in Newark; and a bloke called Albert.

The Cottage remained connected with transport after the departure of the Whitney's, when it was taken over – and extended by about a third – by Eric Talbot, who built-up a garage business on Norwell Lane next to where his Dad lived, while his wife Shirley became arguably the first of Muskham's modern women by running a women's hairdresser's in Newark (opposite the Parish Church) while rearing daughter Linsey.

The Cottage was eventually renamed Little Acre, which caused a wry smile among village oldies who contemplated that if Whitney's fuel tanks had gone up, there would have been larger achers. By the start of the 21st century The Cottage had been increased in size by a third or more, in keeping with many of the homes in the village.

CHURCH LANE
AINGARTH: KINGS WHO RULED SCHOOL

The occupants of the semi-detached houses on the right hand-side of Church Lane shared the same water pump but nothing like the same outlook on life. Jack Dent and his kindly little wife Doris were as meek and mild as Norman King and his sister Florence were confident, confrontational and controversial.

Jack, as all men christened John seemed to be known in the '50s, was born in Newark and educated at the Guildhall Street School when all schools catered for all age-groups. After serving his apprenticeship at J. Ransome & Company, he worked at Ransome & Marles for all his working life – five and a half days a week, rising through the ranks to become senior foreman in the light turnery department. Neighbours spotting him labouring in his vegetable garden at weekends would never have guessed he'd been brought up as a townie. It stretched from the corner of the Dents' half of Aingarth to the Main Street and provided all the vegetables a family of three could ever need.

Doris stayed home to bring up their son, Donald, and served on the committee of North Muskham Women's Institute so conscientiously that she made headlines in the *Newark Advertiser* on 3 December 1958. The reason: she wrote a letter inviting Roma Parlby, the editor's daughter who compiled the women's page(s), to speak to the village WI on Thursday 12 February 1960. Dear Doris made Roma feel like royalty! She wrote in her letter: "The date seems far ahead but knowing what a busy person you are, I thought I would write in good time". Roma wrote in her column: "I felt very flattered. I doubt if royalty is booked for personal appearances very much further ahead than a year and a quarter".

Jack (full name, John Thomas Dent) died after a short illness in Newark General Hospital at the age of 60 on 4 June 1960. By this time, Donald was in the Royal Navy, serving on HMS Albion in the Far East. Back on the home front, Doris May Dent battled sugar diabetes with cheerfulness for several years before dying, aged 78, on 19 March 1977.

Mr. and Miss King – 50 years on, it remains impossible to call such formidable characters by their first names – were the headmaster and deputy headmistress of North Muskham County Primary School for more than 40 years. They ruled with the proverbial rod of iron; and, once Jack Dent's neatly plashed hedge had been replaced by a fence, it became apparent that the Kings

1. The Main Street

really had considered themselves royalty. For revealed in all its glory in their back garden was the only outside lavatory in Muskham that was trimmed with castle-like turrets.

Norman James King, educated at the Queen Elizabeth Grammar School, Mansfield, retired in 1957. He was also a Church of England licensed lay reader for 25 years. Miss King, too, played more than an academic part in village life: among other contributions, she served on the committee of North Muskham Women's Institute, and was the branch treasurer in 1953.

THE NOOK: LOYAL BILLY KEEPS ON WORKING

As befits a painter and decorator who loved gardening, Billy Gascoigne inherited from his folks one of the most picturesque cottages in the village. It was a comfortable distance from the increasingly noisy Main Street, further cushioned by Aingarth and a high wall that ensured absolute privacy. It faced south (and the Church where Billy sang in the choir as a lad) to assure its occupants of the best possible, relaxing outlook.

Not that Billy was totally relaxed. Typical of workmen of his generation, he was loyalty itself to his bosses, though apprentices under his wing in the 1950s remember his acid tongue as much as his valued advice. He joined F. Bingham and Son, plumbers and decorators, at Sutton-on-Trent in 1909 and, if anything, became more of a stickler for propriety and hard work with each passing year. By far the longest-serving worker the firm had – ever – Billy took an hour or two off in January of 1959 (he was aged 71 yet still working full-time) to receive a cheque from his boss, Mr. Stuart Bingham, "as a token of appreciation" for his 50 years of service.

William James Gascoigne died in Hawtonville Hospital at Newark aged 81 on 12 September 1969. His wife, Annie, too ill to go to his funeral, followed him on 16 December the same year. She was 80 and died at the home of their daughter, Margaret, a ladies' hairdresser who had married Ken Cossel, a young workmate of Billy's (more of them later).

BACK ON MAIN STREET
PREFAB: HOME IN AN ORCHARD

Jim Shearer and his wife Renee began to bring up their two young children in a prefabricated bungalow built after the Second World War in the orchard between Church Lane and the semi-detached cottages occupied by the families of his brother-in-law, Jack Guy, and Percy Spafford.

Jim, one of the few heroes to serve during the Second World War as a rear gunner in a Lancaster bomber and survive, initially worked at the Old Hall

Farm and reared his own pigs in brick-built sties in the orchard between his prefab and Church Lane.

Renee, who also looked after her widowed mum, Mary Priestley Key, as well as her son Robert and daughter Jean, was a typical part of the fabric of the village. In her spare time, she looked after magazine swaps for members of North Muskham Women's Institute in the 1950s (when not every housewife could afford such luxuries as *Woman*, *Woman's Own*, *Women's Weekly* or *The People's Friend*).

Mrs. Key had been born in 1900 in Crab Lane, one of the offspring of barge worker Henry Guy and his wife Sarah. While Sarah took the pledge of abstinence from alcohol on 26 November 1905 (her great-grandson Stephen keeps the declaration as a family treasure), Mrs. Key was equally prim and proper, reaching the status of Superintendent at the village Chapel.

The Shearers eventually moved to the poultry farm and smallholding near the Norwell Lane crossing; but do not worry that they had been cramped or handicapped for mod-cons in their prefab. They had a bathroom long before the older cottages around them and used to allow their nephew, Stephen Guy, to have a soak after he played football matches for North Muskham in the early 1970s when the pitch was in the swampy field immediately to the north of Mackleys Lane. And where there was once one railway carriage-shaped prefabricated bungalow surrounded by enough grassland for half the village to play ad hoc football matches of an evening, there is now the compact estate known as St. Wilfrid's Close.

SEMI-DETACHED COTTAGES: FULL OF CHARACTERS

Two of the village's greatest characters, Percy Spafford and Jack Guy, reared their families in the semi-detached cottages at the junction of Main Street and the unnamed lane equidistant between Church and Ferry Lanes.

Percy Spafford and his wife May were both inspirations to sport in general in the village and to North Muskham and Bathley Cricket Club in particular. Percy continued to play, as a hard-hitting batsman and sharp-eyed fielder, well into his middle age while May was a crucial tea maker (and never short of the odd short, sharp phrase of advice for the players). Older son Clarence not only followed Dad into the cricket team and on to the selection committee, but also had the good sense to marry a lovely lass from Cromwell, Joan Bass, who was the team's scorer. What younger son Raymond lacked at cricket (and it wasn't eagerness), he more than made up for at football, becoming the rock around which the North Muskham defence was built in the Newark and District Minor League. Daughter May had the good sense

1. The Main Street

to marry a cricketer, in 1949 (but as they lived in Balderton to be near the Lincolnshire Road Car depot from which he worked as a bus driver, he was never allowed to represent North Muskham and Bathley CC).

Once the kids were off their hands, the Spaffords moved to the new bungalows built in Trent Close in the early 1960s. Esther May Spafford died aged 79 on 9 January 1990. Percy celebrated his 90th birthday with a balloon flight before passing away, aged 91, on 25 November 1997.

The Guys occupied the 'other half' of the cottages. Edward Guy was succeeded by his nephew Jack Guy, his wife, Ethel, and two sons, Richard, born in March 1947, and Stephen, who arrived in April 1951.

As sharp of wit as he was short of stature, Jack was the village's ultimate cheerful chappy – though he had more reason than most to have a chip on his shoulder. For though he had been christened Albert, his mum always called him John (which is why all his playmates, workmates and friends came to know him as Jack). He even went through North Muskham School from the age of 5 to 14 as John Guy without problem until he had to produce his birth certificate to prove he was old enough to leave what passed for the education system. As soon as Head Teacher King clapped a beady eye on 'Albert Guy', he held a hasty investigation, came to the conclusion that the hapless Albert/John/Jack was to blame for attending school under a false identity and gave him one stroke of the cane for every year of the 'deception'. What a leaving present!

Much later in life, the man with three names ran into identity trouble again. Albert Guy won a prize in a raffle run by the Newcastle Arms landlord, Frank Neath. Having immigrated from the Socialist Independent Republic of South Yorkshire in the early 1960s, the somewhat dour Frank was not impressed when the man he knew only as Jack Guy turned up to claim his reward. Such was the confusion and stand-off, Albert/John/Jack had to nip home for his birth certificate before Frank relented... though he always bore a slight suspicion that he'd been 'done' by the ever-mischievous Mr. Guy!

Stockily built, Jack invariably bounced about like a ball, and his slightly high-pitched voice gave him the perfect impish tone. Born in Trent Cottages down Crab Lane – the third generation of the Guy family to reside there – he wed Ethel in 1946, when he was working for the "War Ag", the Government-funded department working to return huge acreage of land to farming after the Second World War; and they lived initially in Harrowby near Grantham and then in a semi-detached house outside Claypole on the North Road to be close to his work.

He caused a hasty evacuation of Newark Police Station in Appletongate one day by turning up with a bunch of unexploded mines in the back of his lorry and asking the station sergeant: "What should I do with these?" The Bomb Disposal Squad was called quicker than you could say: "Stop messing about, Albert/John/Jack Guy!" When the police stopped running and had the breath to ask questions, it transpired that Jack had unearthed the potentially lethal load while helping to clear Balderton Airfield to make way for Balderton Hospital (which this century became Fernwood).

To the relief of all, the post-war reclamation work ended without further mishap and Jack brought his family back to North Muskham when he got a job working for Winter Knight, who was coming towards the end of his reign at Burridge Farm. After a short spell in one of the two Burridge Farm Cottages at the far end of Crab Lane, the Guys succeeded Uncle Ted next door to the Spaffords.

Jack became a driver with Notts Highways Department and always made sure the roads out of North Muskham were thoroughly gritted on frosty mornings and ploughed on most snowy ones. While children doubtless thought him a kill-joy for ensuring they could get to school, adults greatly appreciated his dedication to his job. Whenever evil weather was forecast, Jack brought his work home in the shape of a lorry laden with grit or salt. As soon as duty called, he would go to work on the A1 – pausing only to make sure the village street had been thoroughly treated as a priority.

After the Spaffords moved to Trent Close, Jack and Ethel had the cottages knocked into one family home. Richard moved away to the Nottingham area to live and work. Stephen kept the cottage in the family with his wife Linda and their own family… and Albert/John/Jack's mischievous tendency lives on in the nameplate on the wall: 'emanon'. Read it backwards.

FERRY LANE
FERRY LANE COTTAGES: FOUR INTO FIVE DO GO!
Four (families) went into five (cottages) in the row just across Ferry Lane from the Newcastle Arms' vegetable garden. The re-adjustment came when the Needham family out-grew No.1, and owner Norman Burch arranged for numbers 2 and 3 to be knocked together to accommodate them. This is how the re-alignment worked in the 1950s:

In No.1, William H James, an insurance agent, and his wife brought up daughter Jean, succeeding Ernest Worthington whose daughter Diana had moved to Newark on her marriage. Jean, approaching the rebellious teenager stage of her life at the time, starkly remembers the shock of moving from civilised Nottingham to a rural location most memorable for its outside lavatory being a haven for rats. Half a century on, she swears she still bears

1. The Main Street

the scar of where her front teeth went through her lip the pitch-black night a rat sent her fleeing in such a panic that she fell flat on her face in the gardens.

She survived – spiritedly in that another of her fond childhood memories is scrumping apples from the laden orchards around the village – to lead a wonderful life with her husband and family in Newark.

In No.2/3, Jack Needham and his family – wife Doris, sons Neville and Brian, daughter Marjorie – were stalwarts of the Methodist Chapel, their faith undiminished by man's cruelty to man. Jack's jobs reflected the evolution of 'Muskham Man' from the land to a more urban role.

First, he farmed at Foxholes for Squire Edge. Having acknowledged what a thankless task that was, he made inquiries about the possibility of a better-paid job on the railways. As soon as the strict Squire heard of this "disloyalty", he gave the Needhams notice to quit their home. It looked as if they would be homeless until a brave farmer in Bathley, Mr. Peatman, defied Squire Edge and offered them a room in his house.

Having settled in Ferry Lane, Jack worked for British Railways until Dr. Beeching's axe cut the workforce so ruthlessly that the 'survivors' ceased to provide a service and floundered in their attempts to function as a business. Jack escaped to the Worthington-Simpson engineering works at Lowfields, Balderton. Throughout these upheavals, he remained devout; and standing firm while it must have seemed all around him were relaxing their morals. He even forbade Brian to play cricket for North Muskham and Bathley CC on Sundays. So the village team had to find another opening bowler for the second match of each weekend. Brian was quietly a bit of a rebel, though, in that, despite winning a place at the rugby-playing Magnus Grammar School in Newark by passing his 13-plus exam, he remained faithful to football and was a powerful and creative inside forward (midfielder in modern parlance) for North Muskham Football Club through its most successful winters.

As the children grew bigger, the Needhams moved from the Ferry Lane Row to the more spacious Rose Villas on Nelson Lane. Jack – real name John – died at the age of 84 on 10 February 1991. Mrs. Needham similarly lived for the Chapel and performed many kind deeds for parishioners aside from running the Bright Hour for decades. She was well into her 80s before she finally parked up the pedal cycle on which she propelled herself around the village and moved into Newark to be nearer Marjorie, who had married Barry Watson in October 1969. Barry was a schoolteacher at the Grove Comprehensive School, Balderton, and as devout a Methodist as the Needhams. Needless to say, the wedding ceremony was at the village Chapel. Marjorie, who had worked at the Co-op (when the Co-op stretched along half of Kirkgate at Newark) after leaving school, looked pretty as a picture in ribbon lace and satin. The new Mr. and Mrs. Watson set up home and brought up their own family in Salisbury Road, Newark.

The Needham boys moved away, too. Neville settled in Epperstone. Brian enjoyed a career in banking in Nottingham before retiring to Ravenshead and frequent rounds of golf. Muskham's last link with the Needham family was sadly severed on 20 November 1999, when Doris died at the age of 86; but there are those who will never forget the qualities the family brought to the village.

In No.4, Gordon Harker and Bet, the daughter of George Worthington, were a chalk and cheese partnership. Gordon was a quietly spoken bus driver with Lincolnshire Road Car, as conscientious as he was conventional. Bet, via one of the most notorious departments at Ransome & Marles' factory and one of the most respected and responsible jobs in the village, became a garrulous barmaid, hair blonded in the candy-floss fashion made popular by film star Diana Dors, lips as scarlet as her reputation. Through all her distinctive career changes, she had a heart of gold and a head for mischief. During the Second World War, not long out of school, she 'did her bit' in the Fitting Up Department at R&M. This was where young male apprentices with sheltered up-bringings were sent by the management to learn an entirely different language and way of life from that taught by their mothers.

For two decades after Miss Gibson from Marsh Lane decided to forego the pleasure of making the mail deliveries, Bet was the village postwoman. She'd bike around, her peaked cap at a jaunty angle amid her mass of candy floss hair, keeping her tongue firmly in her cheek as she pedalled through groups of gossiping villagers, urging them to: "Let the Royal Mail come through!"

The most royal thing about Bet was the rumpus she always seemed on the verge of. There was, for example, the Wartime night when she was biking back over Norwell Hill after a convivial evening at the Plough Inn. Bladder bursting, she hopped off her cycle and disappeared into the pitch darkness among the trees. Presently, the eerie silence was pierced by a scream. A male scream! Bet had stumbled – literally – upon a soldier on manoeuvres. Whether he faced anything more startling when he actually went to War is not recorded. But this particular exercise was well and truly blown. And as the soldiers silently regrouped for the march back to base, all they could hear was the hysterical laughter of a blonde (or possibly two) free-wheeling down the hill towards Foxholes in much the same carefree fashion she brought to life as a whole. She eventually lost the post job amid allegations that she had

1. The Main Street

committed the cardinal sin of reading other people's mail. In truth, she had probably glanced at a couple of holiday postcards and ventured the thought: "So-and-so's having a nice time – wish I was there". But she was genuinely hurt by the fact that a fellow villager should think so ill of her as to get her the sack from a job that clearly gave her much pride.

That said, she wasn't so distraught as to shrink from public view. There were those who viewed her as a poacher turned gamekeeper when she became a barmaid; but her popularity at the pumps in the public bar of the Clinton Arms Hotel made Our Bet one of the main attractions in Newark Market Place during the '60s. Such were her winning ways that she never had to catch her husband Gordon's bus home. There always seemed to be a Baxter's taxi ready to go her way from their base in the Clinton Yard. Out she would get in Ferry Lane, high heels clicking, fashionable skirt swirling… the epitome of an It girl defying the onset of middle age!

In No.5, Arthur E. Brumpton, who lived in the end cottage closest to the river, had two key roles. His full-time job was with Ransome & Marles in Newark, making more ball bearings than any other factory in the world. On Saturday afternoons and light evenings in the summer, he would earn a few extra pence by acting as barber for any man needing a short back and sides. Whisper it, but he never charged even the minimum being recommended by the barbers' union, which was 1s 9d (8 and threequarters pence) until Easter of 1955, rising to 2s (10p) thereafter. Arthur's brother – always reverentially referred to as "Mr. Brumpton" by we children – was an equally unforgettable character. He was born with feet so deformed that they pointed inwards. Yet he spent his working life as a road repairer, walking the villages diligently making sure the byways were not only free of litter but were also well drained (tasks that local authorities seem to be incapable of fulfilling 50 years on). Arthur was survived for many years by his wife; and their son Alan continued to live in No.5 into the 21st century.

Indeed, Alan had been a source of great pride to the village in the 1950s: he was so clever that he earned a degree at Cambridge University. Alas by the time of his death half a century later, he had become a recluse and the family cottage had become a rather macabre museum of 'the good times'.

BACK ON MAIN STREET
FERRY LANE COTTAGE: WHAT A PICTURESQUE PRESENT!
It went on sale a few months before the Coronation. It was bought for £550 and was occupied by a Pearl Insurance Company agent called Mr. Dawson until 1955 when Ken Cossel bought it for his young wife Margaret with a

gesture that was as romantic as it was breath-taking. Margaret, nee Gascoigne who had spent her childhood at the cosy family home in Church Lane, recalls: "All the years I'd grown up in North Muskham, I'd always said Ferry Lane Cottage was where I wanted to live. Whenever Mum and I were waiting for a bus at Ferry Lane corner, I'd gaze at that Cottage and wish… I couldn't think of a nicer place to live. When Ken and I married, we lived in Sutton-on-Trent until our daughter Katherine was four months old. Then Ken came home one night and said: 'You know your cottage at Muskham?' I said: "It's not my cottage!' He said: 'It is now – I've just bought it'. He'd been told by my Dad earlier that day that there was a For Sale sign up and, after he'd finished work, he'd gone down to Muskham and bought it on the spot".

And they lived happily thereafter. The move took them close to Margaret's parents, which suited all of them in an era when families instinctively stuck together. Five years later, Ken and Margaret moved to one of the new bungalows built alongside Main Street between Ferry Lane and Mackleys Lane, and became village fixtures. Ken, who had worked for Walton's at Sutton, felt it would be more economic to live in a new property while he built up his own painter's and decorator's business. Margaret, a trained hairdresser, raised Katherine through Muskham County Primary School and the Lilley and Stone High School, Newark, to a career in newspaper advertising. And when they went to catch the bus to Newark, she always looked fondly at Ferry Lane Cottage… "I could have stayed there forever", she says. "But I suppose it was more practical to move".

Kenneth Kench Cossel died, aged 74, on 19 April 2001. Margaret continues to live in the village, on Main Street hardly 200 metres away from 'her cottage'. Katherine and her husband, Martin, a farmer, brought up their own three children at Coddington.

HOLLY COTTAGE: SLAVING THROUGH THE SADNESS
The cottage at the corner of Main Street and Nelson Lane, known to current generations as *Costalot*, was occupied by Irad Price and his wife, Fanny. Mr. Price was frequently to be found in his vegetable garden, which stretched from the back of the cottage in an inverted V-shape alongside Nelson Lane, which was much narrower and twistier then than now. The couple had five children, sons named Stanley and Philip and daughters Grace Beryl, Joyce and Barbara, who was married just before Easter 1955 to Douglas Ball of Lawrence Street, Newark.

The next time the family published an announcement in the local papers, it was a much sadder occasion. 'Rad', as he was known to all, died.

1. The Main Street

The next time was sadder still. Grace passed away on 29 March 1959 after a long illness, aged only 35, leaving a husband, Jim Bentley, and four young children – Julia, Jennifer, Meg and Chris – at home in Staunton Road, Newark. The word "cancer" was so feared, it was never mentioned.

Of the other Price children, Philip married and brought up his family in Norfolk; Joyce married Edgar Ward; Stanley and his wife Shirley ran a shop in the village for a while before moving away in search of a more viable life; and Barbara's marriage was so fruitful that, when last heard of by her friends in the village, she talked happily of her grandchildren.

As for Fanny, she survived until 15 May 1972, by which time she was 79. And as her home was visible from three sides (and Nelson Lane was much closer to it until the changes wrought by the by-pass), she gave an unwitting demonstration that a housewife's work was never done. Monday morning, for example, would see her firing up the boiler in the wash-house between the cottage and Nelson Lane. Soon steam would be mixed with smoke as she did the washing in the warming water, dried it through the mangle, and then pegged it out on the line down the garden path. The afternoon would be spent ironing, keeping the old iron warm enough by lodging it on its special shelf close enough to the coal fire as necessary. Other days would be set aside for sweeping throughout the house; polishing the furniture and furnishings (remember, brasses had to be Brasso'd every week!); changing the bedding and getting it washed and dried in the days before mechanical assistance was invented or affordable; baking the pastry for the week; and doing the family shopping on Market Days. Sunday was hardly a rest: there was the family dinner to cook… followed by the washing up.

The cottage has been considerably extended since the 1950s, when it was a basic rectangular two-up, two-down facing Main Street. Nelson Lane was much closer to the side gate than became the case when the School was built opposite. In the days before the majority owned cars, one of the Prices' benefits to their community was their generosity in allowing people from Bathley to leave cycles in their backyard when they caught the bus to Newark.

BEHIND FERRY LANE COTTAGE: LITTLE SHOPMAN AND HIS BIG FAMILY

In the corner of the patchwork of fields that became Trent Close, in the '50s, stood a rickety store. After Stan and Shirley Price departed, the shopkeeper was a Jack-of-all-trades called Herbert Mitcherson, who lived in a very thin, tall mill-house at the far end of what became Hopyard Lane, Bathley, and whose family grew so big, it expanded into a bus that he parked in the garden. Herbert was a clever man, by all accounts. Smart enough to make his own teeth (out of wood!) rather than risk a visit to one of the less than gentle dentists operating in Newark at the time. He was a cobbler who charged little in days when his customers had to make do and mend (re-soling shoes that had developed holes; hammering in segs to prevent heels completely wearing away).

And Herbert was also one of Syd Milnes' staff at the North Road Garage. But he was once confounded by a parson driving a Trojan car, who stopped for re-fuelling and asked helpful Herbert if he would also be so kind as to check the oil and water. Up went the front bonnet – and up went Herbert's voice: "B****y hell, mister – your engine's dropped out!" In his defence, this was an age when cars could be any colour so long as they were black (as Henry T. Ford had informed the world from the first mass production line in the '30s); when engines were placed in the front; when the novelty of hiding engines where the boot should be was laughed at as denying the driver a substantial metal cushion in the event of a crash. Then, though, as now, accidents were something that happened to the other driver.

THE WILLOWS: FARMING FAMILY AT HUB OF VILLAGE
The influential Staniforth family was in mourning at the time of the Coronation. The patriarch of the farming dynasty, Joseph William, had died at the age of 77 on 20 January 1953. For once, the perimeter wall that hid The Willows, its grounds and its farm buildings from public gaze seemed a fitting veil over sadness. For most of the time, it made the hedge-lined Main Street seem suddenly urban and claustrophobic – all the more because the front garden wall grew into cattle shed walls all the way round the Waltons Lane corner. But the family (which had settled in North Muskham from Ossington) was much loved and admired, and there was hardly a dry eye in the Church Hall on 18 July 1953, when North Muskham WI staged a Grandmothers' Night. Mrs. Staniforth acted as President for the evening – wearing a dress that had been in her trousseau 50 years earlier.

While the Staniforths had a son William (who was 62 when he died on 29 December 1967), two grandsons, Guy and Barry (Old Magnusians who in the 1950s were prominent members of Newark Rugby Club) and later a great-grandson, Philip, to continue the family business in the heart of North Muskham and later at Grange Farm, South Muskham, and Kelham Hills, The Willows became something of a females' stronghold.

Joseph's widow, Mary Louisa, continued to play a part in village social life virtually up to her death, aged 88, on 15 May 1963. It had fallen to Mrs.

1. The Main Street

The Willows in its last days as a farm, Rockery House and Cherry Cottage and (bottom right) the corner of Mackley's Lane that was once a pond.

Staniforth, as President of North Muskham WI in 1952, to take the decision to postpone their fifth birthday party upon the death of King George VI. When it was finally held on 21 February (it was a tea to which all members contributed), the ladies made their bid for a bigger gathering place than the Church Hall by ensuring the *Newark Herald* report included: "It was regretted that it was not possible to invite members of other institutes because of a lack of room".

There was no shortage of room, or hospitality, at The Willows, however. It was the venue for a country dancing party, organised by the WI, on 1 August 1953.

And, when the North Muskham Parochial Church Council was faced with a £900 bill for repairs in 1957, Mrs. Staniforth instantly invited them to stage a money-raising garden fete on the front lawn of The Willows. It raised £55, too – marking it one of the greatest successes in the village's money-raising history. It was also one of those memorable occasions when much of the village pooled its resources. For example, Mrs. Bowles, the landlord's wife at 'The Ferry', looked after the ice cream and minerals stall. The white elephant stall was in the hands of Mrs. Davenport from up Nelson Lane and her daughter, Sybil. (That was no white elephant! That was the Sybil who was to become the Reverend Davenport.) Flowers and produce were sold by Mrs. Cec Pollard and Miss Gibson. Cakes were dispensed by Dulcie Charles and the lady from the big house up Vicarage Lane, Mrs. Muddell. Mothers' Union needlework by Mrs. Billy Gascoigne and Mrs. W. Whitby. The treasure hunt was controlled by Mrs. Frank Swannack, whose five-year-old son Billy had

had the task of presenting a bouquet to Mrs. John Hole, the nice lady from Caunton Manor who performed the opening ceremony.

And fittingly on the day The Willows became home-from-home to the entire village, the refreshments were provided by the Streeton sisters, a group of ladies who knew the lay-out of the farmhouse rather better than most.

The Staniforths had given safe haven to the sisters, who endured a more tragic life than most families. Their father had died "by his own hand" – which at the time was deemed a crime rather than a cry for help – in the working mill that had crumbled in Mill Lane when they were young, in the 1930s. Their highly respected brother, Edgar, was only in his 40s (and only recently wed to Olive Longmate from Carlton Lane, Sutton-on-Trent, after a long, long courtship) when he suffered a fatal heart attack in January of 1946. Edgar, who was the manager of J. T. Wilkinson and Sons, the jewellers, in Church Street, Newark, was such an accomplished organist that he played regularly at Sutton-on-Trent Church and occasionally at Newark Christ Church. There were four Streeton sisters who lived at The Willows in the 1950s, and one who had got away and become Mrs. Hollingworth. Whatever their marital status, the village knew them as 'The Miss Streetons'.

Emily (Mrs. Buckley), the middle one of the five, had been widowed. But she was an expert dressmaker and, despite suffering noticeably from a bad back, cycled daily to Newark to work in what looked from the Market Place like an ornate, two-storey fairy castle but was in reality an exceptionally well-lit working environment for its seamstresses: Bainbridge's, which stretched from near the Arcade to the Clinton Arms Hotel.

Miriam Streeton, the youngest-but-one, drowned in the River Trent on 15 March 1961. The family tragedy became public five days later at the inquest conducted by the Newark District Coroner, Mr. Claude Mack, a dapper gent with grey hair greased to his scalp and a smile that seemed out of place at times but put many a heart-broken witness at ease. Emily was the 'star witness' at Miriam's inquest.

Her's was a dramatically understated story. The sisters took it in turns to serve the others cups of tea in bed of a morning. On Wednesday 15 March, it was Miriam's turn. "About threequarters of an hour after I had had the tea, I went downstairs", continued Emily. "The hearth was tidied-up. But my sister was nowhere to be seen. Her nightdress and dressing gown were on a chair in the hall, which was quite usual because she tended to dress in the living room". Having looked around the rambling house and failed to find her sister, Emily went to the Church, thinking she may have gone to the Communion

1. The Main Street

Service. She was not there. Emily, trying to control her growing anxiety, called on friends nearby. She wasn't with them, either. Emily went down to the river. She couldn't see her on the towpath...

Quite what time they got up wasn't said at the inquest but after her detailed search of the centre of the village, Emily called the police... and it was only 8am when Police Constable G. H. Ricketts was asked to organise a more detailed search. At 2pm, Miriam's body was found. Poor Emily told the Coroner that her sister had been depressed of late but had never said she wanted to end her life. Probably that was the most heart-breaking aspect. The sisters had shared everything throughout their lives. Yet such was the "stiff upper lip" philosophy at the time, Miriam had kept secret the most important thing in the whole of her world.

Married sister Charlotte Mary Hollingworth, the oldest of the sisters, was 76 when she passed away on 7 April 1964. Her husband died on 17 December 1969 aged 82.

Mabel moved to live in Charles Street, Newark, but was made an associate member of North and South Muskham Mothers' Union by friends determined that she must not lose all contact with the village. After all, the kind heart had made it her business to tend to the flowers for the War Memorial within St. Wilfrid's Church for many years. One cannot help but ponder whether there was one fallen hero in particular she remembered; after all, she would have been in her mid to late 20s during the First World War, as were most of the eight men who sacrificed their lives "For God, King and Empire" as the memorial in St. Wilfrid's Church says. The eight are:

Private F. W. Boulton	Gunner J. Knowles
Sgt. E. Gascoigne	Private G. Talbot
Private J. A. Guy	Private C. B. Walton
Private J. T. Hough	Sergeant F. Ward

Mabel Streeton died in Newark General Hospital at the age of 80 on 28 April 1969, taking with her the mystery of whether she had carried a torch for any of the village's lost heroes of a half-century earlier.

Annie Kathleen (Kathy to all her friends), the 'baby' of the family who had become Mrs. Frederick Hooper late in life, was 83 when she died on 26 July 1986. Freddie, who had spent much of his working life with Kelham Dairy and continuing as a member of the North Muskham Church bell ringing team long after failing eyesight left him almost blind, followed 18 months later, on 28 January 1988 aged 77.

Meanwhile, the Staniforths' successes in moving their operation from Ossington to North Muskham and then to South Muskham was graphically illustrated in March 1955 at a special sale held by auctioneers Turner, Fletcher and Essex at the Newark Attested Cattle Market. The top price of 98 guineas (£104.90) was paid for a pedigree Friesian cow-in-calf from J. W. Staniforth & Son of South Muskham. The beast's name, 'Ossington Honeysuckle the IV', earmarked her as a member of the fourth generation of the increasingly admired stock. Honeysuckle's North Muskham crew yard was eventually erased and replaced by four family houses facing Main Street between The Willows and Waltons Lane.

WALTONS LANE
This winding route from the Main Street/Mackley's Lane junction to the North Road was named after the family who extended a one-man business to a company with a workforce of 800. Unfortunately from North Muskham's perspective, Edward Dennys Losco Walton, known as Denny to all and sundry, revealed his tycoon tendencies more lastingly in the wake of his move up the Great North Road to live at Sutton-on-Trent.

His father, Edmund Charles Walton, founded the firm after immigrating from Australia. Described as "a horticultural builder", he responded to a small advertisement in the *Newark Advertiser* on 24 April 1889: "To be sold by private contract, North Muskham, Beehive Works, with sawing, planing, and other machinery. A good opening for a joinery business". What a prophetic small ad! His business developed at such a rate that he attracted joiners from all over the UK, to lodge wherever a room could be found in the village cottages, and expanded his manufacturing units until they spread halfway to the North Road by the turn of the century. So respected was E. C. Walton that he was elected one of the original eight members of North Muskham's first-ever Parish Council on 5 December 1894. An inkling of his patronage survives in a *Newark Advertiser* report from 25 March 1899 that 42 of his employees were entertained to supper at the Lord Nelson Inn. The report adds: "Host Richmond provided an excellent repast. The rest of the evening was spent in a social manner, with music and singing".

By 1905, the Waltons family firm had grown to such an extent that it included a huge social room, an "institute". More than 120 crowded into it to celebrate the opening of the new Methodist Chapel in September that year. And while St. Wilfrid's Church was closed for massive – and overdue – renovations from March 1906 to May 1907, services were held in Mr. Walton's institute.

1. The Main Street

He didn't have to wait to get to heaven to reap rewards, either. He won the highest reward at the 1905 Manchester Exhibition for "the best-designed poultry house and appliance" – one of many accolades earned by the company at such events in cities all over the UK in the age before newspapers, televisions and the internet allowed entrepreneurs to spread their sales messages.

Unable to expand any further in North Muskham, Waltons sold their plant on 6 February 1908, vacated their mini-community of buildings and moved to Sutton-on-Trent – to a site sandwiched between the main railway line and the Great North Road that made it doubly easy for him to dispatch his sectionalised wooden buildings far and wide.

But E. C. Walton & Co chose North Muskham for the site of the first Government-subsidised bungalow. It was built in eight weeks in October and November 1920. The walls were expanded metal with a cement covering. The roof was asbestos tiles. The first occupier was one of the family's sons, E. D. L. Walton. Denny was born in 1887 (a year before the foundation of such blessed institutions as county councils and the Football League). Far from content to rest on his father's laurels, he was in his 20s when he showed his own mettle. Despite being rejected as unfit for service in the First World War (1914–18), he still managed to spend four-and-a-half years fighting on the North-West frontier in India (and so became possibly the first person from our little village to confront the ancestors of the Taliban). He became an innovative legend in his own lifetime but was only 67 when he died, on 10 April 1954, after moving to the grander family home in Sutton-on-Trent, Tudor Court.

CHERRY COTTAGE: PICTURE POSTCARD IN THE GARDEN

The Brown family, occupants in the 1950s of the little cottage tacked onto Rockery House, used to deliver milk in tin cans from the North Road Farm when it was occupied by Grandma Doncaster, who proudly kept on the herd of 100 milkers that had been built up by her late husband.

The longest surviving member of the family sired by William Brown, Vera M. C. Brown was born in 1910 and lived to the age of 89 in the picture postcard cottage surrounded by the land-tillers ancient and modern who were at the heartbeat of the village. (More of the modern part – horticulture – when we return to Main Street.) William, who hailed from Wisbech in East Anglia and met his wife Louisa while working in Essex, was one of the many joiners and carpenters lured to the village by Waltons. They were aged 48 and 34 respectively at the time of the 1901 census, when they already had five offspring: Langwith (14), Margaret (11), Stanley (8), Evelyn (5) and Wallis (9 months).

Cherry Cottage, which was named after an earlier occupant called Mr. Cherry, looked out across Waltons Lane on a little building just past Staniforth's farm buildings, in which Muskham's defences were organised during the Second World War. It was the inauspicious, hastily-found headquarters for Special Constables including Billy Bourne, Harry Clipsham, Frank Davenport, Billy Gascoigne, Jack Needham, Harold Phillips-Moul, Ray Rippin and no doubt several more whose names have been lost with the passage of time.

Vera Brown left North Muskham in 1978 and retired to a flat in Balderton.

ASHFIELD: 40 YEARS IN THE SAME JOB

Fred Osborn, a fitter at Ransome & Marles for more than 40 years, moved from his home town of Grantham to North Muskham in 1941. He wed Geoff Partridge's distinctively-named daughter Almena (her friends called her 'Mena'). The newly-weds moved into her parents' place – the first Waltons-built bungalow the stroller would come across, on the right-hand side of the lane about a third of the way from the Main Street towards the North Road. Like innumerable factory workers of the era, Fred was a keen gardener.

The Osborns had a daughter, Joan, who seems to have gone to the Coronation fancy dress as a magician (well, she wore a pointy hat). When she grew up, she became Mrs. D. Marshall.

As for her Dad, Frederick Thomas Osborn was only 64 – a few months short of retirement and the prospect of many more happy hours in the garden – when he died in Newark Hospital on 7 December 1966.

SILVERDENE: HOME TO A BUS DYNASTY

The founder of Wright and Sons, coach operators, of Lincoln Road, Newark, lived in the larger of the two Waltons-built bungalows – the one that was originally built in 1920 as a show home and occupied by the leader of the firm that devised and constructed it.

Charles H. Wright was a big, stout man who bravely launched his company in 1926, when the country was virtually paralysed by a national strike, and continued to take an active interest in its progress until only shortly before he passed away, aged 89, on 23 January 1963, one of many Muskham victims of a particularly harsh winter. In the 1950s, the company ran services from Ollerton into Newark by a variety of routes – including one (just one!) to Bathley and back on Wednesdays and Saturdays; and vied for the outings trade to the seaside, etc.

By the time of his death, Mr. Wright had been a widower for the best part of 14 years, his wife having died on 1 February 1949. He had made his two

1. The Main Street

sons, Leslie and Frank, partners in the company and it continued to thrive throughout the second half of the 20th century and, as Travel Wright, into the 21st after moving from its long-time home at the foot of the Lincoln Road railway bridge in Newark to the town's Brunel Industrial Estate.

BACK ON MAIN STREET
ROCKERY HOUSE: FIELDS OF FRUIT AND VEG
The imposing south-facing house at the junction of Waltons Lane with Main Street was occupied by the Field family, who ran a thriving fruit and vegetable shop in Newark. Much of the produce for the townies was produced in the market garden that stretched along Main Street and up Waltons Lane. In addition to greenhouses and seemingly endless plots of vegetables, they also had room for a tennis court – at the time, the ultimate sporting sign of affluence – where sundry village folk would be encouraged to play.

Thomas Field was probably as close to a retail tycoon as Muskham possessed, but you'd never have guessed his status as he rode around on his bike in the 1950s, by which time he was in his 60s. Born in Somerset, he never lacked confidence in his commercial potential. He opened his first shop with a partner in Sheffield before setting up his own business in Newark in 1910, when he was only 23 years old. He wed Miss Marian Smith of Rolleston and they became a mighty fine team.

Marian was "noted for her specialisation in floral work" according to her obituary in the *Newark Advertiser* after she died on 28 September 1956. A measure of the esteem in which the family was held can be gleaned from the fact that, before their next football match in the Newark & District Minor League, North Muskham's under-18-year-olds stood, heads bowed, for a minute's silence as their instinctive mark of respect. The equally well-liked Mr. Field died at the age of 80 on 12 April 1967.

The Fields had two daughters. Celia married Mr. G. B. De Borde and had two children, of whom Roger and his family lived in a bungalow in the old family grounds at the time this book was composed. Marion remained single, devoted to the family business until it closed and to The Rockery until her death on 18 January 1995.

SUNNYDENE: OWL IN AN IVY BUSH
Harold Corbridge had married a Walton, one of the daughters from the building family, leaving at home in Sunnydene his intelligent spinster sister Bertha Corbridge with their father, who was head of the village school at Weston. Bertha was a pupil-teacher in the era before students had to go away

to college, when it was sufficient for them to learn classroom control, etc, from another teacher. Pater was one of the old school, recalls Peggy Granger, who in the 1950s took special interest in such characteristics as she embarked on her own teaching career.

For example, come 3.45pm when the children were supposed to go home, he would sometimes keep them in until 4.15pm, explaining that he did not want them to grow up to be clock-watchers.

As soon as Miss Corbridge was deemed knowledgeable enough to teach children at home, she revealed herself to be much more understanding. For example, children as young as three would go to her, especially if their mothers were working in the fields picking potatoes or mangles, or singling sugar beet or helping with the harvest. Little more than babies, they would take their favourite dollies for company. Some teachers would encourage the tiny, terrified children to grow up by throwing dolly on the fire, whereas kindly Miss Corbridge would sit dolly in a chair until it was time to go home.

In the days when many loving parents were prepared to pay for special tuition of their offspring, Miss Corbridge was known to her mischievous young ladies as "the owl in an ivy bush". And why not? After all, owls are terribly wise. And such was the extent of Miss Corbridge's shock of curly hair, who could be sure a canny creature was not nesting in there..? The fact is that she taught upstairs in a bedroom, which she referred to as The Schoolroom. Marian Dye's memories are less of the lessons, more of the meals that Miss Corbridge used to prepare on her paraffin stoves: "Ginger jam and rice pudding. She seemed to have rice pudding in an oven every day". Of an evening, she would read the library books delivered to her by the children from North Muskham School at the behest of Head Master King. And Miss Corbridge tested her mind every Friday evening by entertaining the Streeton sisters for a game of whist.

HOLME VIEW: QUIET START FOR HOSPITABLE FAMILY

Arthur Gleed, the occupier of the second half of the two terraced houses just past the northern end of Fields' garden that fronted along Main Street, was the '50s forerunner of a family that contributed hugely to village life for most of the next 50 years. He was related to the Duncans – Mr. and Mrs. and their son Pete – who followed him in to the house.

Mrs. Elsie May Duncan died in her 84th year in 1991, by which time two generations of her relations, the Pratts, had played large parts in the village's social life. George Pratt and his wife Minnie succeeded Len Barrett at The Crown in the late '50s. Its clientele was increased far beyond the village

1. The Main Street

boundaries by George's workmates from his day job at Hoveringham Gravel (not to mention the attraction of the Pratts' blonde and bubbly daughter Jean, who worked days in the pharmacy at Boots the Chemists in Newark then spent her evenings dispensing pints and dousing the romantic hopes of countless over-ambitious adolescents). The Pratts eventually moved to the Lord Nelson.

MAYFIELD: ECCENTRIC SURVIVOR OF BETTER DAYS

Miss Mary May was an eccentric reminder of the rapidly departing era when class and appearance counted for much more than capability and ability. In her designer clothes and with her nose in the air as she walked around the village, looking down on the inhabitants with barely disguised disdain, she was obviously the survivor of a family that had enjoyed better days and had left ample provisions for her to survive without working for a living. Beneath her steely facade, Mary obviously had a heart: she spent the Second World War years doing her bit for charity by acting as honorary secretary of the local branch of the British and Foreign Bible Society.

In a village of crueller tongues and sharper minds, middle-aged Mary and her widowed mother might have been mistaken for a couple of panto dames when they stepped out of their substantial, but gently crumbling detached house with its expansive views over the undulating Trent Farm meadows and the river towards Holme. While Mary never looked worse than sharp, her mother, an extremely large lady, is best remembered for the less than elegant sidestep she was forced to employ whenever she struggled to embark the utility bus that took her on shopping expeditions to Newark. Mrs. May was listed as the chief occupant of the house in the 1950 *Kelly's Directory*. Mary was the sole occupant by 1958, when the *Directory* was next up-dated.

What few knew was that maybe Mary had a good reason to shut her mind to the realities of life. She could not have been terribly old when her father, Eustace Henry May, went off to the Great War. An Old Magnusian who had played football and cricket, and been a powerful athlete, in his youth, he was gassed. As with thousands of Allied soldiers enveloped by strange-stinking clouds while they were trapped in the trenches in Belgium and France, it was a lingering death. Mr. May finally succumbed on 14 January 1926. He was only 41 years old; and at his funeral at St. Wilfrid's six days later, all the bearers were ex-Servicemen who had been with him in the trenches. "Great sympathy was felt for his wife and two daughters", said the *Advertiser* report of the funeral. The women would have swapped all the sympathy in the world for a few more years with Eustace Henry. And, of course, the sympathy drifted away in much the same way as that poison gas cloud of 1917.

BELFIELD: DUTCH MASTER OF SUGAR FACTORY

No Common Marketeer or pro-Euro campaigner of the late 20th century could have dared dream of a more vivid contrast of ancient and modern than the occupants of Mayfield and Belfield, which was built in 1901 by E. C. Walton, who gave it his wife's maiden name.

The Belfield occupant of the 1950s, Wilhelms De Vos had brought his family over from their native Netherlands in the 1930s to work at the Kelham Sugar Factory. Hard as it was to imagine the rest of the world could teach The Great British Farmer anything at all, especially while our islands were slowly emerging from the horrors of the First World War, a small group of Dutchmen was enlisted at managerial level to ensure the factory produced sugar more efficiently, and in sufficient quantities for it to be freed of rationing at last.

In an era when 'the campaign' – as sugar beet gathering has always been known – was strictly restricted to the pre-Christmas half of winter, it seemed as if every 'campaign' set a new productivity record. This in an era when tractors were much less powerful and much more primitive and when trailers were more like slightly glorified wheelbarrows compared with their monstrous successors that grew large enough to shatter entire agricultural drainage systems, flatten historic networks of ditches and obliterate hedges that provided welcome shelter on windy days in country lanes.

True, the smoke and steam billowing from the Sugar Factory chimneys must have contributed horribly to the pea-souper fogs and smogs that made the increasingly busy North Road even more of a danger as traffic volumes increased (and Mr. De Vos's big thick Churchillian cigars added modestly to the haze wherever he went). But as the British Sugar Corporation thrived and its electricians became clever enough to emblazon the company name in red and white lights across the front of the attractive building (in the years before the addition of huge drab silos made it look like a Soviet rocket base of the Cold War era), it was possible on crisp and clear December nights for fathers to persuade the children: "It's Santa's factory. Imagine how hard the elves are working!" Down-to-earth mothers were just happy to think that, almost a decade after the end of the War they would at last have plentiful sugar to sweeten the Christmas fare.

Wilhelms and his wife had been equally productive at home. There was no mystery as to why they had purchased such a big house, from Mr. Herbert Banks Friend (who was so grand that he employed a housekeeper, Miss Sarah Hallam from Middle Holme Lane, Sutton-on-Trent).

According to a consensus of counts by their neighbours in the '50s, there were no fewer than *nine* De Vos offspring:

- Pat married a Mr. Baker from Cross Street, Newark;
- Sis wed one of Stanley Noble's sons. Stanley sold freshly cooked cakes and pies, warm as they were tasty, from a shop at the corner of Newark Market Place and the Arcade and had a shop-cum-restaurant on Kirkgate;
- Another daughter went to live at Upton after her wedding;
- Hanni married a bank man;
- Wyk started a joinery business;
- then there was Rosie…
- and Marie…
- and Tony who became a schoolteacher…
- and Jo (pronounced Yo). He was the likely lad who specialised in socialising while all his siblings were slaving. The life and soul of many a party at the Ferry or the Nelson or the Crown (whether it be the Crown at North Muskham or Bathley). Not that there was anything malicious about him. He just liked to have fun.

In other words, the De Vos family gave North Muskham a glimpse of most of what Europe had to offer years before many, if any, of us could afford to even dream of a holiday abroad. And it was a much more convivial image than the War had left in our consciences.

POST OFFICE: HEART OF THE VILLAGE

Marian Dye, who became initially indispensable and ultimately legendary in the second half of the 20th century, had extra good reason to remember Coronation Year. It was when she presented her husband John with their firstborn, a daughter, Ann. Their son, Andrew, followed two years later.

Both Marian (nee Story) and John spent their lives at the heart of North Muskham. Marian was born in 1925. Her parents ran a grocery store that also became the Post Office from the time it moved from the Gibsons in 1937. Her father, William Story ran a productive small-holding in the fields between Main Street and the North Road (not to mention the village horse betting syndicate whose hushed yet heated deliberations enlivened many a dinner time before innocent young Marian was deputed to contact the bookmaker… all this subterfuge in the years before betting was legalized!). John's family had moved out of Trent Farm, its base for decades, when Charles Dye died. Marian was educated, along with her older sister Renee, at the Winton Private School (up an alley beside St. Leonard's Church on Lombard Street, Newark) and then Newark High School for Girls (later renamed Lilley and Stone as a Comprehensive). The girls, who had a younger sister Jean, would travel on Thomas's bus and, while at the private school, would be taken for lunch to The Temperance Hotel near the Corn Exchange.

Marian was naturally grief-stricken on 23 July 1950 when her mother, Frances Idonia Story, died at the age of 58. The closest the mild-mannered Marian ever came to being intemperate was some years earlier, in 1938, when it was decided the public telephone would be placed outside, in one of those nice red kiosks that became a symbol of modernising Britain. Until then, the public phone had been situated on a wall inside the Post Office – so anyone could use it… provided it was during opening hours. Once the contraption was in its kiosk right outside the front windows of the Post Office, it became much harder for John and Marian to ensure their babies had a good night's sleep.

In the years when very few villagers had their own telephones (there were exactly 22 in North Muskham in 1950), the kiosk became a gathering place: people would pop along to phone a friend or relative, bump into the next caller, start to have a chat, and before you knew it, half a dozen were gossiping away whether the Dyes wanted to hear it or not. As private cars became more fashionable and affordable, the situation worsened: drivers would leave their engines running while they made their calls. So it wasn't all sweetness and light, being at the heart of the village. Not that John or Marian let it put them off.

The village lost much more than a postman when John passed away at the age of 61 on 18 September 1979. For years, he had been in the habit of dropping in on old folk who lived alone, even on days when he had no mail for them, just to make sure they were in good health and wanted for nothing. He also regaled them with tales of the unexpected, such as the windy day on which he inherited a new flat cap as he cycled along the North Road back towards the village from Billy Bourne's farm. "It flew off the back of a lorry and landed in my letters carrier", he explained twixt puffs on his pipe, sparks flying onto his woolly jumper, threatening to set him alight. His listener would pat his chest to extinguish the smouldering, have a laugh with him – and look forward to the next morning's visit, irrespective of whether he actually had mail for them.

Despite spending hours more than was strictly necessary on his round – his chats and checks would now be deemed the job of social services – John also ran the family smallholding. His potato field eventually became the Willow Drive development. Upon his death a seat on the village playing field became a tangible memorial to John.

And another memorial seat appeared, this time at the junction of Main Street and Nelson Lane, all too soon, after young Andrew's life of being as valuable to the village as his Dad was ended in a road accident on the old

1. The Main Street

North Road at South Muskham. Marian still had as neighbours her daughter Ann, in Chapel Yard, and Andrew's children Lee and Lydia in a house built behind what used to be Kemp's Cottages for old folk in need of charity help.

SILVERDENE: HEROISM, MUSIC AND MEMORIES

In the former Plough Inn pub between the Post Office and bustling Chapel Yard lived one of North Muskham's extended families: War hero Cliff Garwood, his wife Rosie, their children Colin (born in 1946) and Mick (who came along 18 months later) and Rosie's brother, Syd Thurman, who became probably the only church organist in the history of the world to earn his own bar stool in his favourite village pub. Syd and Rosie were the offspring of Samuel Thurman, last landlord of the Plough.

It was entirely fitting that the family should span village life from serious church services to pub sing-alongs: a century earlier, the Plough Inn had been the venue for inquests into sudden deaths in the village. Coroner W. M. Newton carried out two such inquiries in eight days in 1856. On 11 May, he decided that the 6-month-old son of George Key had died of natural causes. On 19 May, he heard that 60-year-old John Norman had died as he sank into his chair on returning home from a Chapel service. Coroner Newton recorded a verdict of 'dead by the visitation of God' according to a subsequent report in the *Newark Advertiser*. A century on, all that remained of such dramas were the old beams around which Silverdene was built.

Somewhat sensationally, Syd Thurman was hauled before the Newark Borough Magistrates on 19 November 1945 to admit a summons of driving a motor car without due care and attention at the junction of Castlegate with the Great North Road on the night of 28 October. Syd, on his way home from a shift at Worthington-Simpson where he was a progress clerk, explained he'd been briefly blinded by a lamp (remember, Britain was still emerging, blinking, from the Wartime black-out) when he collided with a lorry. He was fined £2 and also ordered to pay costs of £7 5s 5d (£7.27), which was a good few weeks' wages.

This brush with notoriety was extremely fleeting. Syd was well on the way to becoming an invaluable churchman. Colin recalls being a cherubic curly-haired five-year-old (author's description, not Colin's) when he first became the organist's little mate. He says: "I used to go and pump the organ at South Muskham. The North Muskham organ was electrically-driven so it didn't need pumping, so I used to sit on a box and look down over the balcony while he played the organ". Uncle Syd's love of the keyboard was well satisfied at home. "We always had a piano", says Colin. "That went in 1968, just before the family left to live in South Muskham. We also had a harmonium and piano accordion".

But playing music was only one of Syd's hobbies. He also enjoyed playing darts and dominoes for the teams at 'the Ferry', where his devotion was eventually recognised by a unique ceremony. To celebrate his 50 years of loyal custom, Syd was presented with his own bar stool.

Cliff's loyalty was such that he served in the Army throughout the Second World War – then came home to spend his working life at Worthington-Simpson. He was never far away from the heat of battle: he fought through Africa with Field Marshal Montgomery's Desert Rats; and at Simmo's, he was a fettler in the foundry.

The lads were brave, too, in their own way. Colin recalls cycling up and down the North Road to and from Sutton-on-Trent School from the age of seven or eight. They used to be able to catch the bus for a start, but when they were aged seven and a half, the County Education Committee deemed they were adult enough to cope with the increasing volume of traffic on the main road. "Barry Talbot was my mentor – he taught me how to cope", says Colin. And, by one of those coincidences that tempts one to believe all life truly is a circle, after the Garwoods and Syd moved to South Muskham, into Silverdene moved... Mr. and Mrs. Barry Talbot and their children!

Sydney Morris Thurman died at the age of 78 on 20 June 1997. He was buried in South Muskham Churchyard next to his sister, Rosie Garwood, who had passed away on 27 March 1988 aged 66. Clifford A. Garwood continued to live in Forge Close, South Muskham, into his 80s in the 21st century. The lads both married, and continued to live in North Muskham for some time.

CHAPEL YARD
BLACKSMITH'S SHOP: A FAMILY AT WAR
Nobody cried "fix" when Mrs. Hutcheson ('Dutch' to everyone in the village) and her son-in-law George Lynn appeared among the prize-winners at a whist drive in aid of the National Society for the Prevention of Cruelty to Children on 21 October 1953. They were regulars at the village's "card nights" and there was never any hint of cruelty among the three generations of the family that shared the house attached to the Blacksmith's Shop at the junction of Chapel Yard and Main Street. But their love-hate existence was the perfect example of a family at war. A visit to Tommy and 'Dutch' Hutcheson, their daughter Dorothy, son-in-law George and grandson John was wonderful entertainment; an endless education in the black art of intimate repartee. Here's an example...

1. The Main Street

Dutch: "I've cooked yer breakfast". George: "Where've you hidden the arsenic?" Dorothy: "Arsenic'd be no good – you'd turn it sour". Tommy: "Shuttupp all o'yer – where's me cup o' tea?" Dutch: "Aaagh, bless 'im. He's deaf – he thinks we're talking about him behind his back". George: "Silly old sod". Dutch: "You'll be old one day". Dorothy: "Not if I've owt to do wi' it". George: "You've nowt to do wi' owt – get back in the kitchen". Dutch: "Is the lad up yet?" Dorothy: "Come on John – two buses have gone already". John (strolling down stairs): "Then there's two to come, isn't there? Where's my breakfast?"

Now to explain… Old Tommy Hutcheson was the village's last blacksmith; and although there were precious few horses to shoe in the North Muskham of the '50s, that did not stop him rising every morning and firing up the furnace in his Blacksmith's Shop. For decades afterwards, the wall bulged out into Chapel Yard, catching the unwary motorist (literally) – a typically unusual monument to a wonderfully determined character whose occupation had perished in the name of progress.

Despite the unsafe appearance of the building, George (his weather eye forever seeking a chance to improve his finances) planted a threequarter-size snooker table in the loft of the Blacksmith's Shop. It was reached via a rickety wooden ladder, the foot of which was guarded by old Tommy's guard dog – a yappy little terrier whose ambition was to extend its lead that vital extra few inches so that it could reach its human targets. As if those dangers were not sufficient, the attic floor was so uneven that one walked downhill to break-off and the table was kept level only by George painstakingly lodging his used Park Drive cigarette packets under each leg. George charged all-comers 1d or 2d a game, which he would pocket surreptitiously with a glance over his shoulder to make sure neither of the women of the house was watching. The all-comers were mainly adolescents seeking warmth and company on a chilly evening but also included a middle-aged little bloke called Danny Stubbs, one of the sometime occupants of a caravan that stood in the back garden of the Newcastle Arms.

Chapel Yard prepares for a day at the seaside (from left) front: Horace Johnston, Bernard Cottam, John Lynn, Allen Faisey. Back: Phyllis Johnston, Mrs. Hallam, Mrs. Munks, Joy Faisey.

There was good reason for George's wariness: he was half the size of his wife, who was as roly poly as her Mum. The only thing they had in common was an adoration of John, who was about 10 at the time of the Coronation and, after education at North Muskham Primary and Newark's new Sconce Hills Secondary Modern Schools (and learning to beat his Dad at snooker), began a career as a tailor by working at John Collier's Newark branch. That he was never late was entirely due to the persistence of his Mum and Grandma, who both had hearts of gold. If teenage John loved anything better than his sharp suits, it was his bed of a morning. So it was just as well four Lincolnshire Road Car buses went through the village at around 8.30am each Monday to Friday. I reckon that when the first bus rumbled past, he opened one eye. When the second appeared, he opened his second eye. With the third, he walked into his clothes and dashed downstairs. And caught the fourth with either Dutch or Dot virtually carrying his breakfast (and him) to the bus stop. Wonderful entertainment for this paper boy, who was paid 2s 6d a week by George to deliver to the whole of Bathley before school – and a tanner extra to man his general store for the rest of a Saturday morning. That tanner (2½p) made the difference between a Saturday night at the Savoy Cinema in Newark and an evening in with Mum. 'General store' is a bit grand for George's shop. It was hardly bigger than a corridor. And he would greet his customers with grumbles such as: "Ain't you anything better to do than bother me?" But he packed in most provisions. And it sure beat catching the bus to Newark if you only wanted a couple of items. It was also safer than the fish and chip shop George used to run. Neighbours would take bets on how long it would be before he blew himself up.

There was an explosion one 'Mischief Night' as the eve of Bonfire Night was known. Some said it was Doug Smalley who had found a fire-cracker left by the war-time soldiers in the Old Hall. He (allegedly) tossed it through the door of the Blacksmith's Shop, it landed in a tin can which acted as an echo chamber when it went off. Only Old Tommy didn't hear it; he simply could not understand why his little haven had suddenly filled with smoke and cordite.

Even more amazing, the family never imploded, But they did provide some amazing entertainment. Come quieter times, John married and moved to live in Bathley.

COTTAGE: WE LOSE THE JOKER IN THE PACK
The Cottams, who lived in the south-facing cottage attached to the living quarters of the Blacksmith's Shop, were the first family to escape when new-fangled council houses began to spring up across the district. It was North

1. The Main Street

Muskham's loss that they moved up the North Road to Cromwell. There was Mr. and Mrs. Cottam and their children – John; the lovely Thelma, who became Mrs. Tinsley when she married a joiner and undertaker who lived at Collingham; and Bernard, the unforgettable Bernard, who was an instinctive entertainer long before it became ritual for children to cheek their elders. Not that Bernard was ever offensive: his victims were invariably left laughing at his sense of humour rather than reeling at his audacity – to such an extent that many of us seriously believed he'd make it as an entertainer.

But, these being the Flinty '50s, when Bernard left school in 1955, there was no way he would be allowed to live on his wits. So he went to work for the East Midlands Gas Board, sweet-talking newly-weds into buying all kinds of new appliances (though even he couldn't sell his wares to his former neighbours, because, of course, North Muskham was never blessed with a gas supply). Even though Bernard committed the enormous treachery of playing football for Sutton-on-Trent at a time when North Muskham FC seemed poised to rule the Newark and District League, he remained enormously popular and became a cause of even greater envy in August 1966 when he married one of his new neighbours in Cromwell, Cynthia Lambert. Alas, Bernard died at a ridiculously early age, 35, from injuries received when he fell while painting the upstairs window of their home.

2 CHAPEL YARD: PETER, 16, GOES TO WAR FOR MUM

The Mussons – Mrs. and her youngest son Peter – lived in the south-facing cottage between the Hutchesons/Lynns and the terraced row. A quiet lad, Peter joined the Army at the age of 16. He went to fight in the Second World War to boost Mrs. Musson's widow's pension of 5 shillings (25p) a week. Peter, who saw service on a Bren Gun carrier in Italy, explained: "I was barely 17 when we landed in Italy and got involved in the Battle of Anzio, but I was nothing special, you understand. There were several lads like me. There was no money for widows and my Dad had died when he was only 36". He was the father of five, too. George, Alice, Alf and Hilda were all older than Peter, who went on: "When I joined the Army, they paid me 7 shillings (35p) a week and half of it came directly back home every week to help my Mam". He also picked up a few pence in pin-money by repairing fellow soldiers' boots – having begun to learn the trade pre-War at Combes in Newark.

Peter wasn't always considered a hero. Years before the Second World War, when the village celebrated King George V's Jubilee with a party in the paddock between Chapel Yard and The Hollies, every child was presented with a commemorative mug. Every child, that is, except Peter. The reason?

The task of distributing the mugs fell to Norman King, the village school headmaster who was feared and respected in equal measures. Mr. King refused to give a mug to Peter on the grounds that, as a young boy, he had been sent to Norwell School. Every day, he walked past North Muskham School, up Norwell Lane, over Norwell Hill to be bullied as an invader from another planet – and back again after lessons and torments – because his Mam refused to submit him to Mr. King's harsh brand of discipline. Peter presumed that, as a punishment for being so disloyal to his local school, Mr. King asked him to pay two shillings (10p) before he could be admitted to Chadd's field where the party was being held. Peter declined to pay. He couldn't have found a spare two bob, anyway. But he did find a gap in the hedge and snook into the field.

By the early 1950s, by a wry twist of fate, Peter was making daily visits to Mr. King's school, as part of his driver's job with Thomas Tours. He was collecting the hot dinners which he then delivered by taxi to the schools at Norwell, Caunton and South Muskham. And he was still upsetting the teachers. "Miss King kept reporting me for whistling", he says. "I was in the habit of whistling wherever I was but she took exception to it, and kept reporting me to Thomases".

And although he moved to work at High Marnham Power Station after the bus business closed down, Peter continued for years to help countless neighbours with their transport – by mending their bicycles at extremely generous rates.

While his Mam died, aged 69, on 20 January 1962, Peter remained a valuable contributor to village life in the early years of the 21st century, frequently making early morning forays from his bungalow on Main Street to mow a considerable part of the Churchyard, where he had buried his beloved wife, Alice, in the mid-1990s. Despite being in failing health, he kept the north side of the Churchyard tidy until only weeks before his death, on 16 February 2003.

CHAPEL YARD TERRACE: SIX OF THE BEST – AND MORE

The occupants of the terrace of six south-facing two-ups, two-downs shared a water pump across the other side of the Yard, had a dash to the row of lavatories at the bottom (no pun intended) end of their allotment gardens towards the North Road, but never lost the instinct for mutual help. These were the families who were, in many ways, at the heart of the village:

The Munks lived at No.3. Jack was one of the platelaying gang on the railway. His wife Hilda was one of the Ward family from down Main Street.

1. The Main Street

Salts of the earth, both of them, always willing to lend a hand, always a part of the social fabric of the village.

Then there were the Faiseys. Joy, fittingly for a Mum who liked to have fun, made sure sons Allen and Tony were up for the Coronation Day fancy dress parade. Allen was a cowboy with the biggest ten-gallon hat and shiniest six-shooter this side of the Great North Road. Tony was a butcher in borrowed apron and straw boater, with meat made out of wood on a lathe by his clever old Grandad who lived at the end of the Terrace.

Joy Hallam had worked for seven years in the Brass Shop at Ransome & Marles before marrying a Geordie called Albert Faisey (known to all as 'Titch' because of his stature) and having the two lads. Her next long-term job – apart from the endless task of motherhood – was delivering newspapers to help her cousin Jim Graves, who had returned from the Second World War looking like his own ghost. He had been taken prisoner by the Japanese at Singapore, spent five years almost starving in a succession of camps riddled with disease and death; and clearly his survival instinct was as great as the faith of his parents, who placed this notice in the *Newark Advertiser* in the appropriate issue of 1945 when they still had no idea whether he was alive or dead:

Pte. J. H. Graves, PoW Japan.
Loving birthday greetings for your 25th birthday, 31 March.
God grant you a safe and speedy return.
From your loving Mother, Father, sisters and brothers.

Five or so years later, Jim inherited the newspaper delivery business from his uncle, Lol Garland – a middle-aged man so conscientious that, when his motor car broke down, he walked from Sutton-on-Trent round North Muskham and Bathley (and probably one or two other parishes) until he was literally worn-out. It never occurred to him not to bother. But he never fully recovered. He died shortly afterwards. Jim was still physically frail. But psychologically he was strong enough to cope with anything, having withstood the horrors of the worst PoW camps – and he had Joy's ever-lasting support and waspish humour to sustain him.

She continued with the daily deliveries for some time after Jim sold the franchise (to use a modern cliché) to George Lynn. Far be it from Joy to allude to George's lack of physical stature, but she was in the passenger seat of his car as he drove along Bathley Bottom one day when she was astonished to see a young mother leap into the hedge bottom, dragging her pram with her. George stopped and got out to ask what was wrong. The lady loudly berated him, explaining that she thought the car was propelling itself because she couldn't see a driver through the windscreen.

Come rain, shine, snow, fog and more rain, Joy always had the knack of bringing sunshine... even though she and her best friend Bet Worthington (the blonde bombshell from Ferry Lane) arrived at the Crown Inn, Bathley, with dark news one night long before street lights appeared on the rural scene. They'd seen a ghost. "It was like a 10-year-old boy", insists Joy, her memory undimmed by the best part of 50 years. "We'd been to the Fox at Kelham and we were biking to Bathley, and just before we got to Sleath's farm, there it was... Came out of the hedge, flailing its arms as ghosts do. We just put our heads down and didn't stop until we got to Bathley Crown". Thankfully, the experience did not deter them. Joy and Bet were life and soul of many a gathering for years to come.

Titch eventually departed for pastures new. Tony emigrated to Australia to make a fine life for himself. Allen married and moved to live in Normanton-on-Trent but remained in touch with the village of his birth. Joy moved to live in Newark but kept an eye on Muskham – from the windows of the bus transporting her to see her brother Ted in Carlton-on-Trent a couple of times a week.

The Johnstons next door ran the football club. Harold, a wiry little bloke who hailed from the north-east of England via service in the RAF was a painter by day, but was much more important on a Saturday afternoon as the trainer, secretary and general inspiration of a team that was entirely his creation. His wife Phyllis (nee Stimpson) was the kit washer, cheer leader and no-nonsense Mum to under-18s and seniors alike. Older son Alan was a dashing forward when he was not on National Service and, later, a journalist of considerable versatility who also found time to establish a Youth Club across the Yard at the Church Hall when the post-war baby boomers threatened to turn into rebellious teenagers. Younger son Horace ('Ottie') was a creative inside forward (attacking midfielder in modern parlance), high-scoring opening batsman for the village cricket team and, in real life, went on to make a career in printing.

The Barratts at No.6, Tom and his wife were the newcomers at Coronation time. They moved in to Chapel Yard after the death of old Mrs. Talbot, 'Grannie Hannah' as she was known to the village. The matriarch of the family that bestowed Herbert, Archie, Bill and young Rosie on the village was 88 when she passed peacefully away on 1 March 1953. Mrs. Barratt was a worthy successor; an ideal occupant of caring, sharing Chapel Yard. "She was a good woman", says Joy Faisey. "She would always help you".

1. The Main Street

Of the Barratt sons, Len wed the Goodwins' daughter Cath up at the Crown at a time when it did not make enough profit to rank as a full-time job. So he was also foreman of one of the gangs that worked in the Highways Department of the local council. And the other Barratt son, Alf, was in the vanguard of an increasing number of young adult villagers who realised they were more likely to thrive in an urban environment. He went to live in Foster Avenue, Newark, when he married his wife, Edna. Having served his apprenticeship as an electrician in Newark, he then went to work at the increasingly important and imposing Staythorpe Power Station, where the nationalised wages were much higher than private contractors could pay.

Chapel Yard neighbours Mrs. Munks and Tony Faisey (plus smarter than the average socks).

The Carnells occupied No.7. For a pair of sisters who never moved far from their roots, Doris and Amy were dogged by despair. Amy moved to the top of the village when she married Bill Cox, but then spent much of her life in a wheelchair after falling down the stairs. Doris stayed with her mother, Lilly, in the Chapel Yard cottage where she had been born – but was killed by a train on her way back from a walk to inspect the council house she was being shifted into at South Muskham. So much for hum-drum lives!

Mr. Carnell had been a kindly Dad. He worked on the waterways and was missed by more than his immediate family after he died in the late 1940s. Joy Faisey remembers that when her eldest, Allen, was two or three, Mr. Carnell used to take him for walks… "he would even take him into Newark and buy him a toy". Maybe, in his mind, Allen was the son he never had. Or maybe the walks were a soothing escape from the harsh realities back home.

Doris was a loyal daughter but always painfully shy. So much so, she wouldn't even go to Newark to get her hair done. She used to pop to Joy's when she wanted a trim… and would always insist on 'paying' with vegetables out of the family garden at the end of the row. Problem was, one morning,

Joy had spotted where Mrs. Carnell had emptied the guzunder rather than take it all the way to the lavatories at the bottom of the garden. "I hope she doesn't pay me in mustard cress", thought Joy. But, sure enough, Doris appeared shortly afterwards bearing a bowl full of mustard cress. "No, no!" protested Joy. "You're too kind to me. Give it to Phyllis! She's got three hungry fellas to feed as well, you know". It was probably as well Phyllis Johnston washed the cress thoroughly as she prepared a salad tea for husband Harold and sons Alan and Horace… or maybe we've at last solved the secret of how the village footballers and cricketers managed to p** on the opposition so often. Whatever, Joy and Phyllis were good enough friends for Joy to confess what she'd seen Mrs. Carnell pour on the cress… and decades later, as Joy walked into Phyllis's 80th birthday party, Joy asked: "What's for tea?" Phyllis piped up: "Mustard cress!"

Meantime, Doris had died, aged 58, in the late springtime of 1967, leaving her old neighbours completely mystified as to how she had managed to *walk* in front of an 80-mile-an-hour express train. She always walked with her head down, sometimes locked so tightly in her own little world that she wouldn't even acknowledge neighbours as they passed in the narrow confines of Chapel Yard or Main Street. On the fateful day, she would have been even more distracted. The Yard cottages were to be knocked down; she was being moved to the new council estate at South Muskham, and had walked to inspect her new home.

Even so, the official story – reported in the *Newark Advertiser* on 3 June 1967 – was starkly nightmarish. Doris walked back from Forge Close to South Muskham level crossing. Once there, she spent several minutes chatting with the gatekeeper on duty, John Black, who lived in Sleaford Road, Newark. She then walked on – into the path of the London-bound express. The verdict was that Doris died accidentally.

The Hallams at No.8 were Joy Faisey's parents. John and Mrs. Hallam lived at the end of the terrace furthest away from the Main Street from 1918; and by 1953 were particularly grateful to still have with them their son, Ted.

Born in 1929, Ted contracted infantile paralysis when he was two. When they admitted him to Harlow Wood Orthopaedic Hospital, set in Sherwood Forest just outside Mansfield on the road to Nottingham, they didn't expect him to survive so they put him in the front row of beds. He had a smashing view of the trees but all he remembers is: "Boy! It was cold. All the time. It was like sleeping in a cart shed. They didn't coddle you in there".

From which you'll gather that, against all odds, he survived. And thrived. Even though he was paralysed from the waist down, he got around – initially

1. The Main Street

on a contraption that looked like a perambulated serving tray. It might have been made for the tobogganists who career down mountains head-first at Winter Olympics except, as North Muskham was even less hilly then than it is now (because there were no bridges over the A1) Ted had to propel it himself. "I used a broom handle that Dad had cut down to size", he says. That brush handle wasn't the only indication of what a clever bloke Ted's father was. John William Hallam was a builder by trade who spent the bulk of his working life with Ransome & Marles after first coming to the area in the gang that built the Tubular Bridge over the railway. His hobby was the new-fangled wireless, and he was a dab-hand at making sets, much to the admiration of those around him.

When it was obvious that, even with his legs in irons, young Ted would need help to get around, John turned his mind and his skills to the problem… and came up with what looked like a perambulated tea tray but was, in fact, a three-wheeled trolley. There were two wheels beside where Ted sat; and one wheel at the front, which was linked to the rest by a pair of old bike forks. To turn the front wheel, Ted would lean in the appropriate direction. Just about the most heart-rending sight in North Muskham was of Ted, with his legs in irons, forcing his first wheelchair through the ruts of the unmade lane that was Chapel Yard, along the village streets and over the Bathley Lane crossing to the football and cricket pitches, where he would watch his contemporaries running around (and be excused if he ever paused to wonder, 'Why me?').

He was 18 when he bade farewell to Harlow Wood for the last time. For 16 years, he'd been in and out to have various examinations, and to have his leg supports adjusted as he grew. Cold to the bitter end, his last stint coincided with the deepest snow for decades.

Not surprisingly, his plight touched hearts. The bell ringers at St. Wilfrid's welcomed him along on their trips to other churches. And, unknown to Ted, Len Barratt and the regulars at the Crown Inn had a series of raffles to raise money for a proper wheelchair that he could sit in. Ted and his sister Joy still argue over how much it cost. It's something siblings are allowed to do after so long watching out for each other. One reckons the drinkers raised £47, the other insists it was nearer £75. Either was a massive sum, reflecting how much Ted was valued by the community. They both agree it was worth its weight in gold. It also had three wheels, big ones either side the seat, a smaller one at the front which was connected to the handlebars by a bike chain. Ted had to reach forwards and upwards to reach the top of the handlebars so that he could both propel and steer the machine by pushing pedals round with his hands.

He was so fully mobile now, he started work at the REME Camp at the bottom of Lincoln Road, Newark, in 1958 (aged 29). His wheelchair had no shelter, but he hand-pedalled it in all weathers down the old North Road past the Sugar Factory and through Newark almost to Winthorpe Airfield, did a day's work, then pedalled back. He can't say what he did for his living because he signed the Official Secrets Act when they took him on – "and you sign for life".

But his achievements are no secret. He didn't just pick up a wage packet; he collected admirers by the day. Not that he expected or received favouritism. His foreman was Reg Dickenson, the captain of North Muskham's football team during its most successful years, who played at left back and tackled with all the ferocity of those weapons they probably made during the week. "Reg didn't treat me as an invalid", says Ted. "More as one of the blokes".

But Colonel Spring at the REME Camp was sufficiently moved to campaign for Ted to receive better transport; and, in time, he became the proud possessor of a three-wheel car with an engine and, equally important, a cabin to protect him from the elements. Ted, now living in Carlton-on-Trent, took early retirement in 1986, reluctantly, when Newark REME closed and its work was moved to Old Dolby in Leicestershire. He explains: "It would have meant catching a bus from Newark at 6am and not getting back before 6pm".

Clever old John Hallam died on 9 March 1963 at the age of 71. His wife, who joined the exodus to South Muskham when Chapel Yard was demolished, passed away on 6 November 1980. She had found herself in good company in Forge Close: most of 'the Yard' occupants had gone with her. They were North Muskham's loss. As early as 13 March 1951, North Muskham Parish Council had agreed there was "an immediate need" for council houses and the Clerk was instructed to enquire from the Rural District Council what prospects there were of any allocation being made. It proved the unluckiest of 13ths: the subject of council houses did not resurface at a North Muskham Parish Council meeting for more than five years. So the Rural District Council never got round to building housing for rent in this particular parish.

PEAR TREE COTTAGE: CASH FOR ALLOTMENTS

Opposite the terraced row lived three generations of a Smith family. First there were Mr. and Mrs. Harold Smith. Then the man of the house became their son, Dennis and his wife Hilda and children, Gillian and Roger.

1. The Main Street

They were preceded in Pear Tree Cottage by the Freestones – and, before them, Johnny Gascoigne and his first wife. Johnny was treasurer of the Horticultural Society and one of his duties was to collect eight shillings (40p) a year from the folk who rented the eight allotments behind the School at the top of the village.

One was dug and cultivated by the schoolboys; and the general theory was that Mr. King took most of the produce home to be cooked by his sister (his reward for teaching the boys the finer points of horticulture, you understand) though his supporters suggest he was also known to offer the odd cabbage to parents without a couple of ha'pennies to rub together – particularly parents of children who happened to be among his favourites. George and Peter Musson tended one allotment in an effort to keep their Mam in potatoes and greens.

CHURCH HALL: AND A VILLAGE HALL PROJECT

The boxlike, brick building that was the focal point of the village for 50 years was originally a Methodist Chapel built for around £290 in 1814–15. With the growth of the Waltons' joinery business and the influx of families from all over the UK, it became too small for its purpose in the early 1900s. So the Methodists moved to a bigger Chapel, built for the princely sum of £700 in four summer months of 1905, and sold their Chapel Yard premises to the Church of England for £40. What value for money it turned out to be!

By the 1950s, it was the venue of pretty well every social activity in the village… from dignified monthly meetings of the Women's Institute to (avert your eyes, ladies) acting as the Saturday afternoon changing room for the footballers, who then had to parade along Main Street, up Waltons or Nelson Lane, across the North Road, along Bathley Lane and over the crossing to the pitch in Billy Bourne's field. The traipse back was better – except on particularly wet afternoons, when it was impossible for the players to keep their cigarettes alight.

There was escapism for the Mothers' Union, too, at a time when very few even contemplated a week's holiday on England's East Coast never mind a flight to sunnier climes: of the MU meetings in 1953, one was an American tea and another featured a talk on missionary work in India. The down-to-earth mums organised a bring and buy sale that raised £3 17s 1d (£3.85 approximately) for overseas missions.

Such were the activities in the Hall, though, in an era when television provided entertainment for only a few hours a night to maybe less than 10 per cent of the population, that it occurred to the most community-spirited

The Coronation Day celebrations that beat the rain... Above: the fancy dress contestants (from left): Top row – chimney sweep Bernard Cottam, mountie Raymond Spafford, coalman not known, cowboy Allen Faisey, tramp Horace Johnston, 'Charlie Chaplin' John Lynn. Second row – usherette Celia Ward, 'Bo Peep' Kathleen Guy, king Mark Lewis (the winner), nurse Harriet Barley. Third row – butterfly Jane Swannack, pirate ? Chadd, paper girl Marjorie Needham, Thelma Cottam, hat girl Barbara Pape, Mavis Talbot, tramp ? not known, pointy hat Eva or Jean Osborn, cook Jill Marriott, 'Bo Peep' Jean Bagguley, Dutch flower girl Judy Swannack. Front row – Jean Pape, not known, 'Britannia Valerie Ward, not known, Jacky Cockerill, 'Red Riding Hood' Donella Smalley, Josie Pape, butcher Tony Faisey.

that A Proper Village Hall was needed. The fact that South Muskham was already saving-up for one had nothing to do with it. It was also deemed irrelevant that the building between the Church Hall and Thurmans' cottage had been initially a boys' club built by the appropriately named Mr. Friend who had lived in Belfield (and was now used as a fruit store). The popular clamour was for North Muskham to have A Village Hall. Only seven years earlier the Parish Council had decided it would not be practical to try to provide one "owing to the size and total rateable value of the parish".

1. The Main Street

But The Village Hall Project was resurrected with a vengeance at a public meeting on 17 February 1955. Its purpose was simple:"to make the dream a reality". Peter Kent, on leave from his exotic job as a pilot with BOAC, provided the down to earth information. Fresh from negotiating with Clipshams to build his new house beside the river at the bottom of Mackleys Lane, he estimated a shell measuring 65ft by 35ft would cost about £700 and internal fittings could be provided for another £300. To raise the £1,000, the nucleus of a committee was formed. There was Mrs. Barbara Swannack, whose husband Frank had obviously served the village well as Chairman of the Coronation Committee. Plus Mrs. Billy Bourne, who was prominent on every women's organisation for miles around. Plus Cyril Marriott, who knew a thing or two about winning whist drives, playing other sports and spotting lovely new bricks surplus to requirements for other jobs. And Harold Johnston, the little Geordie who was turning the village into a football power in Division Two of the Newark and District League. Lest they felt the pressure of expectancy too great – and the mood of the evening was 'whatever South Muskham can do, we must do better' – they were empowered to co-opt one representative from each of the village organisations.

Alas, what ensued was more Nightmare off Main Street than making the dream a reality. South Muskham Village Hall opened in 1958, followed a few months later by Norwell Village Hall. North Muskham muddled along with the Church Hall. Alan Johnston started a Youth club there in 1957, usually attracting 18 to 25 youngsters on a Wednesday evening. In the Parish Magazine of March 1958, an article presumably written by the then Vicar, the Rev. Hilary A. Dunn, paid this tribute:

"It is one of the few Youth Clubs we have ever come across which seems to run quite happily of its own accord, though it is only fair to say that a great deal of this is due to the quiet efficiency of its excellent secretary, Alan Johnston, who more or less 'sees to' everything. Although the girls are in a distinct minority, they more than hold their own and succeed in providing us each week with first rate sandwiches and tea… There was a riotous Christmas party towards the end of January. The young ladies provided enough eats to feed nearly the whole population of North Muskham. We did our best but there were still acres of sandwiches and cakes left over at the end, so it was suggested that the Vicar might go round for the next few months bestowing it all upon the 'old people'. (We didn't think this at all a good idea and we weren't quite sure that the 'old people' would, either!) Other attractions included some of the most rumbustuous dancing we have ever seen (the girls being airborne for much of the time) and all sorts of games, culminating in a sort of break-your-shins, oh-mind-my-nylons hockey competition, in which the girls certainly gave as good as they got!"

If only the village as a whole had been so hearty! Far from harnessing all this enthusiasm into a brand new Village Hall, the socialisers watched the Youth Club disappear once Alan's work took him to live near Nottingham, and sort of adopted their old village school (and renamed it the Woolhouse Hall after its original benefactor) as a slightly bigger meeting place than the Church Hall once the new school was built at the junction of Main Street and Nelson Lane. Despite various patch-up jobs, the Woolhouse Hall began to crumble around its users' ears in the late 1970s. Simultaneously, as luck would have it, a new organisation, the North Muskham Playing Field Association had persuaded the Staniforth family, by now ensconced in South Muskham, to let it have a massive field between Nelson and Waltons Lanes (less the outer strips on which bungalows would be built alongside Main Street and Waltons Lane). Once it was discovered that the changing rooms could take the form of a wooden shed large enough to call The Village Hall, the dream of 1955 took totally unexpected shape.

But the erection of a purpose-built centre for the community did not commence until 2008.

BACK ON MAIN STREET
TRENT FARM COTTAGE: NOW YOU SEE THEM...
A succession of worthy folk and their families lived in Trent Farm Cottage, just across the Main Street from Chapel Yard, without necessarily working at Trent Farm. As traffic volumes increased during the '50s, the occupants doubtless cursed the fact that the place was so close to the road (which would help explain why there was a more rapid turn-over than in many other properties) though folk waiting for the bus to Newark had reason to be grateful for the shelter it offered from the cold nor-easterlies.

For many years, it was home to Jack Hessle, a bespectacled little middle-aged mechanic who worked for Frank Swannack, who hired out agricultural equipment such as combine harvesters to farmers for miles around. Jack was the proud owner of an Austin 7 car. It was so ancient, it had gate gears, and the gear lever and hand brake were sited between the driver's seat and the door rather than in the centre of the vehicle. But it was his pride and joy.

He was followed by the Chester family from Ossington: Ray, a farm hand who set to work on the scattered acres of Trent Farm (some fields were as far away as the hills between Bathley and Caunton), his dark haired and formidable wife, daughters Rosemary and Elizabeth plus son David. Mrs. Chester was busily engaged in the social life of North Muskham WI by 1957.

1. The Main Street

When they moved on to South Muskham's nice new council houses, they were briefly succeeded by the Faisey family of mum Joy and her sons Allen and Tony (Titch having decided to take a job up North). Fresh out of Sconnies (Sconce Hills Secondary Modern School) Allen worked briefly at Trent Farm, sadly at a time when small farmers were beginning to feel the pressures of profit lines. Allen recalls being summarily dismissed for 'deserting' his tractor in a field atop Bathley Hill one day. All these years on, it still rankles that Farmer Jepps never stopped ranting for long enough to listen to Allen explain he had had to leave the tractor to go in search of a can of water because its radiator had leaked dry.

Then came the Briggs family: Martin, his wife and two daughters, Gill and Ann. While the parents eventually became the village newsagents, both of the girls qualified as teachers.

TRENT FARM: INNOVATIONS, POLITICS – AND STRUGGLES

The reign of the Dye family had ended by the 1950s. But it is worth recording, if only to add substance to the importance of Marian Dye and her offspring to the community. Robert Dye had such foresight that Trent Farm was frequently the venue for demonstrations of new equipment back at the start of the 20th century. In 1903, more than 100 farmers from around the district accepted an invitation from the Muskham Co-operative Society to inspect "the 20th Century manure, lime and fertiliser distributor made by the J. S. Kemp Manufacturing Company of Newark Valley, New York, and for which Mather and Co of Newark and Southwell, are the local agents". Robert Dye and his wife Mary had two sons, Robert junior born in 1883 in Leicestershire and William two years later in Long Bennington before they moved to Muskham.

The good news was that Trent Farm had about 1,000 acres. The bad news in the days of horse-drawn machinery was that they were miles away, up the hills towards Caunton and Norwell; a huge drawback for a dairy farm in the days when the milkers spent most of the year out in the fields and were led in twice a day for milking. Indeed, many were still milked by hand in the '50s, when new-fangled milking machines were treated with suspicion by dairymen and cows alike.

Once the Dye family had left, Tom Ullyott preceded the Jepps family, who delivered milk around the village. The Ullyotts had a daughter, Janet, who earned a place at the Lilley and Stone High School and became one of the young bell-ringers at St. Wilfrids. While Tony Jepps fretted about how to make money out of milk, his wife became secretary of the village branch of the Newark Division Conservative Association at a time when it proudly announced it had doubled its membership even though the population of the village had fallen. Their daughter Alison was among the top prize-winners at Muskham County Primary School in July 1968; and the following year, Mum and her mates appeared to have Socialism on the run with a typically conservative approach. Their social calendar included a day trip to Blenheim Palace and a cheese and wine party. Wot? No whist drive! Alas, the farm was not proving as productive; and once the Jepps moved on, Trent Farm became a base for other businesses, such as haulage, before the farm house was demolished and replaced with a grander property, and the farm building became residences.

THE HOLLIES: HIGH FLYING DAUGHTER OF AIRMAN
The smaller farm across Main Street from Trent Farm evolved to the Chadd family via the Dyes. Mrs. Mary Chadd was the younger sister of John Dye of Post Office fame. Her husband Geoffrey had served in the RAF with distinction during the Second World War and returned home to work for the 'War Ag', the Government department tasked with maximising the productivity of Britain's green and pleasant land at a time when rationing still limited what one could buy.

Of their three daughters and son, Sally was not only the youngest and the only one to remain in North Muskham once she became an adult, but the most memorable. Even when she was at North Muskham School, she told playmates that she was going to be the Prime Minister.

She pursued her worthy ambition in that she met the then Prime Minister, Margaret Thatcher, when she stood as the Conservative candidate for Greater Glasgow in the 1984 European elections. Sally was not elected; but she continues to hold onto the family base at The Hollies into the early 21st century.

THE COTTAGE: QUIETLY GETTING ON WITH LIFE
George Dobbs was not among the high-profile villagers. He pretty much kept himself to himself, which made him typical of a 1950s 'man about the house'. He helped with good causes when asked, like in the summer of 1957 when he manned the roll-a-ball stall at a Church garden fete on the front lawn of The Willows.

He was elected onto the Parish Council in the same year without having to go through an election campaign, filling what was described as a casual vacancy. But generally he contented himself with working his shifts as a fitter and turner at Ransome & Marles – alternating between days and nights – and

1. The Main Street

keeping his garden productive enough so that his wife did not have to drag huge amounts of shopping from Newark.

Rather than be in the old cottage on her own when George worked nights, Mrs. D used to enjoy having her young niece Margaret Gascoigne to sleep over; another example of how extended families helped each other along.

BUTCHER'S SHOP: PRIME CUTS AT THE DOOR
Across Main Street from the Dobbs' cottage, Arthur Walker and his wife Violet ran the butcher's shop at the southern end of the row of cottages between the entrances to Trent Farm and Manor Farm.

Although there were some suspicions about the age of a few joints of his fresh meat – usually pertaining to how long it had lain around Winter Knight's farmyard down Crab Lane – it obviously did Arthur no harm. He lived to be 90.

Villagers too busy (or cautious) to actually visit the shop could benefit from home delivery: at one stage, Tom Charles used to take meat round on his cycle. The service was welcome in an era when housewives had to carry their shopping from Newark on the buses; and into the 21st century, a glimpse of the old shop remains in the shape of the two halves of the iron grilling over the door from which Arthur hung his beef and lamb for all passers-by to view.

BUTCHER'S COTTAGE: HUB OF THE WARD FAMILY
The Ward family was pretty much based in the cottage behind the butcher's shop (and just in front of Mr. Walker's slaughterhouse). By the '50s, the family had spread to all points of the village; and the cottage was inhabited by brothers George and Bert, both farm labourers; both physically aged before their time by the sheer effort of earning their crusts; but both fondly remembered by descendants such as their niece Val, who became Mrs. Donnelly and moved to South Muskham.

Bert was salt of the earth for Billy Bourne.

George cycled daily to and from his toils at Winter Knight's farm, flat cap pulled down to his ears and eyebrows, shoulders hunched against the wind/rain/sun/sheer effort, sucking on his pipe, looking for all the world like a slow motion *Popeye* of comic book fame. He was obviously a loyal servant: when Winter died, George was left £200 in the old farmer's will – an amazing 'thank you' from an employer whose tight fist was legendary (as we will learn when we reach Crab Lane).

One hesitates to guess who inherited the windfall from George. "He was a horse racing fanatic with my Dad", whispers Marian Dye, revealing only now one of the village's best-kept secrets in the days when gambling was not only frowned upon but illegal unless conducted in a certain way. North Muskham's way was to employ the young Marian to telephone Pennington's at Newark (in these days the public telephone was actually inside the Post Office), utter the code "LWP" and place the bets for quite a few menfolk. Alas, winners were few and far between.

GENERAL STORE: OPEN ALL HOURS FOR 50 YEARS
Stepping into the shop run by Arthur Rogers and his wife Florrie was akin to a shrouded visit to the dying embers of the British Empire. The image was aided no end by the Indian brandy in the window. At least, I think that's what it was – the window always seemed to be misted by much more than spray from the passing traffic. Once you'd stumbled inside, the shelves seemed a history lesson, appearing to contain decades worth of soaps, tins and jars. They were fabulous (but fading) evidence that Florrie had run the shop since she married Arthur in 1910. And to her enormous credit, even though she was in fading health for several years, she kept the emporium open until her death, at the age of 73, in 1962.

And here's a thought that obviously escaped the minds of the health and safety executives of the day: throughout the winter months, Mrs. Ada Bagguley, who lived in the semi-detached cottage that formed 'the other half' of the shop, used to do her washing up in her back kitchen standing on a plank of wood which was balanced on two bricks. It was her way of being prepared for the Trent finding its own level through the brick floor. The tale was recounted by Peggy Granger, who was sad to add: "All the family died of TB".

For those not terminally ill or marooned by floods from circa 1910 until motorised buses made his service redundant, Arthur Rogers took a carrier's cart to Newark every Monday, Wednesday, Friday and Saturday, terminating his service at the George and Dragon pub on Castle Gate. For years, one of his regular duties was to take Mrs. Story's dirty washing from the Post Office to Mrs. Broderick, the washerwoman, at South Muskham.

It was obviously one of the more versatile carts: Arthur also found time to deliver coal in competition with Jimmy Nickerson's horse and dray in an era, pre-central heating, when every household was warmed by solid fuel – be it best quality coal, nutty slack, new-fangled coke (which was said to contribute less to the smogs of each winter) or scavenged wood.

1. The Main Street

A dramatic portent of travelling trends had arrived in a field rented by Arthur beside the North Road on 3 October 1934. An aeroplane – a 2-seater Fuss Moth – made an emergency landing in the field. The locals took the surprise in their leisurely stride. Its wings were folded back, it spent the night between the petrol pumps and mechanics' shed at the North Road Garage – and, after refuelling, the pilot continued his journey next morning.

Six years later Arthur made headlines in the *Newark Advertiser* again as the owner of the last horse-drawn carrier's cart in the area. The story related that he used to carry 14 or 15 passengers every trip "but has carried none for the last two years".

And by the 1950s an increasing number of travelling shops were making emporia such as Florrie's all-but redundant. Lunn's had a lorry that traversed the village selling household goods (floor polish, wash powders, scrubbing brushes, etc, etc) and paraffin for the lamps that preceded electric lights in the houses.

Groceries were also a battle-ground of the delivery vans. Holland's had regular customers. So did Mason's (no relation to the family we are about to meet at Manor Farm). Meat? Take your pick of Browns from Norwell or Brewitts from Carlton-on-Trent. Foster's battled with the van from the Newark Co-operative Society (simply known as 'The Co-op') for the privilege of selling bread door-to-door though many housewives baked their own bread, along with jam tarts, scones and, for extra-special occasions, cakes – usually on a Friday so that they were fresh for the weekend.

They all saved housewives carting huge loads on the buses in an era when very few people owned cars. Not that the deliverymen ever bothered to come round the village on Market Days (Wednesdays and Saturdays). It seemed to be every housewife's duty to 'pop into town' twice a week.

Here is a list of the cost of foodstuffs in the 1950s as wartime rationing ended (remember, there were 12d to the 1s and 1s equals 5p now).

FIFTIES FOOD BILL

Item	s.	d.	Item	s.	d.
Beans (baked)	1	6	Bananas	2	0
Baking powder		7.5	Breakfast cereal…		
Biscuits (crackers)	2	2	Quaker Oats	1	8
Biscuits (wholemeal)	2	2	Rice Krispies	1	3
Butter (New Zealand)	3	11	Shredded Wheat	1	0.5
Margarine (Velto, 1lb)	2	0	Weetabix	2	0
Lard (2lb)	3	4	Cake (sponge, iced)	1	9

Item	s.	d.	Item	s.	d.
Cheese (1lb)	*1*	*3*	*Peas (processed)*	*1*	*4*
Kraft triangles (box)	*1*	*3*	*Pickle (Branston)*	*1*	*9*
Cocoa (1lb)	*3*	*8*	*Plums (Victoria, tin)*	*1*	*10*
Coffee (Nescafe)	*3*	*0*	*Pork luncheon meat (tin)*	*3*	*5.5*
Custard powder	*1*	*9*	*Raisins (1lb)*	*1*	*4*
Flour (plain, 4lb)	*1*	*11*	*Salt (drum)*	*1*	*2*
(self-raising)	*1*	*6*	*Sauce…*		
Golden syrup (tin)	*1*	*9*	*HP, bottle*	*1*	*6*
Gooseberries (tin)	*2*	*4*	*Tomato k'chup*	*1*	*6*
Gravy salt (Symington's)		*11*	*Salad cream*	*1*	*0*
Icing sugar (1lb)		*11*	*Salmon (tin)*	*3*	*0*
Jam…			*Sardines (tin)*	*1*	*2*
Apricot	*2*	*11*	*Soup (can, tomato)*	*1*	*4*
Raspberry	*3*	*6*	*Suet (packet)*	*1*	*1.5*
Lemon curd	*1*	*7*	*Sugar (2lb)*	*10.5d to 1s 2d*	
Jellies (two)	*1*	*8*	*Sweet pickle*	*1*	*11*
Milk (evaporated)	*1*	*5*	*Tea (99, a quarter)*	*5*	*8*
(sweet)	*1*	*7*	*Tinned fruit*	*1*	*9*
Mincemeat (jar)	*1*	*9*	*Tomatoes (tin)*	*3*	*0*
Onions (pickled, jar)	*1*	*9*	*Vinegar (a pint)*		*7.5*
Peas (dried)	*1*	*3.5*	*Liver salts (Andrews)*	*2*	*6*

Chocolate was a treat: biscuits 2s 1d for half-pound packet; Penguins 1s 2d for 4. You'll note sugar yo-yo'd wildly depending on the season even though the factory was so close.

Household goods were necessary to all house-proud wives: blue bags 1s for 4; candles 9d for 6; furniture polish (Mansion) 1s 6d; matches 2d a box; soap – (Wright's Coal Tar) 1s 2d for 2 tablets; shoe polish (black) 11d a tin or Tonette 6.5d; stain remover (Thawpit for greasy collars) 1s 6d; starch (Robin's) 1s 6.5d; window cleaner (Mirrorglow) 1s 3d. And then there was a choice of wash powder – Dreft 1s, Omo 1s 10d, Persil 1s 9d, Rinso 1s 9d, Spell 1s 11d, Tide 1s 11d.

Sadly, when Florrie Rogers was interred in North Muskham Churchyard early in the winter of 1962–63, Arthur was too ill to attend the funeral service. The chief mourner was their only son, Cyril. The shop died with her.

1. The Main Street

MANOR FARM COTTAGE: A KINDLY TEACHER

The Marsh family could be excused if they did not celebrate the Coronation with 100 per cent fervour. For in the year Elizabeth became Queen, the unmarried daughter of the family, 45-year-old teacher Lois May Marsh became paralysed.

They had moved up the street from Trent Farm Cottage in 1951 (the father of the family, Sam Marsh used to work at Trent Farm); and had reason to be proud of all three of their girls. Edith, who worked in Larkins' solicitors' office in Newark, married Jack Peel and they set up home together in one of the little cottages in Vicarage Lane that eventually became disused after a haulage company moved in next door. Mabel, who as a school-leaver worked for Mr. and Mrs. Story at the Post Office from 7am till as late as they liked, married Jack Trickett and moved to a cottage opposite Bob Hough, the threshing machine owner, in Bathley. Then she got a job in the kitchens at North Muskham School, where Lois taught as compassionately as the Kings were strict.

Lois used to go for long bike rides with the Storys' older daughter, Renee, and bore her increasingly debilitating illness for years. She first fell seriously ill as the Second World War got seriously underway in 1940, but stuck to her task of teaching the village children. She was the kindly lady who introduced the five-year-olds to the finer arts of learning before Mr. and Miss King added their harsher touches. Even though she was diagnosed as suffering from multiple sclerosis, she also helped look after the youngsters at St. Wilfrid's Sunday School. Lovingly tended by her mother, Ellen (who went on to live to the age of 87), Lois finally succumbed on 7 January 1963, a full 23 years after she initially began to feel poorly.

By poignant coincidence, only three weeks after her funeral at St. Wilfrid's, it was confirmed that the village school where she had taught so conscientiously, would definitely be closed. Nottinghamshire Education Committee announced it was planning to buy a field in Main Street for £3,000 and build a new school to replace both of those that had served North and South Muskham for so long.

Mother Marsh passed away on 25 April 1973. She had been a widow for 12 years: Samuel had died in his 79th year on 16 March 1961.

MANOR FARM: A RARE EMIGRATION

The greatest trauma for North Muskham in the month of the King's death was the news that the occupier of Manor Farm, William Mason, was "going abroad". Hardly anyone moved much further away than Newark. But the rest of the village took it as proof of what they'd always thought – that he was "a bit different" from them – when he let it be known that he was emigrating to Tasmania. He instructed Edward Bailey & Son, auctioneers, of Newark to dispose of "live and dead farming stock and household furniture", to wit 1 dairy cow, 13 strong store pigs, agricultural implements and machinery. In truth, Mason wasn't badly missed. Villagers' chief memory is of a man who committed the anti-social act of locking a clapper-gate in an effort to prevent people walking along the riverside near his house. Worse, he used to fell trees for no good reason. In a featureless landscape like North Muskham's the crime of lopping probably merited deportation to the colonies!

The land had already been auctioned by Bailey's on 23 January 1952 at 3.15pm precisely. Imagine the huddle of furtive bidders as dusk descended to meet the mist rising from the Trent in the grounds of the neat, white-washed farm house with its spectacular views over the river to Holme and, to the west, over its own pastures to the Main Street and the Grange. Oh no you can't! Not any more. Not since the Manor Farm House was demolished one Saturday teatime towards the end of the 21st century to help make way for a new development. The demolition gang did not even pause to erect a 'Manor Farm Was Here' plaque where in 1952 stood what the estate agents called "an important small freehold productive agricultural property with comfortable residency, substantial buildings, orchard and gardens". Bailey's were able to boast that Mr. Mason had installed mains water and electricity (while some neighbouring farmers continued to make do with a well in the yard and paraffin oil lamps). The house also boasted modern drainage and telephone (though that was very new – he wasn't listed with a phone number in Kelly's Directory of 1950).

There was also more land than many farms possessed. The High Trentside Pasture extended to an area of about 16.630 acres. There were also five lots of "fertile arable and pasture land each having hard road access and extending to a total area of about 43.850 acres".

It was all bought by the Dunn family, who came from Derbyshire. The unmarried John Needham Dunn moved in with a bachelor brother and a spinster sister. As if to emphasise their shyness, they were debited with totally blocking up the riverside towpath. It had been vital in the age when barges were pulled by shire horses. By the 1950s, the barges were powered by chugging engines. But the towpath was a Sunday afternoon magnet for strolling families. Mr. Dunn died at Manor Farm on 29 October 1961.

The vast majority of Elizabethan Muskhamites agree that the contributions to the community of Mason and Dunn were not a patch on those of their predecessor, Ernie Vickers, who used to traverse the village on the best-stocked bike imaginable. It had a basket at the front and a box at the rear, packed with vegetables as well as milk. Sybil Davenport remembers that Ernie also had "a lovely little wife" who was equally considerate.

SYCAMORE COTTAGE: HARVESTING CORONATION CELEBRATIONS

Frank Swannack (pictured) arrived in North Muskham as 'Mr. Sunshine' – a rotund, smiling, ruddy-faced agricultural contractor armed with the latest harvesting machinery – and found himself immortalised in the village's folklore as The Chairman of the Coronation Celebration Committee. His problem was that, whereas the farmers who hired him to cut their crops made sure he was rarely less than knee-deep in work, the village was drastically less productive in ideas as to what ought to happen on The Big Day.

The Parish Council had the first debate on 21 October 1952 and decided to pass on the challenge. The official minute recorded:

"The matter was discussed at great length, and it was decided to call a public meeting in the Church Hall at 7.30pm on 20 November to ascertain what form these celebrations should take and to form a local committee of representatives from all sections of the village. The Clerk was instructed to arrange the meeting and send out invitations to the various bodies".

At a time when street lights were still three years away from North Muskham, it was probably asking a bit much to call such a meeting in the dank darkness of the foggiest month of the year. Squire Edge (in effect, the Lord of the Manor who lived at Foxholes on the way to Norwell) took the chair and, in addition to Parish Councillors, there was a good company of members of the general public present. Among the suggestions received and discussed were: ringing a Coronation peal on the Church bells; contributing towards the purchase of new bells; planting trees; presenting mugs to the children; building a kitchen in the Church Hall; and buying a public seat (possibly because the Parish Council had missed out on a Battle of Britain commemorative bench a couple of years earlier).

After much discussion, it was decided to form a committee to sift through the idea. On it would sit two Parish Councillors, two members of the Women's Institute, two members of The Public and Squire Edge as the ex-officio member.

They opted, after due deliberation, for tea for old people in the School, sports for children, tea for children, evening social in the school – all set off by a fancy dress parade through the village to The Grange park. Then they set about paying for it… for the hire of the School, prizes for the fancy dress and sports winners, food for the teas and refreshments, and entertainment for the social.

Whist drives (as ever) did the trick – though nobody noticed at the time the irony of a King kind of ruling them: Sam King went home to his smallholding in Vicarage Lane with three prizes! The January drive in the Church Hall enabled Mr. Swannack and his committee to bank £10 even after they'd given prizes to that lovely young Thelma Cottam, Mrs. Kent senior, Mrs. Handley from Bathley, Sam King, a Mr. Betts and a Mr. R. Sansome (which was probably the weekly paper's way of spelling the surname of a member of the Sampson family from Norwell)… and Cyril Marriott went home with a chicken after winning the raffle. Nice touch, that: Cyril and Reg Bell had been MCs for the evening. The February whist drive was even more successful. It raised £11 6s (£11.30). And there were more prizes. They were won by Miss Miriam Streeton, Mrs. Hempsall, Mrs. Hakes, Sam King (again), Ted Blore and Les Staples. Booby prizes went to Norwell, won by Mrs. Sampson and Mr. Graham. The Raffle was won by Mr. Evelyn Clipsham and Ted Blore. And the prize for the lucky ticket went to… surprise, surprise… Sam King.

The remaining monthly money-raisers were obviously equally successful. For after The Big Day and Even Bigger Night and The Dry Day's Sports, the village was invited to another Public Meeting in the Church Hall on 7 July 1953 – to decide how to dispose of the balance left over from the Coronation Celebration Fund! This despite the village raising £35 9s 8d (£35.48) at yet another whist drive for the East Coast Flood Distress Scheme. Squire Edge was there, of course, along with fellow Parish Councillors Bourne, Bell and Clipsham. But the village must have been pretty well partied-out (or busy in the garden) because only six parishioners attended. It was agreed, to nobody's great surprise, to plant a tree and provide a public seat. The Squire, it is recorded in the Parish Council minute book, "kindly agreed to dedicate a piece of land, free of charge, in front of the Grange, where the tree could be planted and have it fenced round, open to the public". The seat would replace the Festival seat that never quite materialised. An extremely high-powered Committee was appointed to make sure it happened, too: Squire Edge, Maurice Barley, Willie Lowndes and Frank Swannack. While the pointlessness of planting a tree in a rapidly developing wilderness seemed lost amid the euphoria of the moment and there was no official mention of how the rain

1. The Main Street

ruined The Big Day, there could be no argument when Billy Bourne congratulated the Coronation Committee on their splendid work. After all, the only thing they hadn't managed was to book decent weather.

As for Chairman Frank, he spoke of the generosity and ready response of the public and expressed the thanks of the Committee for their support. The Swannacks' only tangible reward was the trinket elder daughter Jane won in the fancy dress competition. Younger daughter Judy kind of equalised in 1961, becoming a Queen's Guide at a ceremony in St. Mary's Rooms, Newark. Little brother Billy proved himself to be an immensely successful (and versatile) athlete at the South Muskham School Sports, held in Bob Swallow's paddock just up the North Road between the School and the last houses in the village. In the events for 10 and 11 years olds, Billy won the flat race, the skipping race, bowling a ball and the high jump but was pushed into second place in the obstacle race by one James Simpson. To complete the family's happy day, his Mum, Barbara, was second in the parents' race – defeated only by the Reverend Snow, who presumably qualified on the grounds that, in effect, he was 'Father' to all of the children.

Meanwhile, the Swannack business blossomed as *The Good Life* met Mechanical Heaven. He employed a gang of five or six, including a tractor driver called George; and Brian Bowles, who used to manipulate one of those new-fangled giant combine harvesters along the country lanes without snagging we children and our secondhand bikes on his spokes. Ted Hallam, the wheelchair-bound lad from Chapel Lane who never allowed his infantile paralysis to hamper him too much, remembers travelling as far afield as Cranwell in Lincolnshire... and has even fonder memories of what a good boss Frank was. Ted recalls one boiling hot day when a farmer's wife refused point blank to fill a flask for one of Frank's men, telling him: "You're supposed to be here to work, not drink tea!" The driver instantly returned to base at North Muskham and found support from Frank, whose attitude was: "It costs nowt to boil a flask of water. Let 'em find somebody else to do their bailing".

It was North Muskham's loss when the family moved up the North Road to Carlton-on-Trent. For in addition to Frank's contributions, the tall, slim and always smilingly approachable Mrs. Swannack was similarly community-conscious. By 1953, she was a vice-president of North Muskham WI and orchestrated their sixth birthday party, welcoming guests from Balderton, Coddington, East Stoke, Farndon, Norwell and Sutton-on-Trent to an occasion that featured a play performed by the Coddington Drama Group (but which was also memorable for all members being asked to bring their own spoon and dish if they wanted trifle). She graduated to the presidency as the 1950s unfolded and the WI became even more popular.

Mr. and Mrs. Swannack went on to spend a long retirement on the Isle of Skye. Jane and Billy both went off to live happily in the USA. Judy and her family play a huge part in village life a few miles up the A1 at Carlton-on-Trent and Sutton-on-Trent.

THE GRANGE: FOCAL POINT FADING FAST

William Hall Lowndes and his family were the last gentry to occupy the most imposing residence in the village during the years when it was sensibly divided into flats and eventually, insanely in the view of many, allowed to fade into oblivion. Some say the Lowndes were the last of a long and largely selfish line of occupants of 'the grand house' who contributed little to village life. Others depict them more as victims of circumstances. So the Lowndes and the Grange were morbidly suited. They were a stunned, moneyed family that had suffered the trauma of having their main base, a farm at Chilwell near Nottingham, badly damaged when an Ordnance Factory blew-up, with the loss of hundreds of lives, during the First World War; it was a residence that had suffered innumerable ups and downs since it first appeared in records in September 1720, sold by Andrew and Elizabeth Capps to Robert Heron, gent, for £363 as "one messuage, farmhouse or tenement with homestead or close adjoining in which the messuage stood, circa four acres". In its pomp in the 19th century, it was frequently let to the well-heeled who could afford to furnish its drawing room, dining room, library, small breakfast room, six bedrooms and two dressing rooms; and staff its six offices for servants, butler's pantry, housekeeper's room, store room, servants' hall, brew-house, double coach-houses, stabling for eight horses, walled vegetable garden, and 24 to 25 acres of land. The Edge family got hold of it along with other chunks of the village in 1836 (hence Squire Edge's eminence in the 1950s). Indeed, during the First World War, The Grange was occupied by a brave Irish lady called Mrs. Cogan who became legend for taming a pet hyena. She was also humane enough to transform The Grange into a military hospital – mainly for troops wounded on the battlefields of Belgium – between 1914 and 1918.

It was far from a grand house by then; but it hardly deserved its harsh fate. After his father died at the age of 79 in 1945, Willie Lowndes attempted to keep the wolf from the door by selling produce out of the walled gardens while many rooms became lodgings for a variety of people – some passing through, others with much to contribute to the village. The rest of the grounds became a wilderness of a park.

1. The Main Street

The Grange flats were highly popular: the Swannacks and Marriotts were two of many young families who lodged there on their way to more permanent and private village properties.

Jill Marriott has mainly fond and fascinating memories of Grange-life as a toddler. Born in 1946 to Cyril, a builder's labourer who became the most successful captain the village cricket club ever had, and Lucy, the little lass who was reared by the Boer War hero who ran the North Road Garage in the 1930s, Jill remembers living in rooms on the top floor, alongside Mr. Lowndes. While Cyril played cricket and acted as the master of ceremonies at village whist drives, Lucy played hand-bells at the Church and tennis at Harry Clipsham's across the road at The Shades. Jill remembers evenings when Dad would look after her while Mum went to dances at Gatiss's Cafe; then when Mum came home Dad would dash off through the Park to the Lord Nelson for a swift pint before closing time. Though Jill was a mere toddler, she recalls Willie – "Mr. Lowndes" as she still respectfully refers to him – as a tall gentleman who would bring her Mum chickens to pluck. She'd load them on a shelf specially created on the axles of Jill's pram, and they would walk into Newark to sell them wholesale at one of the many butcher's shops that took fresh goods. Meanwhile, Willie would laden himself with fruit and vegetables grown in the Grange gardens and greenhouses, and take the bus to the Castle Station and the train to Nottingham, to barter at the Sneinton Wholesale Market.

Jill Marriott and one of the Grange monuments.

The rest of the old house fairly heaved with folk who reflected the rapidly changing ways of middle England...

Mrs. Bawtry-Williams was a little old lady with a manner as imposing as her name. "Being a toddler, I used to love to run along the corridors", says Jill. "If I met her, she would snap, 'Walk! Just walk!' But I had to accompany her to the Church when she used to take flowers to place on her husband's memorial. It was inside the Church, and she would sit looking at it for what seemed like hours before we walked back down the street".

Mrs. Bray and her sister Miss Turner were genteel residents; kind enough to make Jill's costume for the Coronation Day fancy dress parade. They

All dressed-up for its last great party: The Grange provides a fairy castle backdrop for the Coronation celebrations as children and adults join in a display of country dancing.

dressed her up as a cook... totally unaware, of course, that she would spend in excess of 40 years of her future life working as a cook at various schools.

Mr. and Mrs. Bill Midwinter represented the new generation. Jill thinks he worked at Worthington-Simpson; and he was definitely a member of the bell ringing team at St. Wilfrid's. Jill is more certain that they eventually moved up in the world by taking one of the new properties in Valley Prospect, Newark. Her memories of other neighbours are more hazy... but there was Mrs. Rogers, who made it obvious that she did not like children by tut-tutting at whatever the toddler did; and a Miss Burns, who was such a grey character that she is just a name. And in the out-buildings was an old chap called Tommy, who liked a drink. How he afforded his nightly trips to the pub, Jill knows not. But she still giggles at the memories of Tommy staggering along the Grange drive, attracting the attention of the resident cockerel who would attack him. It was a ritual that awoke her with such frequency that it was all part of life's rich pattern.

Material opulence was still apparent in the out-buildings, too. Ted Hallam, a regular visitor from Chapel Yard on his tea-tray of an invalid carriage,

1. The Main Street

remembers the woodwork in the stables being of polished oak with shiny railings setting-off the top of the woodwork. One part of the building had been modernised to accommodate a petrol-paraffin driven pump with two wheels – made, he thinks, by Ruston's of Grantham – to pump water out of a big well and into the house.

But that was about as far as modernisation went, apart from another area of the stables becoming a garage for some of Frank Swannack's farm machinery. The Marriotts moved to the terrace up the North Road and, in the end, the property that could/should have been the heartbeat of the village could no longer be sustained by 'young Willie'.

Marian Dye's fond memories of visits to The Grange best explain why the Lowndes never came near to making enough money to maintain the place in anything like its former glory. She says: "Mum used to send us up there to buy tomatoes out of the greenhouses. Both the old chap and young Willie would give us a bunch of grapes. They were lovely, nice and warm, fresh out of the greenhouse".

While Marian might have been describing the Lowndes as well as their grapes, the cold commercial facts were that the bills were increasingly hard to pay; and it became immaterial that the Grange had been listed as of special interest under the 1947 Planning Act.

As if the old house was trying to scream from the rafters that it could still have a use, one of its final flat-dwellers donated her body to scientific research when she died in January 1957. The gesture became evident the following April, when solicitors publicised the will of Miss Katherine Annie Johnson. She left her body to the Ministry of Health for scientific research, £676 13s 3d (£676.66.25) in cash to relatives and a Regency couch to Mr. and Mrs. Wilson Wing of Baltimore, Maryland, USA.

The vultures had already swooped. When 'Young Willie' Lowndes died, Jill Marriott remembers her parents debating how much the lovely old furniture would fetch at auction. After all, Jill herself remembers the tastefully furnished music room, reading room and library. Strangely, though, all the furniture disappeared, as if by magic, as if the ghost of 'Young Willie' had risen and somehow accomplished a midnight flit. There was much mystification among villagers; but nobody in authority cared enough to actually launch an inquiry into how the furniture disappeared. Nobody cared much about the house, so why should they concern themselves about a few sticks of furniture that had apparently grown legs and walked?

It is fitting that the following sad little story should appear at the bottom of Page 13 of the *Newark Advertiser* on 6 November 1963:

Coronation Village

Grange down
Unused and not maintained for several years, North Muskham Grange is to be demolished. Although listed as a building of architectural and historic interest, it is, says Nottinghamshire Planning Committee, "of no special interest to the general public".

Southwell Rural District Council do not object to the demolition and no action is to be taken for the making of a building preservation order.

By coincidence at the time when The Grange and its splendid park were being demolished, the Parish Council's search for a Village Hall was entering its second decade, North Muskham and Bathley Cricket Club had been forced to disband for lack of a pitch and North Muskham Football Club was also looking for a home base that was not susceptible to flooding from the Trent. Oh, and the garage and transport cafe were being shunted to a spot that was inaccessible to all but the most daring of village motorists.

The Grange became a private housing estate with no social amenities of its own.

THE SHADES: 'MR. HARRY' BUILDS A COMMUNITY CENTRE

By painful coincidence, the bespectacled pensioner living across the road from the Grange quietly spent hours building a Community Centre – up the North Road at Sutton-on-Trent! It never seems to have occurred to North Muskham to ask him to do the same for them, though it is doubtful he would have declined.

Harry Clipsham doubtless blushed at the appearance of a lovely story and picture about him in the Newark Advertiser of 28 October 1959 (page 10, to be precise). It was headed 'Big building task at Sutton for Muskham veteran', and the accompanying photograph revealed Harry looking slightly embarrassed behind his spectacles. But the story was well worth telling. At the age of 71, he was building Sutton-on-Trent Methodists' new community centre "brick by brick, often completely unaided". The 84-foot by 25-foot building included a stage and ante-rooms; and Harry worked from 7.30am to 5.30pm (noon on Saturdays, not at all on Sundays) to get the job done, helped "occasionally" by his son Harry and two labourers. The real point of the *Advertiser* story was to highlight the fact that, after only six weeks, the building was big enough for a commemorative stone to be laid in the wall by the entrance. The point that probably grated with anyone wishing for a village hall in North Muskham was that Sutton-on-Trent Methodists had raised £2,500 in 18 months and were confident of finding another £1,000 by the time Harry finished the job. When the centre was opened in May 1960, Harry was invited to hand over the key –

1. The Main Street

which he did with such typical modesty that he did not appear in any of the pictures of the occasion published in the local papers.

Mr. Harry lived with his wife Lillian and son Harry in The Shades, which stood in splendid isolation – three fields away from School House, a couple of grassy paddocks clear of the drive to Manor Farm, over-looking the sadly decaying grounds of the Grange… and cheek by jowl with an item of special architectural and historical interest which even North Muskham Parish Council forgot the village possessed. It was/is the Village Cross; and it was the object that heaped special mirth on the Parish Council in 1952. At their meeting on 21 October, a letter was read from the Ministry of Housing and Local Government, drawing attention to the Cross and the Village Stocks. The Councillors' reaction was to instruct their Clerk to ascertain where these were situated in the village. Despite this indifference/innocence, the remnants of the Cross remained visible into the early years of the 21st century though the stocks were never traced.

There is also a pertinent comparison to be made about the byways around the dignified old cottage then and now. Long before a highway planner possessing no empathy with rural life aimed a bridge over the dualled A1 directly at The Shades (and local authorities compounded the black comedy by encouraging a haulage company to grow in the vicinity), there was a grassy lane from near the side-gate to The Shades that slid off (beside the Cross, as it happens) towards the river Trent. Hugh Kent remembers he and other village children used it as a safer route than the North Road to Lodge Farm, where they used to practice their cricket and, on less hectic occasions, learn to enjoy the intricacies of fishing (albeit in a much dirtier, more polluted Trent than was the case by the 21st century).

Harry Senior – "Mr. Harry" to all respectful villagers needing to specify which of the four Clipsham brothers they were referring to – worked (surprise, surprise) for the family building firm, his agility seemingly unhindered by a stiff knee which forced him to walk in a most ungainly manner. Neither did the impediment ever prevent him leading an extremely active life for a man who had passed his 60th birthday by 1950. Many an evening would find him working in his vegetable garden, its neatness and high productivity merely emphasising the neglect around the big house across the Street. He also found time to construct a miniature wall maize that was a magnet for young visitors. And then there was Mr. Harry's massive lawn. It was not only big enough to be a tennis court. It was a tennis court for a time, and looked as immaculate as Wimbledon every July.

But Mr. Harry would always dash away from work on a winter Saturday to catch Thomas's special buses so that he could watch his beloved Notts

County play football. His dedication to the Football League's oldest club through thin, thick and thinner was so extraordinary that he became more famous at Meadow Lane than many of the footballers in the days after the heady era when Tommy Lawton and Jackie Sewell attracted crowds of 50,000-plus to matches. Despite his 'gammy leg', Harry never dreamed of sitting to watch his football. He always stood close to the front of the terracing near the touchline. Eventually, the club made a special presentation to him in acknowledgement of his loyalty to them.

But when he got home after his moments of fame at either Sutton or Meadow Lane, the chances are that Lillian ensured he remained down-to-earth by greeting him with: "Wipe your feet!" For she was an enormously house-proud lady, who scrubbed her floors once a week yet still felt obliged to protect them by laying down newspapers for her visitors to walk on.

Harry died, aged 81, on 4 March 1970. His wife Lillian was 98 when she died on 10 September 1991. Young Harry, clearly a chip off the old block, married and lived in the village all his life, in a bungalow he built in Crab Lane.

SCHOOL HOUSE: NORMAN MOVES WITH THE TIMES

The Camerons were the historic occupants of the School House, a slim dwelling on the right-hand side of the imposing educational establishment as you faced it from Main Street. Although Mrs. Cameron had died, aged 87, on 17 September 1945 (and her husband had pre-deceased her), one of their daughters was still in residence during the 1950s. By then, she was Mrs. Wykes and she and her husband, Stan, had two sons – Norman and David.

Quite where Stan had gone by 1953 cannot be reported. It was one of those mysteries that were not discussed; certainly not when young ears were flapping! John Stanley Wykes, to give him his full name, wed Evelyn Margaret Cameron when both were aged 22 at St. Wilfrid's just before Christmas 1926. They had two sons; but nobody seemed to know where their Dad had gone. The consensus of the period was that such domestic arrangements were private among those involved, especially when they involved such a respectable family as the Camerons.

And it was quite logical for them to take in a lodger in Coronation Year: A typical gentle giant of the period, John Harris (pictured) should have been

1. The Main Street

preparing to succeed his father as the head of the family building firm in Grantham. Instead, his love of the land drove him to become a labourer for Mrs. Wykes' brother-in-law, Billy Bourne, across the fields to the north at Lodge Farm.

More than half a decade on, John had retired to Collingham but retained vivid – and extremely fond – memories of his labours in the years when tractors were replacing cart-horses but mechanisation still had some way to go to replace human muscle.

For example, root crops would have to be hoed by hand – a task shared between the full-time farm hands and any women and children prepared to slave for a pittance during the school holidays. Bales were hoisted onto carts on twin-pronged forks wielded by the menfolk, who worked from dawn till dusk to gather in the harvest before summer's sun gave way to the inevitable thunder storms. Then the same men would use the same forks to unload the carts and carefully build stacks in the farmyards.

This task took on a particularly painful turn for John after he dislocated a shoulder while playing rugby union for Newark (for whom he was an exceptionally mobile flanker). "I knew I was in trouble when I picked up a bale and my collarbone slid under my chin", he reflected. Even though John suffered this agony *after* spending time in Harlow Wood Orthopaedic Hospital supposedly getting the problem sorted, you'd have thought he would have leapt at the chance to get back to his Dad's business. Nothing could be further from the actuality! He persevered with the energy-sapping, often painful life of a farm labourer until Billy Bourne's death closed the chapter on what he considered to be an idyllic existence.

As a member of the North Muskham and Bathley cricket team – and of virtually every social event connected with the village in general and the Lord Nelson pub in particular – 'Gentle John' was the epitome of 1950s community spirit.

The Wykes brothers were not nearly so out-going but still played parts in enhancing the quality of life. Norman Wykes was one of Thomas Tours' drivers when everyone was clamouring to get on the buses for their holidays or day trips. Later, when cars took over from buses as the transport of choice, Norman drove lorries, making a living out of transporting materials for the rapidly-growing building industry; and he and his wife reared their son, Michael, in the family home.

SCHOOL: WAS IT REALLY SO STRICT?
No building represented North Muskham's lack of unity better than the County Primary School. It stood on a bank overlooking the triangle of green

formed by the Main Street sweeping in from the North Road and Vicarage Lane; and was surrounded by a hedge at the front and, on all other sides, a high wall which encompassed everything – rear of classrooms, playgrounds, outside lavatories – giving the impression that there was no escape. Ever!

But it was not its elevation, nor its fort-like appearance, that made it so daunting. It was its Head Teacher, Mr. Norman King. I have to confess vested interest: I was sent to South Muskham Church of England Primary School because my father had taken such exception to the unsympathetic way in which Mr. King had treated his first three children. Charlie, Hilda and Annie had been aged eight, six and four when their mother (my dad's first wife, Tess) died. Precisely how their trauma was treated at school, I was always deemed too young and innocent to hear. Suffice to say that, after I passed my 11-plus, I passed the front door of the Kings' home dressed in my Magnus Grammar School uniform twice a day for five years – frequently when he was outside collecting water from his pump or cleaning his windows. Not once did Mr. (or Miss) King give me so much as the time of day.

Not that I was alone. Among my pals at South Muskham School were several North Muskham children… Judy Swannack (she and I frequently took on the rest of the school at football and won), Harriet Barley, David Clipsham, Mavis Talbot to name but a few. We were taught the five Rs – reading, writing,

The children prepare to tuck into their Coronation tea.

1. The Main Street

'rithmetic, right and wrong – in a friendly, relaxed atmosphere by some extremely kindly ladies. Mrs. Eastlake was our Head from 1950 to 1955, when she left to accompany her husband, an Army Captain, to Singapore. On her final afternoon, there were some lovely speeches by Barbara Allen, one of the oldest pupils; Mrs. Barley as one of the most articulate parents; and the Rev. Rigden on behalf of the Governors. Mrs. Eastlake's parting gifts were a travelling case and some jewellery.

A kindly, plump, matronly lady called Mrs. Billyard became Head with Mrs. Jones as her deputy. Equally important as our teachers, Mrs. Cooper who lived across the road was our dinner lady, cleaner and general daytime mum-to-30+. Oh, and she must have got up early because she always made sure the huge pot-bellied cast-iron fire was roaring hot by 9am on the most miserable of mornings. Even when the school became something of a dangerous spot in the mid-50s, with lorries frequently failing to negotiate the southbound curve of the North Road into South Muskham and tippling into the school grounds, parents became no more noticeably biased towards North Muskham School.

Yet scores of children enjoyed their time being taught by Mr. King, his (equally strict) spinster sister Florence, and their assistant teachers in the four classrooms. In addition, Mrs. Turner, the wife of the poultry farmer at Bathley, would pop in and teach the girls to knit while Mr. King would pass on horticultural skills to the boys in the allotment garden.

Money was also raised so that the children could be bussed on an annual adventure to the seaside – Skegness or Mablethorpe, usually, with a halfway stop at Wragby for some impractical drink such as lemonade that had the effect of making the rest of the journey a stomach-churning (at least) nightmare. A whist drive organised by the staff in aid of the Scholars' Outing Fund in 1953 attracted 21 tables (that's 84 card-sharps!) and produced the following winners: Mrs. Whitehead, Mrs. Blundy, Mrs. Lynn, Mrs. Pinder, Mr. Allison, Master Alan Franklin, Mr. Spafford and Mr. Hugh Kent. A guessing competition for a dressed fowl (one that's been plucked and is oven-ready, not one with clothes on) was won by Mrs. Maxted and the holder of the lucky ticket was Mr. Whitehead. After incidental expenses had been met, the balance remaining was approximately £20.

And the Kings were never slow to generate positive publicity. For example, the *Newark Advertiser* report of the school Christmas party in 1954 said: "After weeks of preparations, the efforts of Mr. N. J. King and Miss F. King were well rewarded. The evening's entertainment was one of the most successful in recent years". The children involved in the plays were Peter

Thurston, who was a major academic star despite spending months in hospital under-going operations; Valerie Ward, whose caring nature led her into nursing; Jean Baggaley, from North Road Farm; Peter and Freda Rogers; Jacqueline Cockerill from the Lord Nelson Inn; Jean James from down Ferry Lane; Josephine Pape from Crab Lane; Michael Peppitt; Jill Marriott who you have just met at the Grange; and Christopher Marrows from Bathley. There must have been a goodly number of satisfied parents in the audience, too: a collection raised £4 15s 9d (that's 4 pounds 78 and threequarter pence in modern Elizabethan currency).

The initial death knell was sounded for both village schools at the dreariest time of year. The *Newark Herald* on 21 November 1953 was quite ruthless about it, reporting:

"When five new classrooms are finished at the Sconce Hills County Secondary School in January, four village schools will be decapitated and 42 children from them will go to Sconce Hills School. The villages concerned are North Muskham, Carlton-on-Trent, Averham and South Muskham". The

Smile folks! Please smile! The grown-ups' Coronation party with Teacher King (bespectacled) the third person from the front of the second row from left.

announcement was made by Alderman J. A. Markwick, the Chairman, at a meeting of Newark District Education Committee. 'Sconnies' had been opened three years earlier and a note to the story explained: "The educational term 'decapitated' means the cutting out of the senior department for children from 11 to 15 in the village schools". In other words, the introduction of the 11-plus examination.

Thereafter, it was only a matter of time before some Smarty would suggest to the Education Committee that there were too few children at North Muskham, Carlton-on-Trent, Averham and South Muskham to justify their continuing as separate entities. It was possible to see Smarty's point, if not entirely sympathise with it. When I left South Muskham School in 1956, there were (I'm pretty sure) 33 pupils. In my form, 1B, at the Magnus, there were 32 pupils. Not that I ever learnt to accept that big was necessarily better.

When the inevitable happened and the two Muskham Schools merged in new buildings at the junction of Main Street with Nelson Lane, the Kings retired and Mrs. Billyard became the first Head Teacher. Typical of this mumsy figure, her chief message at her inaugural parents' evening was: "The standards set in the home are the standards the child will bring to school". And now they would all take the same standards home from school...

ROSE COTTAGES: NO, YOU CAN'T HAVE YOUR BALL BACK!
Annie Price, who lived to the ripe old age of 91 before she died on 23 April 1981, kept the schoolchildren over the wall in the school playgrounds alternately amused and terrified. Long after the Second World War hostilities ended in triumph, life-long spinster Annie continued to battle with all and sundry. She and her brother 'Rad' were the offspring of farmer John Price and his wife Sarah, who died in her 83rd year on 29 March 1945; and Annie was never more refined than earthly unsubtle.

Always dressed in black, she gave a wonderful impersonation of the wicked witch who figured in the children's fairy story books; and would substantiate the image virtually every playtime when a ball ventured out of the playground and onto her patch with the cry: "I shall burn every one!" And whenever Mr. King decided to add his Head Teacher's weight to the children's cause, calling on her to return the ball, he was similarly seen-off with a verbal flea in his ear and left in no doubt that he should do more to make the little horrors behave. The children, accustomed to being on the wrong side of Mr. King's rough tongue, loved that bit of playtime!

Annie was also an extremely vocal guardian of the six or seven allotment gardens tended by villagers in the area just beyond her row of cottages and the school wall. One allotment belonged to the School and was ostensibly used by Mr. King to help teach the children the basics of horticulture. And perish the thought that most of the produce found its way onto the dinner table at Aingarth! It can now be exclusively revealed that Peter Musson, the Norwell School pupil who tended one of the other allotments for his widowed Mum, would occasionally "borrow" a cabbage or maybe a handful of taties from the school plot… "only if ours weren't ready, you understand", he added in his defence. "They were only borrowed, really".

The Wass family also lived in these cottages for quite some time. Their father, Robert Wass, worked at Lodge Farm for the Bournes. The family's link with the village ended when their kindly daughter Kate wed a Lincolnshire farm worker and moved to Caistor. One wonders if they were related to "a man named Wass" who made it into the local newspapers in 1805. As the result of a quarrel it was said he entered his home and vowed never to come out again. "There he remained for 30 years and, despite all entreaties, never emerged alive".

In another cottage, hidden from the road by the School, lived the Bradley family. The patriarch, Tom, reached the grand age of 95 before he passed away in Newark's Hawtonville Hospital on 22 February 1958. His son, who worked for Trent Navigation, moved to live in William Street, Newark, when he married. After Tom's death, Mr. and Mrs. Bradley Junior inserted a notice in the *Newark Advertiser* to thank Dr. Reed, Dr. Collis, Nurse Clipsham and the staff of Hawtonville Hospital "for kindness shown to their father during his illness".

Interestingly, they also thanked kindly neighbour Mrs. Amy Cox "for untiring attention". This was the wheelchair-bound Amy, who lived between the Village Green and the North Road. You'd have thought she would have been burdened enough by her own problems without taking on another's worries. That she helped care for old Tom Bradley speaks volumes for the community spirit instilled in her during her childhood in Chapel Yard.

CARPENTERS' ARMS: MEND MY BIKE FOR A PINT

It was fitting that Joe Edlin should live in a former public house. He liked a pint, and earned many by repairing the bikes of friends and neighbours. It was a vital chore which he later handed down to the oldest of his three sons, Brendan, who worked at Ransome & Marles.

Of the other sons, Harry, was a farm labourer for Percy Jackson at the Ness. He earned the nickname "Pedals" because he would use virtually every bike ride home as an opportunity to do a bit of scavenging in the hedgerows, which were always kept neat and tidy, on the North Road in search of beer

1. The Main Street

bottles in an era when he could still get money back on "empties". The other Edlin brother, Bill went to live at Normanton-on-Trent.

There were also daughters. Fanny married a bus driver and moved away from the village. Ethel was disabled and, sod's law being what it is, was the last survivor of the family to live in their house.

When the A1 was widened, the sturdy house survived – just – though the Carpenter's Arms sign had finally worn off the side of the cottage that faced the School. Quite how the planners managed to squeeze round the cottage to create a northbound lane from the village to the new filling station between the southbound A1 carriageway and the house remains a mystery that has confounded many a traveller seeking a bed at the Travel Lodge. In reality, it belongs to Ronnie Milnes, who inherited the filling station and kindly allows others to use it. But for visitors to these parts, it is a much more secretive road than the old drinkers at the Carpenters' Arms could have negotiated!

LIPSTICK COTTAGE: QUIET FOLK AT NOISY CORNER

The little old cottage at the increasingly busy junction of Main Street with the North Road, which had to be knocked down when the A1 was widened, was officially named Oak Tree Cottage because of the huge tree that guarded it

Lipstick Cottage – above, as seen from Main Street, attached to the taller Carpenter's Arms.

Right: the view from the Old North Road with the hedge in the foreground, Rose Cottages in the left-background and (right) the towering Oak Tree that gave the cottage its real name.

from just behind its trimly-cut hedge, and the prim and proper occupants would probably have sued those who nicknamed it "Lipstick Cottage". The reasons were obvious: it was painted white like the powdered face of the modern Miss of the 1950s; but its front door and window sills were vivid red.

The long-time occupier Herbert Woolley, the elderly and rotund grandfather of the Edlins, is remembered as a quiet little man who regularly took out library books dispensed from the School by Mr. King. After Mr. Woolley passed on, into "Lipstick Cottage" came another quiet gentleman, John Bushby, and his wife. The amiable couple eventually moved to the first of the bungalows to be built in the fields towards the Shades when the lovely Lipstick Cottage was smudged out by the road builders.

It was by far the smallest building to disappear in the name of progress.

2. CRAB LANE TO FERRY

Turn left out of the Crown Inn and you'd find characters in every cottage – plus the remnants of the route taken to the Trent barges in the horse-and-cart era by countless traders and farmers from the villages over the hills beyond Bathley…

MAIN STREET
SALT 'N' PEPPER COTTAGES: A REGAL BUILDER
AND GARDENER
His name suggested he was closer to royalty than anyone else in North Muskham but fittingly for a man who lived in one of the most imaginatively-nicknamed houses on Main Street, Harold Phillips-Moul's lasting legacy to the village stemmed from his skills as a builder rather than his intriguing ancestry. The second half of the surname can be traced back to French nobility before the Revolution. But far from resting on such lofty laurels, Harold worked as a builder. Among his more noticeable creations were the wall round North Muskham Chapel and Thomas's Bus Garage, which later became a workshop for a thriving company of double-glazers before being erased to make way for houses. And he was respected for his gardening at home so much that he was treasurer of the village Horticultural Society for many years.

As befits a family with a hint of royal blood, the Phillips-Mouls traditionally had two homes – but both were in North Muskham. In 1939, Harold and his family moved from Crab Lane to the distinctive Salt 'n' Pepper Cottages (so-called because, then as now, half of the building was white and the other half red) between the Crown Inn and Thomas's house. Harold had obviously inherited diplomatic skills from his ancestors: he and his wife Janet sent son Ron to North Muskham School and daughters Shirley and Gill to South Muskham School.

Harold Phillips-Moul reached the age of 86 before he died on 8 July 1978. His wife, Janet Margaret Ronald Phillips-Moul, was 93 when she died a decade later, on 15 August 1988. They are both buried in South Muskham Churchyard – poignantly close to one of their sons, Harold, who was only 43 when he passed away on 22 June 1967 after a short illness, the beloved husband of Maureen and father of Michael.

BUS GARAGE: TOURS, TORMENT AND TEARS OF LAUGHTER

Long before television encouraged the country to laugh at a televised sitcom called *On The Buses*, North Muskham was entertained by the everyday deeds of Thomas Motor Tours. John Thomas (for that was the name of the company founder) and his son Syd (who was born in 1915 and grew into a genial giant never afraid to tread on officialdom's toes in his desire to please his customers) always gave the impression of being a family at war and yet they captured perfectly the post-war mood of hard-working folk wanting to spread their wings and simply celebrate being alive.

Syd, born with the First World War a few months old, fought in the Second World War. John, who had been fighting in Mesopotamia with the Royal Artillery within months of becoming a Dad, was a policeman in Sheffield until he and his wife, Nellie Elizabeth, moved to Newark in 1925. He launched his motor company with a single car and, by the time he and Nellie celebrated their Golden Wedding on 18 October 1963, had nine buses – all creamy white and of increasingly sleek design, visible proof of the acceleration of modernisation.

In between those milestones, when the time came for the bus garage to be built, Harold Phillips-Moul did the bricklaying while the drivers acted as his labourers in between their stints out on the road. During the War, the buses were commandeered to transport troops around the country while the bus garage became a base for a troop of Horse Guards.

The youngest of the drivers, Peter Musson, back from fighting in the War himself, took part in the drivers' expedition to Aldershot to reclaim the buses from the Army, in 1948–49, and the mix of community service and commercial enterprise that went into reinvigorating the business. One of Peter's daily tasks was to take hot dinners round the local schools in Thomas's taxi (or a bus, if the taxi was busy earning money elsewhere). The meals were cooked at North Muskham School and packed into silvery containers that retained heat (but probably leaked flavour) as they were driven to the village schools at South Muskham, Caunton and Norwell.

The buses took folk on day excursions to an increasing number of venues… even if they didn't always run smoothly.

2. Crab Lane to Ferry

Probably the most practical problem came when the workmen's service bus broke down on Trent Bridge just beyond South Muskham one morning early in the 1950s. John, who was driving it himself, leapt out of the driving seat, wrenched open the bonnet and fumbled furiously among the various parts of the engine. Finding the broken bit and recognising it was beyond instant repair, he uttered a few oaths, hurled it into the swirling river below and promptly set off back towards the garage – leaving his passengers to walk to work.

Not that everything ran well with Lincolnshire Road Car, the "big brother" competitor of the family firm. In March 1951, the Parish Council noted: "There was no improvement in the bus service for the village in spite of representations made last summer to the East Midlands Traffic Area. The Clerk was instructed to communicate with them again in an endeavour to obtain an improvement".

At the Parish Council meeting in October 1952, Syd Milnes raised the question of complaints received from local people left behind at the Sugar Factory by the Workmen's Bus from Newark. It was left to the Clerk to write to Lincolnshire Road Car, "putting forward the complaints, with a view to future avoidance of these circumstances". These were the days when there were many more workers than seats on their buses. But the inference from the Parish Council was that Thomas's could have done it better than the Road Car, given the chance.

Thomas Tours went to great lengths to help folk escape from such commuter problems and the harshness of life in general; and sometimes, misfortune merely added to the entertainment of days out. Like the one to Heathrow Airport to see the planes in 1952, an era when the phrase 'package holiday' meant sandwiches wrapped in greaseproof paper by a kindly seaside landlady on the East Coast. Two eager young men from the village, Colin Granger and John Cottam, arrived at the bus garage good and early – and walked into one of the celebrated Thomas family arguments. "Syd was filling the bus with fuel", says Colin. "The old man was arguing with him. They were always at loggerheads. Anyway, Syd tired of the row and drove off – without realising that the fuel pump nozzle was still in the bus. It distorted the end of the fuel pipe and, no matter how they tried, they couldn't get the cap back on it. So they rammed a piece of wood in and off we went. Once we got to the airport, we began to forget about the early morning excitement as we drove round the buildings and hangars, on our guided tour – until the bus ran out of fuel as we drove down the main runway! I seem to remember Syd also had trouble restarting it after the refuelling stop at Biggleswade on the way back. We finally got back to Muskham at 1am. It was certainly a day out I'll never forget!"

Which leads one to wonder whether it was entirely coincidence that a show by *The Crazy Gang* (the leading comedians of the era) was the destination of a Thomas bus trip to the theatre in London in the early months of 1952. The all-in price: 24s 6d (£1.22½).

For those who could not afford to spend so long on their enjoyment, there was a trip to the pantomime at Nottingham Theatre Royal, *Puss in Boots*. The all-in cost (of the return coach journey and a stalls seat) was 7s (35p) for adults or 5s 9d (28¾p) for children.

Come 1953, they laid on excursion after excursion to London in an attempt to meet the local demand. For eight days solid in late April, Peter Musson and Reg Ward took parties to London to ogle the Coronation Route. The price for adults was £1 return, and the demand was relentless. Peter recalled: "We'd set off at 6 in the morning, get there 10-ish to 10.30, and not be home till midnight or later. We were only allowed to go at 30 miles an hour and lorries were restricted to 20. So if we got behind one of them, that was that because the main roads were hardly wider than Muskham Main Street is now; and there were no by-passes round the towns – we had to go through all of them".

Peter was enormously relieved when Reg was called upon to drive the excursion on Coronation Day itself, with Syd Thomas as his relief driver and

Syd Thomas, smiling in the foreground, surrounded by some of his day-trip passengers.

2. Crab Lane to Ferry

Hilda among the passengers. They departed from the London Road car park in Newark at quarter past midnight on 2 June, arriving in central London at 5am so that the day-trippers had time to find their vantage points. Syd and Hilda sat in their deck-chairs on The Mall all day, soaking in the rain, but nevertheless delighted to be soaking up the sights. The return bus tickets cost 17s 6d (77½p) for adults or 12s 6d (62½p) for children. As for young Musson, the driver they left at home slept for most of the big day: "I was tired out by all the earlier trips".

During the 'Works Fortnight', when every major employer in Newark closed down (alas, not necessarily during the school holidays, leading to a huge but temporary increase in truancy), Thomas Tours offered day-trippers a choice of four or five venues a day: Skegness, Bridlington, Derbyshire, Wicksteed Zoo, Luton Hoo... Cotswolds, Blenheim Palace, Yarmouth, Mablethorpe... Norfolk, Hunstanton and Sandringham, Bridlington, Skegness... Stratford-upon-Avon Flower Show, Matlock, Windsor and Maidstone, Skegness... Malvern, York and Harrogate, Wicksteed, Bridlington... Great Yarmouth, Cotswolds, Skegness, Kedleston Hall and Belper River Gardens... Windsor and Maidstone, Mablethorpe, York and Harrogate, Bridlington... Luton Hoo, Dovedale in Derbyshire, Great Yarmouth, Skegness... Norfolk Tour, Cotswolds, Skegness... Blenheim Palace, Hunstanton and Sandringham, Windsor Castle and Maidstone, Skegness... Skegness, Stratford, York and Harrogate, Trentham Gardens. The fares? 8 shillings (40p) would get an adult to Skeggy and back; 5s 6d (27½p) was the child's fare. Windsor Castle was the most expensive of the summer's hot spots: 16s 6d (82½p) for an adult, 11s 6d (57½p) for children.

But the real hub of excitement was the Bus Garage. Imagine the scene each morning at the height of the holiday season. From around 4.30am, cleaners (usually middle-aged ladies and for a few summers including Nora Smalley and Ivy Frecknall) are like ants inside the vehicles, emptying ashtrays of the previous days' nub-ends, apple cores and chewing gum; washing the floors clear of stale food, empty fag packets, regurgitated food, sand, grass, mud; finding all manner of surprises left on the luggage racks. John and Syd would be hosing down the exterior of the buses, easing them out of the garage to the fuel pumps, inevitably arguing over who would move which. The drivers would arrive... Reg Ward was No.1; he would have the juiciest drives each day; Norman Wykes, Dennis Lowe and Peter Musson were just as obliging and reliable so far as the regulars were concerned; Syd could be relied upon for the most entertaining running commentary on progress... Who knows? It could have been him who inspired the invention of microphones to help drivers to communicate with their passengers! It was certainly his philosophy to treat every other driver on the road as an idiot.

They were always busy behind the scenes, too, seeking to find new venues for their customers. For 8 shillings (40p) folk flocked to Nottingham Theatre Royal in the autumn of 1953 to watch a Yorkshire comedian and wireless star called Wilfred Pickles in a revue called *The Gay Dog* (in this age, 'gay' meant happy and 'dog' was a raffish fellow). But Thomas the passenger-pleasers upset the regulators of the increasingly competitive passenger transport business, the East Midlands Traffic Commissioners. After years of running 'football specials' to Notts County and Nottingham Forest home matches, Thomas Tours were suddenly limited to 20 matches a season in December 1954. Syd protested that they had already run excursions to 21 matches that season. But the licensing authority refused to give Thomas a road service licence for an express service between Newark and Nottingham after one of their keenest rivals, Wm Gash and Sons, objected on the grounds that the excursions were competing with their normal service. Not that Syd had gone down quietly: the Commissioners had spent three days hearing argument and counter-argument – on 26 May, 27 September and 24 October – before delivering their verdict as a kind of Christmas gift.

Syd dusted himself down and a few months later beat off strong objections from British Railways for the right to run up to three buses to Bridlington, Filey and Scarborough during the 'Works Fortnight'.

There was another drama in 1957, reported in the *Newark Advertiser* on Wednesday 13 March. Bus driver Brian Howard and six anglers were treated in hospital for shock after their coach slid into a 10-foot deep drainage ditch in Lincolnshire. It seems 23-year-old Brian was edging the 7ft 6in wide coach down a 9ft-wide lane when he met a boy cyclist pedalling in the other direction. The boy didn't give way, so Brian drove onto the verge not realising that, only a few days earlier, it had been dug up for the laying of an electricity cable. In slow motion, the bus slid into the icy water. Most of the 22 fishermen (from Worthington-Simpsons' factory at Lowfields, Balderton) were soaked… and engineers were still trying to drag the bus back onto dry land three days later.

By this time, Syd was so well respected by the business community at large, he was the senior vice-president of Newark Tradesmen's Association; and was their official spokesman when the Press sought comment on that year's Budget. Surprisingly, considering the encouragement it would give private motorists, he felt the Chancellor was right to take 1s (5p) off the price of a gallon of petrol. As if that wasn't an indication of his kind heart, he also

2. Crab Lane to Ferry

loaned one of his drivers (not named here) £40... and then had to take him to court to get it back when the man walked out on his job.

But not all in the transport industry were as genial as Syd. No respect was shown to Reg Ward or his 40 passengers during a bitter strike by service bus drivers and conductors in July 1957. Reg had driven his party as far as Lower Tean near Stoke-on-Trent on a Sunday trip to Bettws y Coed in Wales when, the following week's *Newark Advertiser* reported, "a group of men stopped the bus and threatened to overturn it if the driver continued the journey". Reg, dedicated far beyond the call of duty, left the comparative safety of his cab to find a public phone and call the Garage for instructions. Syd's first reaction was to insist that the Staffordshire Police should escort the bus to and from its destination. But anarchy reigned on bus routes throughout the country on that weekend and there was no way even Syd could persuade the law to set such a precedent for a bunch of day-trippers. So Reg had no alternative but to turn his bus round and take his shaken party home.

While the menfolk treated each day as a fresh challenge, it was entirely in keeping with their combative natures that they should register Thomas Motor Tours as a limited company on Armistice Day, 11 November 1957. There were just two directors: John and Syd. Hard though they worked and argued, nobody ever really stood a chance of coming between them!

Old Mr. Thomas remained proud to the end of the company, too. On a rare trip as a passenger in the '60s, he was mystified when 'the hat' was passed round on the journey home. When it was explained that a collection was being made for the driver, John Thomas was outraged. "My drivers don't need charity", he asserted. "I have always paid my drivers a living wage". The driver in question remembers making a special mental note of the amount in his next weekly wage packet: £13.

Away from the buses, Syd also found time to serve as a manager at North Muskham County School from 1952, and the Thomas' wives hardly stayed home quietly. Nellie was active in Chapel life, especially as secretary of North Muskham Bright Hour, which provided gossip decades before afternoon television was even a dot in its inventor's screen. She was equally important to the village WI. A *Newark Herald* report on 18 July 1953, records: "Mrs. Thomas Snr read the minutes and announced that the Handicrafts Class would begin on 15 September". It wasn't the only instance of WI practicality: in November, they had a cookery demonstration on using scraps of food, which "proved most useful and was extremely interesting". And for six weeks early in 1954, the WI organised evening classes at the village school on "art and design in the home". In due time, Syd's wife Hilda became an equally influential member of the WI.

Sydney Thomas died, aged 63, in 1978. Hilda, his statuesque wife, moved to a newly-built bungalow on Waltons Lane in retirement – coincidentally (?) opposite the founder of Wright and Sons, another of Thomas Tours' great rivals in the heyday of bus trips. Hilda was 88 when she died in 1987. The family maintained its voice, though! Their daughter, Susan Saddington, is the village's representative on Newark and Sherwood District Council and Nottinghamshire County Council in the early years of the 21st century.

COTTAGES: LIFETIMES OF DEVOTION
The row of cottages that backed onto Thomas's driveway were as joyous as they were God-fearing... except for one dreadful period in the summer of 1922 when the head of the family was killed on the railway and the district coroner decided to hold the inquest in his grieving home. Thomas Bellamy, a Methodist lay-preacher, had worked for the Great Northern Railway for 25 years, and had risen to be foreman of the gang of six platelayers on the local length. He'd been up towards Cromwell early on the morning of 6 July, making sure that platelayers George Kirk, who lived in Bathley, and Harry Frecknall, who would later move to Bathley, were getting on with mowing the grass beside the line. It seemed an incongruous task on such a Thursday morning, when the showers, driven by a strong southerly breeze, were so drenching that they kept driving them into one of the little wooden huts scattered along the track for just such a purpose. But it was vital if they were to minimise the fires that were bound to be started by sparks from the passing steam engines come the drier times in August and September. As one shower ended, Tom decided he'd nip home for breakfast while the grass dried sufficiently to be scythed. Off he set, walking round the curve towards Bathley Lane crossing, head down into the wind. Minutes later, his two workmates heard the shriek of a steam engine's whistle. Instinctively, they dropped scythes and ran. Quarter of a mile down the track, there were the sparks and smoke of a skidding, halting engine. By the time they got to it, it had reversed to beside the prone body of Ganger Bellamy. He'd obviously not expected it; a light engine travelling from Colwick to Doncaster. Neither the driver leaning out of one side of the cab, nor his fireman with his head out of the other side, had seen him until it was too late to brake because of the curve of the line.

Only two nights later, the mourning household was taken over for the inquest. It was usual in days when few had transport to take the formalities to the folk – there would be an inquest into a drowning four years later at the Crown Inn for no better reason than the then landlord had helped fish the

2. Crab Lane to Ferry

body out of the Trent – but one can only imagine the feelings of Tom's 44-year-old widow, Eliza Ellen, as she strove to control her grief, console her children, and prepare for the arrival on that Friday night of the Coroner, Mr. F. B. Footitt; and the jury of which Mr. H. B. Friend from Muskham Grange was the foreman; the locomotive inspector from Doncaster, Mr. C. H. Davies; an inspector from the Police Department of the GNR at Grantham, Mr. D. Curnock; a solicitor enlisted by the National Union of Railwaymen to take care of the interests of their members involved, Mr. W. H. Franks; the key witnesses – the two platelayers, engine driver and his fireman; plus a couple of reporters from the *Advertiser* and the *Herald*; and the Coroner's officer. It was, to all intents and purposes, a useless exercise.

Aunt Nell, as his widow was known to all of the village, assured them that Tom's eyesight and hearing were good. But nobody could explain why Tom had decided to walk on the down-line (as the north-bound track is called) rather than on the path beside it. Coroners' courts weren't interested in speculation, so neither George Kirk nor Dad dare suggest he was so conscientious, he was probably using the walk home to check the rails for defects. The jury returned a verdict of accidental death... and expressed deep sympathy with the widow and family.

Aunt Nell, a widow at the age of 44, lived for nigh on another 40 years before succumbing in the bitterly cold, foggy winter of 1962, on 25 February... four decades in which happy, wholesome family values glowed from her cottage, and those next door.

As the Roaring Twenties revved up the enjoyment factor, her daughters, Edith and Kathleen, became key members of the Muskham Mummers along with the likes of Edgar Streeton, Florrie Rogers, Norman King and his sister Florence, Harold Phillips-Moul and Harry Clipsham. In the days before television, before even radios were affordable in every home, even before Thomas Tours took busloads to the theatres of Nottingham or Lincoln or further afield, villagers had to make their own entertainment; and the Muskham Mummers toured the surrounding area putting on shows for whoever would watch.

Thirty years on, come the 1953 Coronation celebrations, the Bellamy family were still in two of the three cottages (the other was empty) that looked out across their gardens to Crab Lane and the flat, boggy fields to South Muskham (long before anyone dreamed of driving a dual carriageway through the rural scenery).

By then, one of the Bellamy daughters was married to William Elliott and lived with their children June and Tommy in the cottage nearest to the Main

Street. William was enormously versatile in his value to the village. Take 1968 as an admittedly belated example. No sooner had he finished making a noticeboard for the Parish Council than he set about organising a fashion show for Methodist Chapel funds. The show, with garments for everyone from small children to ladies' out-size, seemed a better fit than the board. It was supposed to be placed beside the Church Notice Board at the gateway to St. Wilfrid's but someone suggested it may confuse the casual reader so, after much debate, it was positioned outside Ferry Lane Cottage... and disappeared as the hedge was allowed to over-grow. Back in the days when Muskham was more green fields than patchwork development, William also owned the field nearest to School House at the opposite end of the village to where he lived. He was 72 when he passed away on 27 October 1971.

His wife was best-known as the Chapel organist whose bravery knew no bounds when they perched her on the front of a horse-drawn dray for Anniversary parades and she played on, apparently blissfully unaware of whether her four-legged friends were trying to tip her out.

While Mr.and Mrs. Elliott had June and Tommy, Kathleen became Mrs. E. V. Warwick and had three children, two sons and a daughter. Tommy, in addition to being a fine footballer for the village team, joined June in helping to run the Sunday School.

June married Tony Suter, an Old Magnusian who worked as an internal auditor at the Sugar Factory, on Saturday 30 July 1955. The service, at North Muskham Methodist Chapel of course, was conducted by the Rev. Frank Onyett of York, assisted by the Rev. W. Hewson Farmery. June had been educated at Newark High School for Girls, then worked as secretary to the Reverend D. Campbell Miller, head master at the Magnus Grammar School, before working in the Newark Borough Surveyor's Department.

Tony Suter was a pretty special bloke... and not because of his full name, Anthony Sidney Warriner Suter. What set him apart from the village lads was that he had spectacularly survived during the Second World War when the Germans sank the ship on which he was being evacuated to Canada. The ship that rescued him was called *Val de Mosa*, so there was no debate about what Tony and June should call their smashing new house, which was built especially for them in the Elliotts' orchard round the corner in Crab Lane. There, they brought up their own family: while son David moved away from the village, their daughter Carolyn continued the family tradition of playing a huge part in running the Chapel Sunday School.

2. Crab Lane to Ferry

CRAB LANE
BURRIDGE FARM: FRESH MEAT A REAL TREAT
Technically Mr. and Mrs. Winter Knight lived in South Muskham. But they made an impact on North Muskham that was/is impossible to ignore. Winter was the only son of Tom and Mary Knight, who recorded in the family diary that they killed two fat bullocks for the 1872 Village Feast, which always took place on the Saturday after 12 September. Adding that the beef went to the Reindeer Inn and the Newcastle Arms, they recorded: "Plenty of food was available at the inns, free to those on good terms with the landlords. Amusements – climbing greasy pole, shooting at clay pipes, dancing in the various clubrooms".

Winter, born in North Muskham in 1878, was three years younger than his sister Miriam but took over the family business as a matter of course. Indeed, he was listed in *Kelly's Directory* for 1912 as a butcher. To his neighbours, though, he was a cattle dealer long before 'wheeler dealer' became a catchphrase. His mission at Burridge Farm was to produce meat that would be sold in the Butcher's Shop down the Main Street. Quite how fresh it was became a matter of debate in the village – particularly after Frank Rowland, the district nurse's husband, claimed to have spotted the same dead sheep in the same spot in Winter's yard on two visits a week apart. His second alleged sighting coincided with Winter discovering it and insisting it was newly dead and therefore could be sold in the shop.

The beast that could not be housed in the brick buildings and crew yard beside the farmhouse were grazed in the marshes from the railway line at South Muskham (no gravel pits or A1 dual carriageway then!) all the way through to the double clapper gates between Reindeer House and the Ferry at North Muskham.

Although he was into his 70s by the early 1950s, Winter's appetite for farming was undiminished; and it was as well that he was in the habit of driving his car through the village in first gear with the engine racing noisily. For the village children had by then become accustomed to his ruse. Ronald Phillips-Moul recalled: "Even when I was at school in the 1920s, if you heard his car coming you hid! His first car was called a Dickey Seat Bean and if he saw you, he'd pull up and say, 'Just come and give me a bit of a hand for 10 minutes'. Ten minutes! You could be taken to somewhere like Normanton-on-Trent to drive beast back to Muskham. Once, he took me through Southwell to fetch some cattle. On the way back, him in his car and me walking, he led us from Southwell to Hockerton and then down the Mansfield road, and it was dark before we got home. And when you got back, he would never have any change to pay you… He was a jovial gentleman but tight as a crab's – er – claw".

Winter and his wife Liz (nee Littler, whose brother was a veterinary surgeon) had four children – two boys and two girls, all of whom flew the nest long before he called a halt to his canny dealing. Indeed, one of the girls married a Major R. Young. *The Muskham Magazine and Cromwell Courier* of March 1958 reported Mr. and Mrs. Knight had decided to retire to Newark and commented: "At least they will be spared the ordeal of seeing much of their land carved into two by the new road". Much of what used to be their land was gouged into gravel pits – without completely burying the legend of South Muskham's first wheeler-dealer farmer.

When Winter died at the age of 83 on 2 February 1962, there was no hint of irony apparent in the *Newark Advertiser* obituary that referred to him as "one of the best-known cattle dealers in Nottinghamshire". But the village boys reckoned they knew exactly what the reporter meant! Elizabeth died at the age of 85 in the Hillside Nursing Home at Newark on 30 September 1968 and, diplomatically, was described in the death notice in the *Newark Advertiser* as being "of Muskham". Close to their joint grave in South Muskham Churchyard are memorials to their oldest son, Robert, and his wife, Anne Elizabeth (nee Parsons, from across Crab Lane at the Old Villa). Robert was born on 24 February 1920 and died in Cape Town, South Africa, on 20 February 1990. Anne (born 8 June 1918) died in South Africa on 9 March 2000.

THE OLD VILLA: DEDICATED EXPORTER BEHIND DEMURE WALL

The big house, originally known as 'The Villa', positioned where Crab Lane makes its right angled turn, has been a prim and proper place in which to rear young ladies since protective father Richard Parsons had 10 rows of bricks added to the perimeter wall during the First World War to deter the local boys from climbing over to consort with his daughters. It didn't deter Winter's lad! And it was not the last time Mr. Parsons saw unusual action during a period of hostilities. In July 1940, when the Second World War black-out was being enforced rigidly to deter Hitler's bombers, he and his wife were summoned for "permitting the display of interior lighting which is visible from the outside". Mrs. Parsons' defence was: "My husband does occasionally do some strange things…"

The join in the wall twixt the old bricks and Mr. Parsons' added layers remains visible all these decades later, though there was added drama in the

2. Crab Lane to Ferry

1950s when the northern-most end of it fell down, revealing an ancient Baptist burial ground that attracted (whisper it, for goodness sake!) grave-robbers and caused so many anxieties that it almost took over from street lighting as the Parish Council's longest-running topic.

'Crab Lane Cemetery' regularly appeared in Parish Council minutes throughout last century. It was "taken in hand" by the village in 1918 when a search failed to discover any relatives of those buried there. The parish councillors themselves paid for the entrance to be bricked-up. Fast-forward to a PC meeting on 7 May 1957: the 10-foot high wall was reported to be in a dangerous state, 15-inches out of upright (which, in centimetres, means it was Muskham's equivalent of the Tower of Pisa). The Nottinghamshire County Council surveyor had been contacted but nothing satisfactory had resulted (in other words, he told the Parish Council: "It's your problem!"). It was agreed that Southwell Rural District Council (forerunner of Newark and Sherwood District Council but based in a fairly modest house opposite the Minster at Southwell) be asked if they could get it repaired.

In due course, the RDC agreed it was a danger to pedestrians and, at their next meeting on 1 October 1957, the parish councillors decided to inspect the wall for themselves. The result of their deliberations was announced at their next meeting on 16 April 1958: The wall should be lowered to five feet high.

So it remains a mystery which ignored souls – and how many – lie forgotten. The only name this author has been able to unearth is Kenneth Mackenzie, who died of a rapid consumption at the age of 20 on Thursday 8 September 1825 and was reported by the *Nottingham Review* to have been "interred in the Baptist Burial Ground at Muskham Villa".

Even though the other skeletons remained anonymous, the Villa was rented by some high-powered families in the wake of the rather eccentric Mr. Parsons as befits a residence that offered splendid views across Burrige Marsh Common (as it was known for centuries) and contained (according to a sales agent's blurb in 1829): "On the ground floor, handsome entrance hall, dining room, servants' hall, kitchens and every other requisite convenience. On the second floor, drawing room, library room and two good-sized bedrooms. In the attics, four good sleeping rooms and store room. Double coach house, stable, well-stocked dovecote, large greenhouse, gardens and pleasure grounds most tastefully laid-out, with paddock. Total: three and a half acres. Also two pews in North Muskham Church". By 1859, it had expanded to also include eight lodging rooms, a water closet, dairy and convenient offices. By 1892, it had grown a wine cellar and an upstairs water supply – seriously futuristic considering that, even in the 1950s, some folk were still using water from wells or outside taps.

First of the post-Parsons occupants in the 1950s were the Palmers. Mr. J. E. Palmer was the managing director of Farrars, the boiler-makers in Northgate, Newark – a businessman with a financial background but a grasp of the need to export that was far ahead of his time. Educated at Lincoln Technical College and the Scottish School of Accountancy in Glasgow, he moved to Newark in 1913 when Farrars became a private limited company. He was made manager in 1919, a director in 1929, and managing director in 1939 on the death of Sir Louis Smith. During the early 1950s, recognising the importance of worldwide trade, he went on a trip round the world to build a large export trade in not only the boilers for which Farrars were famous but also for fish-meal plants. Back home, he was a vice-president of Newark Chamber of Commerce and president for a time of Newark Rotary Club. Unsurprisingly, he had little time to spend on village affairs and had moved to live at The Firs, London Road, Newark, by 1957 when he retired as MD of Farrars but remained on the board of directors.

By the time the 1958 edition of *Kelly's Directory* was compiled, the occupier of the Old House was listed as Dorothy Golding. In fact, she was the housekeeper, living in a flat in a far corner of the house while her husband was serving in the RAF. Her employers were the Crabtree family, who had a son Reg and a daughter who wed Keith Whitehouse, a Newark optician. Mr. Crabtree was a great socialiser, frequently to be found in The Crown when he was not busy working as a manager at Newark Gravels, based in Grove Street, Balderton. They were taken over by Hoveringham Gravel in the 1960s, a deal that was to spark the appearance of gravel pits – later to be called fishing lakes – that dramatically lowered the water levels and reduced the flooding risks in both North and South Muskham.

Coincidentally, the wall of the burial ground fell into Crab Lane in December 1962. Vandals broke into the brick vault and exposed the skeletons. The Parish Council arranged for the erection of a fence, but that did nothing to protect the site from trespassers. Enquiries were made of the British Council of Churches and the Baptist Union of Great Britain but no owner could be found. This is not surprising: the Nottinghamshire County Archive has the deeds dated 16 and 17 January 1810 stating that for 10 shillings (50 pence) brewer John Reynoldson, late of Newark and now of Bromley, Middlesex, leased to John Stephenson of Liverpool, William Guyton of Bromley and William Mabbott of Newark land "formerly part of Pye Yard Close" Eventually a new wall was built and the site was left to disappear beneath a tangle of nettles and weeds.

2. Crab Lane to Ferry

ELM TREE HOUSE: PERSONALISED PLATES – AND A TV!
Herbert Talbot had a lorry with personalised number plates – HHT – years before it was fashionable for many folk to own transport more expensive than a pedal cycle. More pertinent to Muskham's interest in the crowning of Queen Elizabeth II, Herbert also owned a television. He bought it the previous November; a giant cabinet with a 12-inch screen that became the focal point for most of the inhabitants of Crab Lane from 9am to 9pm on 2 June 1953.

It was just as well most of the neighbours crowded into the sitting room. If many of them had stayed at home and tried to boil an electric kettle, the screen would have shrunk as a result of the extra burden on the power supply. Middle son Alan explains: "We were at the end of the line for electricity supply to the Lane and if anybody put a kettle or anything else on, our TV picture used to shrink. Dad complained and they eventually made a circuit to cure that problem". In fact, it took the East Midlands Electricity Board four more years to complete what it called "a scheme for reinforcing supplies" to the locality. The EMEB proudly announced to the eighth meeting of the Nottinghamshire Local Committee of the East Midlands Electricity Consultative Council in Nottingham in April 1957 that the voltage had been improved. The Committee, not totally impressed, expressed satisfaction at the improvement affected but decided to review the position in the district "from time to time".

The fluctuating supply was the second reason why it was as well that Herbert had had the wit to buy the TV seven months ahead of The Big Day. First came the alarming discovery that the chimney of The Cottage (as it was then known) was not high enough for the aerial to pick up reception from a transmitter high in the Lincolnshire Wolds, so he had to buy a "double extended pole" which was duly planted not far from the back door of The Cottage and picked up the black and white signals... provided nobody switched on a kettle. Mind you, the electric price structure in 1953 encouraged consumers to use more. The first 84 units were charged at 4d (slightly less than 2p) each, all units thereafter were charged at seven-eighths of an old penny each. And housewives wishing to forego the pleasure of cooking in the black-leaded oven beside the coal fire could rent an electric cooker for 12 shillings (60p) a quarter.

Not that there was time or room for cooking on Coronation Day. The Talbots' youngest son Barry recalls of the crush: "The television was in the far corner of the room, below the windows that look out over the marshes. I sat on the nearest corner of the table first thing in the morning and never moved all day for fear of losing my place".

Alan adds: "Mum made sandwiches for everyone and stacked them on the back of the table. We all sat there, glued all day". Open house was second nature to the Talbots. "Everybody knew everybody else in those days", recalls Alan. "For example, we used to have a pig. We'd kill it on a Saturday and there'd be fries and all sorts going round".

From which you'll gather the Talbot influence stretched far beyond that momentous day in 1953 – though it might have ended almost before it had begun. No sooner had Herbert and his young brood moved in than The Cottage shipped 5 feet of flood water in the early months of 1947. "Dad made a raft and floated around the garden rescuing the hens out of the apple trees", says Alan. "Then we went to stay in the big house across the road and watched from the attic windows to see whether our new home would be washed away".

The frightening experience did not deter them. Successive floods merely strengthened the family love affair with the 300-year-old cottage they proudly renamed Elm Tree House. The elements also probably had something to do with the black humour that helped the boys weather the storms of strict school teachers; not so much at South Muskham School when they were little but at Sutton-on-Trent, where Alan and Barry were moved as early teenagers to avoid being sent to Sconce Hills Secondary School at Newark. "We couldn't go on the buses to Sutton without paying so I biked", says Alan. "Eight miles there, eight miles back. Plus, some days, woodwork at Tuxford. And maybe a football match".

Barry, who was deemed too young to bike along the increasingly busy North Road to Sutton School, remembers: "If we behaved, we were let out for the 3.10 bus back home. If not, we had to wait till 4.10. I used to while away the time playing football with Mo Jordan on the lawns". *So you weren't always good, Barry?* He smiles: "Got caned twice one day. Can't remember why I got it in the morning. Then at dinner time, I squirted the head teacher, Mr. Whiteoaks, with a water pistol. It was a case of mistaken identity. I was in the boys' toilet. I heard footsteps. Thought it was the bigger lads coming to get me. So I fired. He asked me if I had anything to say about being caned for a second time. I said I did: would he mind doing it on the other hand this time cos the right one still stung. He did".

But Barry wasn't a bad lad really. On leaving school at 15 (in April 1953), he went to work as an apprentice joiner for Ernest Coleman at Balderton. "Stayed there 20-odd years", he says.

When Alan left school at 15, he earned an apprenticeship at Stephenson's, farm machinery manufacturers and repairers whose works were sandwiched between Newark Castle railway station and Nicholson's engineering works, whose clock tower eventually became a focal point for a Waitrose supermarket. Working hours? "You started at 7.30am", says Alan, "and you sometimes worked until 2.30 the following morning if there were farm repairs to be done. And no matter what time you finished, you had to be back there to start again at 7.30am".

Their oldest brother Ralph also avoided going to "Sconnies". Once it became clear he would not be allowed to stay at South Muskham School until he was 15, he was moved to lodge with an auntie in Newark so that he could qualify to attend Barnby Road Secondary Modern School. He went on to become a builder, creating a business that was carried on by Barry's son, Martin – from the house occupied by Syd Thomas – in the 21st century.

As for Herbert, he had left school at 12 and went on to make his living as a haulage contractor in the days when lorries had a maximum speed of 18mph, a weight limit of one-and-a-half tons, and travelled on single carriageway roads that meandered through, rather than round, every city, town and village in the UK. So work for Herbert was pretty much a game of patience, particularly during the period when he carted two loads of gravel a day from Teale's at Carlton-on-Trent to build the famous Ship Hotel at Skegness; and when every load he delivered for the Wartime aerodrome at Ossington disappeared instantly into the liquefied clay. Deliveries were rather more exciting to the RAF airfield at Bottesford… "The bombers were circling round and Dad had a pole on the back of his cab with a yellow flag flying so the pilots could see us", says Alan.

Herbert's lorry was also a priceless form of Wartime transport when he spent his nights patrolling with No.1 Platoon of the 11th (Newark) Battalion of the Notts Home Guard. One of the bravest forays by our version of *Dad's Army* took place one freezing damp foggy night when they had a phone call claiming German paratroops had been seen creeping around the Kelham Hills. Pausing only to load the back of his lorry with his platoon, their guns, garden forks, walking sticks and anything else that could – at a stretch – be a weapon, Herbert ventured up into the hills… where somewhat apprehensive reconnaissance revealed that the shadowy figures were not heavily-armed invaders but meandering cattle.

Come peacetime, Herbert spent enough time at home to develop a super garden, between his cottage and the Fleet, which was as easy on the eye of the folk passing by as it was nutritious for the boys clustered round the kitchen table. He won the prize for the best rose at the 1966 show organised by Muskham and District Horticultural Society and was presented with the Crawley Cup. And annually repaired it after the inevitable floods.

ROSE COTTAGE: TRAGIC MOTHER AND A HERO SON

The Beckett family endured a kind of heartbreak that was all too familiar in the early 1950s – yet they still produced one of the village's greatest sporting heroes. There was nothing particularly exceptional about the man of the house. Sid had fought through the Second World War, and had now returned to his work as a general labourer with the council – out from 7.30am till well gone 5pm Monday to Friday and from 7.30am to past noon on Saturdays.

It was what he came home to that was so sad. His wife, Rosina (one of the Phillips-Moul family) lived in a wooden shed in the garden in the forlorn (and ultimately vain) hope that such exposure to fresh air would cure her of one of the great killer illnesses of the age, tuberculosis. They called it TB or consumption. They opened special hospitals dedicated to the treatment of sufferers – the local one was on the Rainworth road into Mansfield. But there was no known cure for it. The medical profession came up with an immunisation against diphtheria, another disease that had seemed incurable; and was beginning to control the outbreak of polio that was attacking children like a frightening plague. But TB claimed four deaths in the Southwell rural district, which included North Muskham, in 1953 and five more in 1954. So for poor Rosina there was no lasting relief in the shed, which was built on railway sleepers to keep it above flood level.

The birth of their son, Rowland had been so difficult that they gratefully named him after the midwife who delivered him (Mrs. Rowland, the district nurse who we'll meet in the terraced row up the North Road towards Cromwell). His grandmother moved in to Rose Cottage to bring him up. And what a job she did!

Rowland grew up to be a credit to himself, his family and the village. He won a place at the Magnus Grammar School, where he played rugby union, and then became a draughtsman at Farrars' boilerworks. To his many admirers in the village, he became a goal-scoring hero at football, most notably during 1954 while he was also doing his National Service in the RAF and getting married.

Shortly after Harold Johnston re-formed North Muskham FC, as early as 16 October 1952, the teenaged centre forward Rowland distinguished himself by scoring all six goals in a match against Orston in Division Two of the Newark and District League. It wasn't quite a perfect six. One of them was an own goal. But that hardly diminished Rowland's achievement. Muskham won by 5–1; and they weren't often that good!

2. Crab Lane to Ferry

And Rowland went one better while on weekend leave early in the 1954–55 season, scoring seven goals at home to Newark United – and this time they all counted for Muskham. The feat earned him sports page headlines in the *Newark Herald* of 25 September 1954.

The next time Rowland Maurice Beckett got into the *Herald*, he was in a page 3 picture in the edition dated 27 November 1954 – marrying Miss Janet Plowright who lived at Elkesley, near Retford, and was on the staff of the Ministry of Pensions and National Insurance at The Ossington, Newark. Not surprisingly, his football team-mates formed a guard of honour as the new Mr. and Mrs. Beckett emerged from North Muskham Chapel. The Rev. W. Hewson Farmery officiated at the choral service; neighbour Ralph Talbot was best man; and the organist was Mrs.Elliott. The bride, the *Herald* reported, was attractively attired in a dress of white figured brocade with long veil held by a head-dress of orange blossom. Her bouquet was of red carnations. The reception at South Muskham Schoolroom was attended by about 60 guests (quite a stretch for the old building, which rarely had more than 35 pupils). The honeymoon was spent at Skegness, the bride travelling in a turquoise grosgrain two-piece camel coat and black accessories. The pair made their home in Farndon Road, Newark. Janet's gain was North Muskham's loss!

WYNDWAYS: KEEPING AN EYE ON THE BUSES
John Thomas, founder of the family bus company, lived with his wife in the house behind the bus garage until Ralph Talbot built them a bungalow in the grounds of the company. He sold Wyndways to Bill Wilson, whose forte was to make grandfather clocks, using as the casings coffins bought from Arthur Parlby, the undertaker and joiner who lived at South Muskham.

BUNGALOW: BUILDING NEW LIFE AND FRESH HOPE
Two condemned cottages stood at the time of the Coronation where "Young Harry" Clipsham, the son from The Shades up Main Street, was to bring his bride in 1955. His efforts in building the bungalow (in which his widow, Sheila, still lives) somehow epitomised the regeneration of this area of the village. It is easy to imagine folk deciding that improvements just weren't worth the effort, what with the Trent flooding so frequently into the Lane.

But Young Harry used all the building expertise instilled in him by his Dad and his Uncles, sited his new home high enough above the Fleet to make flooding highly unlikely – and quietly inspired countless others over future decades to improve their properties to make the most of the superb views over the Fleet and the Trent in the most tranquil part of the village.

CROWN COTTAGES: BUSY BEING GREAT PARENTS

Two young families boasted hard-working fathers in the semi-detached cottages at the bottom of the field and orchard between Crab Lane and The Crown.

Harry Talbot worked full-time as a railway platelayer on the local gang. And he also found time to rear pigs and grow sugar beet – sometimes with the help of his railway mates when it was harvest time, always with the help of his wife, Addie (short for Adeline).

Born in 1910, Addie moved with her parents to North Muskham aged 12. When she left school three years later, she began work at Mumby's clothing manufacturers in Newark, cycling there and back every day in all weathers. She only gave up the job when she wed Harry in 1942; after all, a woman's place was in the home in those days.

Except Addie's place was also at Harry's side when he fulfilled his ambition to possess a small holding. Initially he bought a few pigs and kept them beside the cottage. Eventually they graduated to buy the field opposite The Crown on Main Street. Harry's brick-built pig sties, which continued to defy the ravages of time into the 21st century, were always stocked well enough to keep Addie busy mixing pigswill when she was not tending for their daughter, Mavis, who had arrived late in 1945 and was ensconced at South Muskham C of E Primary School by 1953.

In 1959, Harry and Addie moved into a bungalow freshly built in their Main Street field – happy as pig rearers in their idea of heaven. After Harry

2. Crab Lane to Ferry

*Celia and Valerie Ward on the prom at Bridlington in 1952...
and their dad, Roy...*

sadly passed away in 1980, Addie continued to serve the village diligently. She belonged to the Women's Institute for 46 years, was Bright Hour treasurer at the Chapel for two decades, made door-to-door collections for charities supporting the blind for 30 years and spent 20 years on the Parish Council. The regimental line of street lights along Main Street from Mill Lane towards the Church stand as glowing testimony to her effectiveness. Addie was 93 when she died on 8 November 2003.

The Talbots' next-door neighbours in Crown Cottages in the '50s were Roy Ward and his daughters... who, Mavis recalls, had a habit of noisily clearing-out his fire grate around midnight.

There was a good reason for this. Roy, one of the huge Ward family that was dotted all around the village, was something of a rarity in the '50s: a male single parent. But the little bloke coped magnificently after his wife departed. He was part of the little army that biked to work at the Newark factories, working five-and-a-half days out of seven. At home in the evenings, on Saturday afternoons and Sundays, he had the energy to keep the cottage smart and the garden productive.

His younger daughter Valerie Ann was the only girl from North Muskham School to pass the 11-plus in 1955. She made such good use of her years at the Lilley and Stone High School for Girls that she went on to make a career as a nurse.

While her older sister Celia moved to Southampton, Val remained close to her roots. Now Mrs. Donnelly, she lives in South Muskham but retains happy memories of her childhood – especially apple scrumping expeditions with friends such as Jean James, ballet dancing with Harriet Barley on the terrace of the Old Hall and putting on plays in front of Roy's garden shed with her friends – and of the virtues instilled by her father.

Roy Ward, as dedicated a gardener as he was a father, died aged 86 on 28 January 1992. But as can be seen from the family picture on page 106 – taken at a wedding in the late 1940s/early '50s – the Wards were a formidable force!

Not all of them lived in the village, of course, but Val can be seen beside the elbow of the lady holding the baby on the right. Bus driver Reg is immediately behind the bride.

No.10: RON AND THE BRASSY WOMEN

Ron Phillips-Moul worked 48 hours a week as a toolmaker for the Ransome & Marles Bearing Company Limited. In the income tax year 1952–53, his gross pay was £458 17s 0d (£458.85) and he paid tax amounting to £19 8s 0d (£19.40). Ron was able to be precise about this because he and his wife Jean saved such memorabilia. And it represented a huge leap in wealth from his days as an apprentice: in 1927, he worked 48-and-a-half hours a week for 8 of the Sovereign's shillings (40p).

By the '50s, he'd helped win a war. It was widely acknowledged that R&M produced the best ball-bearings in the world; and Ron had been one of their bravest toolmakers. Not just because he survived the bombing of the factory, either. He also emerged relatively unscathed through the 'battle of the sexes' that male apprentices always seemed to lose. Ron explained: "When apprentices were 18, they had to go for special training. The short straw was the Brass Shop because they were all women in there. Everybody dreaded the Brass Shop because they used to rub grease on unmentionable parts of apprentices to let them know who was boss. Of course, I got the Brass Shop. On the first day, I learnt more about life than in my previous 18 years! I'd never heard a woman swear until I got there".

Once he'd survived that, beating the worst Hitler could throw at him and his mates was chickenfeed. The worst came one dinner time. It was 7 March 1941: "There were some roof spotters who sounded a bell. We rushed to the shelters. We heard the plane come over and drop its bombs, about 50 yards from where we were. After they exploded, the enamel lights came down the length of the shop. After the 'all-clear' blew, we went out and tidied up. They said, 'You young 'uns had better go home. We'll send for you when we need you'. They didn't want us to see some of the sights in there.

"My bike was near the gatehouse at the Beacon Hill end. I'd got down the side of the railway when this plane came over, spitting machine gunfire. It

2. Crab Lane to Ferry

seemed as if it was following the railway line from Grantham. I stood outside a pillbox, transfixed, watching it drop three bombs. Then I dived in the air raid shelter. When the all-clear blew again, I biked home. We had to go back to work about a week later. 'Cleaning up', they called it. That wasn't nice. They never said how many died but it was too many".

Come peacetime, there were few concessions for War heroes. Unless you count cheap tickets for the men and women squeezing on to one of three Workmen's Special buses that passed through the village at around 5 past 7 every morning, Monday to Saturday. Thomas's bus set out from Norwell and aimed to beat to Muskham the two Lincolnshire Road Car 'competitors' that had begun their journeys at Tuxford and Sutton-on-Trent. Ron paid four-and-a-half old pence return (about 2p) for a 'Workmen's Return' ticket. In an era when more than 8,000 were in the engineering industry in Newark the buses were packed.

The wages were so good that, years before it became fashionable for families to buy luxury goods on tick, Ron and Jean were able to save and acquire their first television for "about £100" from Coynes, a huge shop in Newark Market Place. The set was manufactured by English Electric and resembled a sideboard in that it had doors that opened to reveal the screen. Their second TV reflected how popularity was reducing prices: it was an Ekco and cost a mere £70.

They also afforded a family: daughter Janice came along in 1955 followed by son Keith in 1958. Their up-bringing was constant as could be. Ron bore a painful illness for many years before succumbing in 2001. Jean continues to live at No.10.

TRENTSIDE COTTAGES: THREE INTO ONE...

There were three cottages (that have now been converted into one) opposite No.10, on the Fleet side of the Lane.

Nearest the Lane lived Reg Ward, one of the legendary Ward family that lived all over the village and the No.1 driver in the Thomas Tours business when it was at the peak of its popularity. Not the biggest of blokes, Reg often gave the impression that he was out of his seat, wrestling with a steering wheel bigger than him, as he negotiated some of the tighter bends on the roads to the coast in those days before power steering made driving a doddle. Reg was only 55 when he died on 14 November 1965.

The Prides lived in the middle of the row: Dad was a county council lorry driver; Mum looked after their two daughters. The entire family eventually moved to live in Newark.

The Taylors who lived in the cottage nearest the Fleet were the parents of Addie Talbot. They had lived in Moorhouse when Addie was born in 1910, in a lovely little cottage beside a stream that frequently flooded. So when they moved to North Muskham in 1922, the nearby Fleet held no terrors for them. Alice Taylor was 69 years old when she died on 17 June 1959. Her husband Herbert was 95 when he passed away 12 days before Christmas 1975.

WOODEN BUNGALOW: FIRST STEP ON PROPERTY LADDER
In the age before credit cards and bountiful bank loans provided instant palatial homes for young lovers, wartime flyer Ken Pape began peacetime life with his wife Dorothy in one of the flats in North Muskham Grange while he settled into a comparatively mundane role as a college lecturer. They had met at RAF Cranwell: Dorothy was a private secretary to one of the high-up officers, having earned a 1st Class certificate in her secretarial exams at the age of 16 in 1933 to follow the diploma in piano playing that had enabled her to become an Associate of the London College of Music a year earlier.

The dapper Kenneth William Pape (who became 'Ken' to everyone in the village) wed Dorothy Margaret in 1941 when only the RAF 'few' could prevent Nazism overrunning the free world. War-work well and truly done by 1947, they enjoyed the peace of North Muskham so much that they spent their spare time building a wooden bungalow at the dead-end of Crab Lane. Even when the sun shone, the Papes' little palace was in the shadow of Ron Phillips-Moul's smashing cottage. When the lane flooded (which it seemed to do pretty well every winter at its lowest point until the excavation of gravel pits in the 1960s lowered the water table), the driest way out was by foot, up the path to Main Street that all the residents spread with ashes from their fires in order to keep the mud at bay.

Mrs. Pape helped the early finances by giving piano lessons to anyone ready to pay 2s 6d (12½p) an hour – and woe betide the child who did not practice thoroughly between the weekly lessons. "It was a nice little bungalow, but she was very strict", recalls one of her pupils, Jill Marriott. "She used to frighten me to death in case I hadn't practiced enough to please her". While Ken's career progressed so well at the Brackenhurst Agricultural College near Southwell that he moved his family from the shadows to the olde worlde grandeur of the Villa, he became increasingly influential in the village. He served St. Wilfrid's as a church warden for 30 years while Dorothy used her musical skills to stand-in for regular organist Syd Thurman whenever necessary and to teach piano to girls at Newark High School.

2. Crab Lane to Ferry

When the Pape family graduated to the spacious Villa at the opposite end of Crab Lane in 1961, they lost little time turning it into 'open house' for various good causes. A coffee evening on the Papes' lawn in the summer of '66 raised £66 for North Muskham Church funds. It was a princely sum indeed even allowing for the thanks due for England's footballers winning the World Cup by defeating West Germany in the final at Wembley Stadium. No wonder Mr. Pape was re-elected as people's warden at the next annual general meeting of the Parochial Church Council. Or that he was voted on to the Parish Council and, in due time, elected as Chairman. His term in charge coincided with Syd Thomas becoming North Muskham and Bathley's representative on Southwell Rural Council, and there suddenly seemed to be a greater urgency about parish pump politics. For example, they joined forces quite effectively in 1968 to stir the RDC into action over inadequate street lighting – which had been a running sore with villagers since it had first appeared a decade and more earlier.

While all of this was going on, the Papes' three daughters were doing them proud, too. The eldest, Barbara, was the only North Muskham child to pass the 11-plus at North Muskham County Primary School in 1953. The other successes, Cynthia Lambert and Suzanne Weatherhead, hailed from Cromwell. In due time Barbara plus her sisters, Jean and Jose, all emerged from the Lilley and Stone High School for Girls at Newark with enough GCE A-levels to go on to further education. Jean returned to the village to teach at Muskham County Primary School for two years from 1966–68 before true love tore her away from the village. Her bridegroom, John Rouse, worked for the National Provincial Bank in Chalfont St. Giles, Buckinghamshire, and they moved down there after their wedding at St. Wilfrid's in the summer of '68. Given away by Ken, she wore brocade and carried red rosebuds and fern. A honeymoon in the Lake District followed the reception at the Villa, which the Papes always called 'The Old House'.

As if that wasn't idyllic enough, the Parish Council took Ken – and his neighbours – into fantasy land in 1969. It launched a campaign to persuade Southwell Rural District Council to turn Crab Lane into a one-way street. The story, which was not published on 1 April, in the *Newark Advertiser* did not reveal whether vehicles were to be allowed into the lane or out of it. Thankfully local knowledge prevailed – the powers-that-be were reminded what used to be Town Street was frequently flooded by the Fleet and the Trent – and Crab Lane remained a two-way *cul de sac*.

In 1981, Mr. and Mrs. Pape had the Old Stables transformed into a fine residence and moved in. Legend has it that the previous human occupants of the Villa's stables were soldiers in Cromwell's army aiming their cannon at Newark Castle during the Civil War.

After Ken died in 1998, Mrs. Pape moved to Norfolk to be close to one of their girls. She passed away at the age of 86 on 9 November 2003.

BURRIDGE FARM COTTAGES: UNCLE ALF TAKES CARE

Recently wed Alf and Rosie Smith lived in one half of the Cottages at the end of the Crab Lane cul de sac, backing on to the tufty grass of Chapel Field. A labourer at Burridge Farm lived in the other half, though nobody seems to remember who he was.

The Smiths had wed in early middle age. Alf, a gentle man from a large family at Carlton-on-Trent, worked at Ransome & Marles. Rosie, one of the Talbot girls from up the village, unhesitatingly took in one of Alf's nieces, Jean, whose mother had wed a Canadian airman and gone to live on the other side of the Atlantic.

Young Jean became a pupil at North Muskham School, riding a secondhand bike far too big for her the length of the village to and from lessons, delivering the Kings' library books to various addresses on her way home some nights. As she got older, she followed her Mum to Canada for a spell, while Uncle Alf and Auntie Rosie moved to one of the nice new council houses on Newark's Hawtonville Estate. But 50 years on, Jean was back in the village – living where she used to go to school close to one of her own daughters, Delores.

NORTHFLEET: WORK BASE FOR MODERN FAMILY

Doug Smalley and his wife Barbara were an ideal kind of modern couple in the '50s. Obeying the diktat of the day to 'get a trade', Doug was developing a thriving business as an agricultural and electrical engineer (and found time to pursue his hobby of racing motor bikes at weekends).

Indeed, Doug and his brothers had spent their teen years building what we would now recognize as trail motor bikes and trialling them up and down the Trent towpaths. Continuing his pioneering instincts into his working decades, Doug was responsible for persuading many farmers to forsake the wells that had provided them with water and modernize to electrically-driven pumps in an age before water supplies and sewage systems became commonplace.

Meanwhile busy little Barbara, one of the huge Ward family, ran the home and, I seem to recall, kept a run full of chickens at the bottom of the garden, close to where the Fleet rippled its way towards the Trent. And they spent the '50s bringing up two lovely daughters, Donella and Linda.

2. Crab Lane to Ferry

MARSH COTTAGES: DEFYING THE FLOODS

Doug's grandmother, widow Ada Smalley was arguably the bravest inhabitant of North Muskham for most of the 20th century. Winter after winter, the river Trent overflowed across the marsh – and into the frail little great-grandmother's cottage. It looked gorgeous in summer, facing south, soaking up the sun. But it nestled so low, it was almost dwarfed by the hedge that curved towards it from Marsh Lane. And it was regularly submerged in the days when the water level was higher because there were not yet any gravel pits in the vicinity. Undeterred by the roar of the water as it crested the towpath and cascaded across the marsh, Mrs. Smalley would not hear of moving... except from room to room in her cottage to stay ahead of the rising tide.

And she had an ally in the substantial shape of the farm labourer who lived in the other half of the cottages. Harry Pilkington worked at Manor Farm, Bathley, well into his old age and cycled home every night with a small enamel billycan of milk swinging gently from his handlebars.

Henry Pilkington, as he had been christened, died in Nottingham General Hospital aged 86 on 31 August 1968. After the death of Mrs. Smalley, the old cottage was demolished but not forgotten. Grandson Doug had the land built up above flood level and oversaw the erection of a retirement bungalow for himself and his wife Barbara.

It was placed at what had been the highest point of Ada's old cottage garden and Doug's lawnmower provided a glimpse of what Town Street must have been like in the days when the main trade route between the Kelham/Bathley Hills and the Trent were via what became known as Hopyard, Moor and Mill Lanes to Crab Lane. Careless dog walkers, who failed to scoop the poop, hardly deserved such good going but Doug gave the impression of being proud of all around him.

He and Barbara called the new bungalow LinDon and it had such a great view over the marsh that more than one would-be developer expressed an interest in building a housing estate. "Only if you put them on stilts", Doug always advised them.

After his death, Barbara moved first to Mackleys Lane and then Main Street.

CHURCH COTTAGES: FOUR FAMILIES LOOKING DOWN ON THE TRENT

"Don't call it a row", I was instructed when Mum, Dad and 12/13-year-old me moved into No.2 in the late 1950s (all the way from Bathley so that I didn't have to walk home from the Lord Nelson public house, where the Magnus School bus dropped me off every late afternoon). The address was most definitely Church Cottages. Not Church Row. Nor even Church Row Cottages. But, to give them their full handle, Church Cottages, Church Lane. (And, in an astonishing sign of the times years later, if dear Dad had not been cremated, he would surely have spun in his grave when Church Lane was renamed Peet's Drive. It is arguably the world's only example of a car mechanic becoming more important than religion!)

Back to 1953, and the owner of the four Cottages that had evolved from a barn overlooking the Marsh was Ada Smalley. Her widowed daughter-in-law Nora lived in the biggest Cottage, a three-up, three-down complete with lavatory that was only two steps away across the jitty from the kitchen door (this in a year when Bingham's at Sutton-on-Trent would sell you a shiny new 16-inch galvanised sanitary pan for £1 3s 6d). And Mrs. Smalley had a wooden garage. No wonder her cottage was called No.1. Widowed at a relatively young age, she was rightly proud of the way her sons turned out: Doug you have already met; Ken developed a motor repair business near

Church Cottages, facing the Marsh, with Mrs. Grantham's cottage behind the high fence on the left; Miss Rodgers next door; us with Dad's flower garden in bloom; and Mrs. Smalley's larger home on the right, closest to Church Lane which took us past Aingarth to Main Street.

2. Crab Lane to Ferry

Bathley Green. And Mrs. Smalley lived a pretty busy life, herself. She was an active committee member of North Muskham WI, never slow to encourage newcomers to join.

No.2, a two-up, two-down with the lavatory in a little shed 20 yards up the garden path, was occupied at Coronation time by the Hacketts: a sister of Mrs. Smalley, her husband and their son, Clifford. When they moved to Newark later in the 1950s, they were replaced by the Frecknalls: Harry, a railway platelayer; Ivy Annie, his wife; and me, their (some say) spoilt son. (More about us if anyone ever writes about North Muskham and the Sporting Sixties!)

In No.3 were Bertha Rodgers, a painfully thin and elderly creaking gate (but shyly pleasant for all that), and her lodger, a man of similar age whose name I cannot recall, who worked for W. N. Nicholson and Sons Ltd at the Trent Ironworks on the opposite side of Newark's Trent Bridge to the Castle, up to the age of 65.

Miss Rodgers (we always knew her as 'Miss Rodgers' and she never corrected us) was typical of her era in that she spent the prime of her life looking after her parents: her father William died on 11 February 1925 aged 71 and her mother Fanny was 75 when she passed away on 1 October 1932. Along the way, Miss Rodgers seems to have become most untypical of her era by giving birth to a son... or maybe she brought-up the boy of a relative. Either way, he grew up to be a worthy member of society and regularly visited her, as did several other of her relatives until she died on 13 February 1971 at the grand age of 83.

Flush up against the Church wall in No.4 were Mrs. Edie Grantham, her daughter Sheila, and lodger George Wain. Mrs. Grantham, like Mrs. Smalley, had been widowed young. A victim of the Second World War almost three years *after* hostilities ended! In the kind of tragic accident that would have exercised modern Health and Safety executives for months and probably led to court claims for millions in damages, her 39-year-old husband, Fred, was killed by a falling wall when Sheila was only five years old.

It happened on the windy afternoon of Wednesday 31 March 1948 on the bleak expanse of a wartime RAF station that was being demolished at Fiskerton, near Lincoln. The massive Nissen huts had been sold off to various interested parties, and Fred was among a working party sent from the Kelham Sugar Factory to take theirs down and trundle it back down the Fosse. He had worked at the factory for 20 years. Not as a builder. He was described as "a diffusion battery chargehand" at his inquest. But, then, another point made at the inquest was that none of the Sugar Factory party were builders. That did not stop them cracking on with the work, though, and they'd stripped the prefabricated sections out of the long sides when the rest of the building collapsed. Fred died instantly amid the mangled wreckage of the steel struts and one of his workmates, Lewis Hallam, aged 47, from Sutton-on-Trent, suffered back and head injuries. It was only when police launched an investigation that it emerged that the walls at either end of the hut had not been cemented onto the concrete base. They had just sat there throughout the War. And while nobody at the inquest risked guessing what caused it to finally fall down, the policeman who investigated said the wind was so strong that afternoon, he couldn't ride his bike into it in bottom gear.

"I should imagine it would be a Jerry-built job", said the man in charge of the Sugar Factory working party, William Henry Elliott, who by coincidence also lived in North Muskham. The Lincoln Deputy Coroner, Mr. H. J. J. Griffith, who conducted the inquest, agreed: "It appears that the buildings were put up in a hurry during the War and perhaps not quite so much care was taken to their construction as to those built at other times".

A verdict of Accidental death was recorded. The Sugar Factory let it be known that Fred was "a valued employee and a capable man at a variety of jobs". The Deputy Coroner passed on the court's deepest sympathy to Edie and Sheila. And that was it, basically.

Off they went back home to make the best of the rest of their lives. Sheila, a quiet and conscientious worker just like her Dad, went on to work in a shoe shop in Cartergate, Newark, before marrying. George was a lorry driver (for one of the breweries in Newark, among other employers) in the 1950s and much later moved in to charitable work for animals after flitting to live in Farndon. Edie, the dedicated mother and housewife, also left the Cottages, which in 1973 became North Muskham's first council houses.

TRENT COTTAGES: NURSE OUT OF AFRICA; AND A MAN OF PROPERTY

The much-travelled Nurse Gwendoline Mary Walker and the entrepreneurial Mr. and Mrs. Cecil Henry Pollard occupied the white-painted cottages between the gardens of Church Cottages and Trent Lodge that frequently had flood water in their front gardens as the Trent, marsh and Fleet became one.

Nurse Walker, as she was universally known, devoted her life to helping others. Fresh out of school in Lincoln, she was the first worker to be taken on at the Lincoln Occupation Centre for mentally handicapped men, women and children when it opened in 1924. Years later, she would recall: "There were five pupils – boys of five, seven and 17 and girls of 11 and 12 – all of

2. Crab Lane to Ferry

differing grades of deficiency but all needing love, firmness and patience. On Friday afternoons, I had some higher grade older girls who could sew and knit, and one who played the piano beautifully. I loved the work and only gave up to train as a nurse for the mission field".

She spent more than 20 years putting her medical expertise to use in Africa. Her home became the Labombo Missionary in Portuguese East Africa, as Mozambique was called. On her return home, she was based in the Maternity Wing of Newark General Hospital, which occupied an imposing site flanked by London Road, Sherwood Avenue and Balderton Gate. In addition, she determined to ensure that new-born babies and their mothers thrived; and, to this end, a Young Wives' Group was so popular in North Muskham that, in 1952, 30 children and mothers enjoyed a New Year tea-party in the Church Hall. Community singing was followed by tea, after which thanks were extended to 'Nurse Walker and her committee' and all who contributed to the success. Alas, celebrations of the third anniversary of the group had to be cancelled because of the death of the King. Instead, arrangements were made for an outing to Calverton Lido in August – which seemed to say everything about the philosophy of Nurse Walker. Can't do it now? Never mind – we'll find another way.

Another example of her practical approach to life comes from Jill Marriott, who was her god-daughter. "Auntie Gwen, as I loved to call her, took her duties as godmother very seriously. She made sure I was confirmed as soon as she and my Mum agreed I was old enough to understand what it was all about. And she insisted on buying me my outfit for the day – a lovely white blouse and white pleated skirt. We used to go to Church with her every Sunday morning".

Nurse Walker ran her clinic for mothers and their babies once a fortnight in the room beside North Muskham Chapel long before whole forests would be pulped to create magazines packed with gadgets and suggestions. "We left our prams outside and waited in a row for baby to be weighed", recalls Mrs. Jean Phillips-Moul. "You'd get a tick on baby's card if they were all right. Nurse Walker would tell you if they should be started on solid foods, and give you all kinds of advice".

But kindly Nurse Walker never forgot her missionary work in Africa. As late as 1967 she was still marshalling the forces of North and South Muskham Mothers' Union to send knitting wool to her replacement as a missionary worker, Miss Shirley Smith, in Murgwanza, East Africa. It was probably the last of her annual parting gifts. Later that year, she bade a fond farewell to many of those she had helped in her second (or, rather, third) working life: she retired as organiser of North and South Muskham Young Wives' Group, which she had founded 15 years earlier. But she was still the MU enrolling member in 1969.

A small memorial plaque to Nurse Gwendoline Walker can be found in South Muskham Churchyard. Beside it is a shrub, planted in her honour, as a symbol that what she started had taken root so healthily that it would flourish for generations to come.

Her neighbour, 'Cec' (pronounced 'Sess') Pollard, was best known in the village as the man who grew beautiful carnations in greenhouses in the paddock behind and beside the Chapel. But his life had been much more colourful than that.

Foiled by the economic depression of the 1920s of any chance of following his father into farming, he worked nights for 20 years at Ransome & Marles' ball bearing factory, all the time craving an outdoor job. To say he prayed for the change in lifestyle would be crass, for he was a devout Christadelphian and read from the Bible every night before he went to work. And even while he continued working nights in the factory, he bought three and a half acres of a scrubby field from Mrs. Smalley Senior and started his horticultural sideline in two 40-foot greenhouses, growing tomatoes and sweet peas as well as the carnations that village folk still remember.

Cecil Henry Pollard died in 1970. His wife, Edith May Pollard died in 1973. Thirty and more years on, three generations of their offspring continued to thrive in the village: son Norman, grandson John and John's family.

TRENT LODGE: FRIENDLY LIFE OF A FARMING FAMILY

The Charles family and Mr. and Mrs. William Key lived in the imposing semi-detached houses that gaze out over the marsh. They got on extremely well, by all accounts. And it was a good job they did because their sleeping quarters were separated by only a curtain at the top of the stairs! "We could run up the stairs in one house and down the stairs in the other house without stopping", recalls one of Mrs. Key's grandsons, Stephen Guy. "The thing I best remember about the house is the huge fireplace in the Charles's front room. Uncle Tom (they weren't actually our uncles but they were as friendly as uncles so we called them uncles) used to stand us in the fireplace and measure us against the mantelpiece to show us how fast we were growing".

Once there were four Charles brothers: Reg, Clem, Tom and Fred plus sister Maddie, the offspring of the late William F. Charles and his wife. By the time the second Elizabethan era began, there were but two of the boys: Fred and Tom, who ran the farm across the Main Street at the Old Hall, plus their elderly mother, Mrs. F. N. Charles. They had two Ford tractors (presumably one each), one of them a 27N identical to one that has been lovingly maintained by Alan Talbot in Crab Lane.

Tom, who served as a special constable for several years, also toted a churn around the village every morning, selling milk. It was one of the most competitive jobs in the parish at the time: his was one of at least four rounds. Others were operated by Ernie Vickers at Manor Farm, Thomases from the Bus Garage and the Clipshams at Toll Bar House. The Charleses also took a momentous decision at one stage in the 1950s to go into pig production in a big way – probably the first exercise in intensive farming in North Muskham.

Sadly, the younger of the brothers, Fred, died at the age of only 49 on 24 April 1958. But "Uncle Tom", as Stephen Guy fondly calls him, continued to breed pigs and also to encourage the youngsters to enjoy themselves: "We had a fort in the orchard. Uncle Tom used to come out and encourage us to play. In fact, he often joined us in games like cowboys and Indians".

And he encouraged the entire family to help him with harvest – not least because some of his fields were as far away as the top end of Hopyard Lane, up the Bathley Hills towards Warner Wood. "Dad and everybody would join in fetching the bales", recalls Stephen. "And they'd always make sure they left a gap in the middle at the top of the load – a kind of igloo – so that we kids could ride back without being spotted. It wasn't particularly safe. I suppose it certainly wasn't legal. But it was fun!"

Tom was 63 when he passed away on 15 May 1969. One can only imagine the feelings of Mrs. Charles at his funeral on Monday 19 May 1969. She had had four boys – and out-lived all of them.

The Keys were a no-nonsense couple, typical of the no-frills era. When William passed peacefully away on 2 July 1957, the death notice in the following Wednesday's *Newark Advertiser* carried this stern instruction: "No flowers or mourning by request". Mrs. Mary Key went off to live in the prefab at the other end of the orchard with her daughter Renee's family, the Shearers.

REINDEER HOUSE: CONTENTMENT IN FORMER HOSTELRY
Bill Abbott and his wife, the sister of the Charles brothers, occupied what used to be an ale house that slaked the thirsts of carters who plied their trade twixt the Trent barges and the villages reached by direct route via Crab Lane, Marsh Lane, Moor Lane and (beyond Bathley) the Debdale and Kelham Hills. Last orders were taken by its final licensee, Charles Richmond, in July 1912, after which it became a fine old house with unlimited views across the marsh and Trent to Holme and, to the distant right, Winthorpe.

But what history its old oak beams had overseen! In 1840 Mormons held revival meetings in the clubroom at the Reindeer Inn, which was at that time lorded-over by the Weightman family. Some Newark men were so influenced by what they heard that they emigrated to Salt Lake City, the heartland of the movement in the USA. The ideology continued to prosper in North Muskham until a new Anglican vicar, the Rev. J. Winstanley Hull, was installed in 1853 and took such a proactive role in "stemming the advances of the Mormons", as contemporary accounts put it, that the movement collapsed locally.

By the 1860s, the Reindeer was the headquarters of an Oddfellows Club; the Evening Star held their anniversary meetings there for the best part of 20 years. A newspaper report in May 1877 noted that even though the weather was wet, "a good number" attended divine service.

But there was nothing rebellious about the occupiers in the 1950s. Bill Abbott had been a 29-year-old police constable in Doncaster when he wed Miss Madeline Mary Charles, aged 26, at St. Wilfrid's on 26 July 1924. Thirty years on, after a full working life with the Constabulary in Yorkshire, barrel-shaped Mr. Abbott gave the appearance of being more serene than divine. He had retired after decades of duty patrolling the streets of Sheffield and looked like a gentle giant of a man as he leaned on his garden gate looking out over the Marsh. Everything in his garden was just grand – literally and metaphorically – and Maddy, as his wife was known, was equally content to be back home.

TRENT BANK HOUSE: AN EXTENDED FAMILY

Don Ansell – the son (or maybe grandson) of the grand house that overshadowed 'the Ferry' pub and overlooked the sweep of the river Trent – was entirely typical of his time. A quiet young man who became much more than a postman to the villagers on his rounds. He instinctively took on the role of a social worker, ensuring that the elderly and infirm wanted for nothing irrespective of whether he had mail to deliver.

He lived with his Dad, Fred, and Mother, Muriel, plus Grandfather, James Wilson, until he married a nurse and moved into a bungalow especially built for them in the corner of their paddock facing the new Muskham School site. It was the precursor to the rest of the paddock and orchard connected with Trent Bank House becoming the development known as Eastfield. As part of the evolution, the part of the paddock overlooking the river became popular with a series of caravan dwellers in the late 1950s and early 1960s, especially as increased wealth made it easier for anglers to travel each weekend from smoky cities for a breath of fresh air.

James Wilson, a railway signalman who had been born in Wiltshire, was 80 when he died on 9 June 1962. Charles Frederick Ansell died on 14 June 1973. His wife, Alice Muriel, died on 24 March 1982. Don and his wife, who had two sons, eventually moved to live in Newark – and probably found a more rural outlook than his built-up orchard in North Muskham could provide – in a dwelling overlooking Devon Park.

NEWCASTLE ARMS: 'THE FERRY' BY ANY OTHER NAME

Harry Bowles was mine host of the public house at the bottom of Ferry Lane – and therefore custodian of the ferry boat to Holme. He chose to operate only rarely, which had got him into trouble with the parish councils of both Holme and North Muskham in 1941, when he was busy enough serving in the Newark Auxiliary Fire Service as well as running the pub. Arguing that the ferry crossing was "a public highway", both councils called on the owners of the pub, James Hole & Co., to keep the ferry open at all reasonable times. The company weighed-up their priorities during the Second World War and replied that "to put an able-bodied man there full time, if such was obtainable, would not be in the national interest at this present time, the number of people using the ferry during working hours not warranting it".

The ferry did not really make a comeback once the War gave way to hostilities in angling matches along the riverbank, on the dartboard in the Public Bar and at the dominoes tables in the Snug. Want a meal? Well, there were packets of crisps (only plain, of course) with optional salt in its little blue bag.

The riverbank was heavily booked by angling clubs throughout the season, and busloads would descend from the coal mining communities of Notts, Derbyshire and Yorkshire and even the steel mills of Sheffield in search of a Saturday or Sunday of fresh air. Not every trip was idyllic. The *Newark Advertiser* on 14 October 1953 carried this heart-breaking story:

A Bolsover woman who nearly 15 years ago saw her two sons drown at North Muskham Ferry while fishing, was persuaded to go to the Ferry again on Sunday with a party of anglers. And she saw the husband of a close friend die on the riverbank. Many of the anglers remembered the tragedy before the War when on Sunday they saw one of their party, Edward Jarvis, collapse. He was 45. When he had been fishing for about an hour, he asked his wife to light a cigarette for him. She did and he then asked her to lay him down. She asked the club secretary to help, but Mr. Jarvis was already unconscious. Dr. David Rider of Newark was called but Mr. Jarvis was dead by the time he arrived.

Lawful opening hours in all pubs were strictly limited in the 1950s: 10.30am – 2.30pm and 6.30pm – 10.30pm Monday to Saturday, noon – 2.30pm and 7pm – 10.30pm Sundays. But there was a special opening of 'the Ferry' on Thursday 9 June 1955 for more than 100 Mothers' Union members at a Deanery Festival. The ladies of Sutton-on-Trent, Weston, Carlton-on-Trent and Norwell had a lovely afternoon. They met at the Newcastle Arms and marched up Ferry Lane and along Main Street to the Church with their branch banners fluttering in the breeze. The service was taken by the Rev. Arthur Rigden (the last major service in the village before his death). The lessons were read by the Rev. Robert Keal from Sutton-on-Trent in his role as Rural Dean, and by the Rev. C. C. Fogerty, Vicar of Laxton. The preacher was the Venerable F. H. West, Archdeacon of Newark, and prayers were conducted by the Rev. L. C. Warner, the Vicar of Norwell. And then it was a case of everybody back to the pub for tea provided by the members of the North Muskham branch of the MU. Among those present were the Deanery President, Mrs. Aldred, and the secretary, Miss Keyworth. Not that the need to use a hostelry for such a quasi-religious occasion hastened the arrival of a North Muskham Village Hall. The next time the Deanery Festival came to North Muskham, in 1959, the ladies were invited to tea in... gulp!... South Muskham Village Hall.

Little wonder that all three of North Muskham's pubs were successful meeting, never mind drinking, places. Especially, in the case of 'The Ferry', once the weather was decent enough to encourage a stroll down the Trent side. Many families worked up their summer evening thirst with a stroll along the towpath as far as Cromwell Lock and back in this era before imperial land owners beside the Trent were minded to build barbed wire barricades.

TRENT VIEW HOUSE: DARK AND FOREBODING SWEETIE SHOP
The village's old coal depot was an unlikely place for the most genteel business in the village. Yet the comfortable house from which the Thompson family operated the North Muskham Coal Wharf for most of the 1800s had by the 1950s become tearooms run by a group of tiny spinster sisters known for miles around as 'the Miss Woods' – Miss Susan, Miss Beatrice and Miss Letitia May. The house, like so many properties in the village, was sideways on to its main aspect (in this case, the river) and faced the Newcastle Arms across the bottom of Ferry Lane. Between Trent View House and Ferry Lane Cottages was another property that had fulfilled a couple of roles. It had been built in the early 1800s as a clubroom for the North Muskham Friendly Society, an organisation that encouraged villagers to use their hard-earned

2. Crab Lane to Ferry

A picnic on the neatly-scythed bank between Ferry and Mackleys Lanes in the years when the only building was a yachting clubhouse.

cash wisely. Later it became a house – and for some time in the middle of the 20th century was occupied by the Longmates. After they departed, it became inexorably part of its slightly bigger, taller neighbour Trent View House.

Although Trent View House faced the sun, it always seemed a little foreboding... probably because of the high walls and foliage around its own wooded lawns that over-powered visitors, especially children, as they climbed the steep stone steps from the towpath that led to the front door, but also because of the shyness displayed by 'the Miss Woods' to their callers. Not that they were nearly as diffident as they appeared; otherwise, they would not have stocked a sweetie shop long after their genteel tearooms became a fad of the past. And none of the sisters stood taller than we children, anyway. In hindsight, it's safe to say they were little ladies with big hearts.

Letitia had died suddenly on 30 April 1957 and was described in the notice in the following Wednesday's *Newark Advertiser* as the "dearly beloved sister of Jim and Bee". There are two inferences to be drawn from this: the eldest sister, Susan had already died; and the impact made by the ladies had far out-weighed that of their brother James. The old house fell into disrepair before mysteriously burning down and eventually being replaced.

3. THE LANES TO BATHLEY

The first road between North Muskham and Bathley important enough to be given a name on maps was what is now known as Moor Lane. It was 'Shackley Dike Road' in the mid-1700s and, though it was never graced with a coat of tarmac, it still stands high enough above the fields and ditches to be recognized as a highway across the boggy moor that separates the parishes. It was an important route between the Trentside at North Muskham, taking traders along Town Street, Crab Lane and Mill Lane to Shackley (sometimes spelt Sharkley) Dike Road and, west of Bathley, Fillingate Road up the hills to the Dean Hall area between Caunton and Little Carlton.

By the 1950s Shackley Dike Road/Moor Lane was no more than a cart track (but still used by farm vehicles and adventurous children) while Bathley Lane and Norwell Lane took all the traffic. These were the folk who brought the lanes to life…

MILL LANE
MILL HOUSE: AFTER THE MILL FELL DOWN…
Geordie-born Ted Bennett was living proof that times were a-changing in North Muskham. He reared his family in the Mill House in the wake of the last of the actual millers in the village – the end of a breed who cut his own throat at the prospect of being forced out of business by improved transport making it easier for farmers to sell their corn to larger organisations capable of offering bigger deals. The windmill, erected in the 1790s with two pairs of stones and two flour cylinders, crumbled in the 1930s.

The last baker to operate it, William Streeton, had died "by his own hand" within its confines in the mid-1920s. Born in Grantham in 1860, Mr. Streeton died of a broken heart, blaming himself for the collapse of a business that had been in his family for generations. In 1886 he had been presented with a valuable timepiece on his marriage "in recognition of his services on the harmonium in the Chapel". He and his wife, Mary, who hailed from South Muskham, had six children – Charlotte, born in 1888; Mabel 12 months later; Emily another year on; Florence in 1893; Miriam in 1895 and Edgar in 1897 – some of whom appear in The Willows on Main Street in this recollection.

Mr. Bennett, on the other hand, was an incomer... the epitome of the modern man. A native of South Shields, Mr. Bennett had joined the Ransome & Marles staff at Newark on demobilisation after the First World War. He worked in the Cost Department, and spent 30 years as its head. The suddenness of the demise of milling as a rural industry is probably best illustrated by the fact that, after Ray Rippin died in 1963, the next occupants of his bungalow near the Crown Inn renamed it Mill View. They were spoilt for choice: to the left were the considerable remnants of Streeton's windmill; slightly to the right, across the fields and beyond the Railway Bridge, they could catch sight of the Bathley Mill on the lane from the Lord Nelson. Alas, neither was working by then; and within a decade, both had disappeared.

Mr. Bennett served on North Muskham Parish Council, becoming chairman at one stage, and spent four years on the Board of Managers of North Muskham School. Similarly, Mrs. Elsie Bennett was immensely practical – as housewives and mothers tended to be in their seemingly endless battle of wits against rationing (which was still so prevalent at the start of 1953 that, at the annual general meeting of North Muskham WI, a resolution was passed that in future members would have to take their own biscuits to meetings). During the early 1950s, Mrs. Bennett was a leading light in the Produce Guild that was one of the practical arms of the WI, having steered their three children well towards adulthood: Enid, John and Eileen.

Ernest Arnold Bennett passed away peacefully in his sleep at Newstead Hospital on 1 February 1958, by which time John was on National Service in Sarawak; and the following month, the parish magazine had this thought for his widow: "We offer Mrs. Bennett all our sympathy – the more because she is one of those rare people who can face up to hard blows like this without flinching. Your calmness and courage has [sic] been an example to us all, Mrs. Bennett".

Mill Cottage has been more than doubled in size since the 1950s (much more tastefully than many other old dwellings in the village).

CROSSING HOUSE: ROOM FOR GENERATIONS
In the small railway house at Mill Lane crossing lived a typical example of how '50s families stuck together in the face of adversity. Jack H. Rushby was

3. The Lanes to Bathley

the 'man of the house' – a platelayer in the gang that tended the track between the main line's junction with the Nottingham-Lincoln line and Cromwell.

His wife broke off her housework as necessary to open the gates by hand on the rare occasions traffic wanted to cross. But human nature was touchingly evident in the Rushby household, when four generations lived under the same little roof. Jack and his wife had a son, George. And when Jack's grandfather Joe died at Norwell, they thought nothing of giving a home to his widow, Ann.

Only a few days after the death of King George VI, Ann too passed away at the age of 87. Another close-knit family, the Clipshams, gave their stockhand Jock Granger time off work to play the organ at her funeral at North Muskham Church.

The crossing itself died in 1959. British Railways had employed a gentleman called Dr. Beeching to make economies. His report on where cuts should be made was so thorough, it became known as Dr. Beeching's Axe.

And it even knocked down Jack Rushby's house! Mill Lane was transformed into an unattended crossing. British Railways withdrew the crossing gate keeper and substituted locked gates. Keys were distributed to owners and occupants of land in the vicinity and "other persons reasonably interested such as the divisional surveyor and the local police constable". At the request of the County Council, they also arranged for the signalman at Bathley Lane to be able to automatically lock the gates whenever a train was approaching. Oh, and they installed a phone so that any frustrated motorist or pedestrian could talk to the Bathley Lane signalman.

It would have been more economical, of course, to leave things as they were for a couple of years. Then, the A1 dual carriageway came along and the Mill Lane railway crossing was made truly redundant. Now, why didn't Dr. Beeching think of that? To be fair to him, he did his best: he moved thousands off the railways and onto the roads.

SHACK/BUNGALOW: JUST WHO WERE THEY?

As the '50s unfolded, the Rushby family opened its arms of friendship wider than anyone in the village had ever dreamed likely. Into a wooden shed in the garden of the Crossing House moved a couple who became known to most of us as 'The Poles'. The word was that they had been among the millions displaced during the Second World War. 'Displaced' meant they had been bombed or terrified out of their homes. We never bothered to find out which; just took it for granted that they never dared to return. It was easy to ignore them. They were well outside the village and, besides, they showed no sign of wanting to mix.

So they set about building a new life – in a wooden shack jammed between the Great Northern railway line and the North Road. They kept themselves to themselves and we kept a casual eye on them – glancing across at their patch as we travelled down the railway bridge towards South Muskham, then glancing away to concentrate on the curve at the bottom of the bridge and putting them out of our minds again.

The man apparently got a job in the foundry at W. N. Nicholson and Sons (where, by coincidence, my grandfather had worked), cycling to and fro on a ram-shackle old machine that made him look like a tramp. She shuffled around with her head down, virtually hiding under her ever-present scarf, as if accepting there was no point trying to converse because hers was a different language to ours. Thinking about them now, they obviously found contentment in any language. Their shack gradually grew into a wooden bungalow. The rough ground around it was transformed, year by back-breaking year, into a productive garden.

Not until November of 1962 did we discover that 'the Poles' were, in fact, from the Ukraine. Each had a concentration camp number tattooed into their arm. And we only found that out after he died of injuries received when his old bike was in collision with a lorry on the North Road not far from his new home. Doctors fought for 36 hours to save him, but in vain.

Only in the report of his death did we discover that the bent old man had only been 54 years old. His name was Iwan Parus. We can only imagine what being 'displaced' had really meant to him and his partner.

But we can be absolutely certain that, if it hadn't been for their labours, there would not have been any sign of life on the Old North Road side of Mill Lane once the A1 dual carriageway had been completed and the old Crossing House had been knocked down.

Even though he never communicated with many of us, Iwan Parus provided vivid, humbling proof that North Muskham contained more heroes than we realised.

MOOR HOUSE: FENDING OFF THE TRAVELLERS

The picturesque appeal of Moor Lane and its aloof house, part-way to Bathley down the cart-track opposite the North Road from Mill Lane, was never the same after the Railway Bridge was built.

For the Old North Road – a *cul de sac* once the old railway crossing had been closed – became a magnet for gypsies, who roamed the countryside in their horse-drawn caravans, gathering a reputation for being light-fingered (whether they earned it or not).

3. The Lanes to Bathley

More amazingly, while most folk were pre-occupied with the outbreak of the Second World War in 1939, Muskham went into battle against a chap called S. Horner from Newark, who had installed some permanent-looking vans, complete with occupants, in the lane towards Downside Cottage. The District Council declared them a nuisance and feared they were using a polluted water supply. A court ordered them out within 14 days. It took them more like six weeks to drift away... and from then on hardly a year went by without travellers settling in the inviting little enclave.

The situation became so bad that Billy Bourne complained at a meeting of the Parish Council on 15 April 1952 about "the nuisance and the damage they caused". The councillors' response hardly reflected the urgency being sought by the neighbours of the gypsies. The official minute reads: "It was resolved that a letter be sent to the Rural District Council asking if they could approach the Police with a view to ensuring that no damage was caused in the village and that they [the gypsies] stayed no longer than was necessary".

All of which made the Moor House seem more like Bleak House to we youngsters who rambled past on our off-road adventures. It was inhabited for decades by the Howards. William and his wife Mary, who ran a market garden, had passed away prior to the 1950s, but one of their five offspring, Lily, remained down the lane. Imagine, though, what a sad house it was on Christmas Day 1957 when word came through of the death of one of her sisters, Ethel, in Highbury Hospital, Bulwell, Nottingham.

A simple phrase in her death notice in the *Newark Advertiser* of 1 January 1958 says everything about what a close-knit family grew up in the Moor House (which was tucked back from the lane at this time behind a neatly-cut hedge and lovingly-tended flower garden. Ethel was described as "darling sister of Mary, Arthur, Grace and Lily".

NELSON LANE
TIN BUNGALOWS THAT BECAME A DEATH SHACK
In the shed that was to become home to generations of cattle, horses, ponies and donkeys, there lived and died in abject loneliness a former debutante known to all villagers as Miss Falkner. In a different world from the palaces and grand houses she graced as a girl in search of an eligible bachelor, she was forced to live in a tin shack so spartan that, in winter, the frost glistened on the inside walls. She was an English lady who lost everything in life... everything except her conviction that she was of the upper-class.

First went the family wealth, lost with the collapse of a business operated by her siblings during the First World War, a few years after they had lost the dominant guiding hand of their father. It seems to have been this double-whammy that slowly but inexorably dragged the Falkners from some of the highest-class gatherings in the land to the desolation of a corrugated tin shed in a field: a brother and two sisters.

The brother was "a real gentlemanly sort", says Marian Dye. He wore spectacles and bestrode the village in a top hat. Gerry was his name, says Sybil Davenport, who was born and brought-up just across the field in the Rose Villas. Many families bestowed pet names on each other; and no Falkner male had been christened Gerry but no matter.

Sybil remembers him as smart, up-right, tall, slim, always well-dressed, with a rolled umbrella in an era when Muskham blokes made do with a peaked cap during the week and maybe a trilby at weekends. Very much the City gent was Gerry. He used to walk to Cromwell every Sunday because he was High Church, and Cromwell was Higher than North Muskham, where his sisters worshipped. And Monday to Friday, he always walked to Newark to work, where village folk presumed he was either a solicitor's clerk or someone in an accountant's office. Exactly what he did is lost in the mists of time... along, of course, with any money he made.

Of the Falkner sisters, one with frizzy hair walked around with her back bent as if it bore the weight of the world; the other gave the impression that she was the really surly one.

One by one they passed away, though quite when, nobody can be sure. By 1950, the final remnants of this once near-noble and undoubtedly influential family were not even important enough to figure in *Kelly's Directory*, which was a kind of fore-runner of *Yellow Pages* (but which drew its publishing line some distance above labourers and skivvies, never mind down-and-outs).

Thankfully, and in keeping with the thoughtful times, one or two villagers kept an eye on the final Miss Falkner. Sybil Davenport used to cut the grass for her in the paddock in front of what was rather grandly called The Bungalow, Nelson Lane. Peggy Granger, who would pop round from her family's bungalow in Waltons Lane and sit with her one night a week, fondly remembers Miss Falkner as "an ex-deb who was presented at court". She told Peggy that her family had fallen on hard times during the Great War and she had had to work as a governess. "She once showed me a lot of beautiful needlework and told me she used to do it while she was sitting with the children at night. But there were some winter nights in that tin shed when we would be sitting there talking and the frost would be glistening on the inside of the walls".

As if she had not experienced enough sadness, Miss Falkner suffered further on 5 June 1960 when her cousin, Miss Mary Edith Brodhurst, perished in a fire in the bedroom of her home, The Grange at Upton. Aged 81, she had a habit of propping newspapers against her bedrail even though she still used candles to light the room, the subsequent inquest was informed.

Coincidentally, both Sybil and Peggy had been concerned that Miss Falkner's haystack beside The Bungalow could easily catch fire with awful consequences. But not even these two concerned young ladies could have envisaged how she would meet her end, at the age of 79. She trapped an arm in a window while trying to shut out the autumnal chill on the night of Tuesday 3 September 1960. A neighbour found her the following morning in what the official police report described as 'a collapsed condition'. A doctor was called but Miss Falkner was already dead. A post mortem examination established that death was due to natural causes. Only when the Newark Coroner issued a death certificate did even her few friends know that she was Miss Ethel Louise Falkner. The report of her death – headed *Fatal collapse at Muskham* – generated three paragraphs on page 9 of the *Newark Advertiser* on the following Saturday, 7 September 1960. There was nothing about the agonising circumstances, just the fact that she'd been found dead. This lady who'd rubbed shoulders with royalty wasn't even worth a full story.

There had been a lot more in the *Advertiser* and its rival, the *Newark Herald*, early in March 1909 when her father died. For Evelyn Sherard Falkner Esquire was a son of Philip Richard Falkner Esquire of Upton Hall. A solicitor for 46 years in the firm that was the fore-runner of Larken & Company, he made his family home in Kirkgate, Newark, and was the clerk to the Newark County Magistrates and to the Commissioner of Taxes for Newark. Aged 67 according to the *Herald* or 66 if you read the *Advertiser* (and they say you can't believe a word you read in the papers today!), E. S. Falkner had lost his wife the previous July and had been in "feeble health" for some time. The family mourners were listed as Miss A. M. Falkner, Miss E. L. Falkner, Mr. Thomas Falkner and Mr. Cyril Falkner while their brother, Mr. Phillip Falkner, was the resident stipendiary magistrate in Steveston, Vancouver, Canada.

Which begs the question: Was it Thomas or Cyril who became Muskham's upper-class Gerry? It can now be ascertained that it was Thomas, for the simple reason that the death of Cyril Richard Falkner occurred on 7 March 1953 at the house he shared with his wife, Joan, in Rolleston Drive, Nottingham. Conscious of his lineage to the last, the death notice described him as "beloved husband of Joan and brother of Ethel, youngest son of the late Mr. and Mrs. Evelyn Falkner and grandson of the late Philip Falkner of Upton Hall". Thomas was listed in *Kelly's Directories* of 1912 and 1914 as residing at 135 Baldertongate, Newark but was not there when it was next published, in 1922.

Presumably this was because he had moved to the humbler surroundings of the corrugated iron bungalow in North Muskham and had, in effect, left the social world to which he had been born. What was noticeable was that E. S. Falkner had played such a formidable part in Newark's life, it took two men to replace him: Godfrey Tallents of Cartergate became clerk to the Commissioner of Taxes while the new clerk to the County Magistrates was John Pickard Becher, of Larken & Company, Lombard Street. No wonder Evelyn's children found it so hard to live-up to his standards!

Not that the demise of Miss Falkner was the end of the tin shed as a family home. Among the families who used it as a staging post towards more substantial accommodation were Mr. and Mrs. Stan Smith, who had a young family. While Stan went on to become chief mechanic to the Lincolnshire Road Car Company Limited at their enormously busy garage in Balderton in an era when the vast majority travelled by public transport, he moved his family to live in Winthorpe… and The Bungalow was relegated to being a ramshackle-looking stable.

ROSE VILLAS: A LADY VICAR IN THE MAKING

The Davenports had moved in to Rose Villas in 1933; and Frank never forgot that the pair of houses had been built for £400 each. He also remembered the date when Muskham Mill fell down. It was Monday 24 August 1936 – before his disbelieving eyes as he gazed across the fields, waiting for his wife Gertie to give birth to their only daughter Sybil. One minute it was there. The next, there was a cloud of dust. The next, there was a new baby's cry. And Sybil herself went on to make a pretty dramatic impact… teaching at the village school, overcoming virtual blindness and even more severe shyness to become one of the Church of England's first female parsons.

Frank was as down to earth as the mill, albeit much less destructible. He rose at four o' clock every morning to bike up the North Road to Cromwell, where he worked on his Dad's farm. First task for him and the rest of the farm hands was to milk 100 cows. Then they got on with the day's work. The cowsheds became luxury homes in the 1990s!

Gertrude Davenport, nee Doncaster, was also of farming stock – from North Road Farm, within sight of Rose Villas. After her dad, John William, died at the age of only 52 on 7 September 1922, mum Ann kept it going until she died on 3 July 1929, aged 71. She had the help of a farm manager, Mr. Geeson, but it wasn't easy: the land was not the richest and seemed to flit in a matter of days from flooded and boggy to parched and blazing (usually thanks to the spark from a passing steam engine). On top of that, she had to deal with the tragedy of Gertie's young sister, Ruth. She danced like a dream; so fluent in her actions that those watching would never guess that she had been born deaf and dumb. Loved and admired though she was, she died young – on 3 July 1929, seven years before Sybil arrived.

By then, hard-working Frank had redecorated the place. When he and Mrs. D followed the diminutive three Miss Woods into the house, they were mildly amused to note that all the wall decorations were placed more at waist- than head-height... though they did preserve paintings of birds flying all over the walls. More evidence that the Woods ladies were little gems as artists were found in autograph books, of all things, packed with paintings and drawings (suitably miniature, of course).

Mrs. Davenport was registrar for North Muskham WI in 1953, the year in which Sybil passed 4 GCEs at the High School. She and her Mum ran the white elephant stall at a garden fete at The Willows in 1957 when the Church faced a £900 repair bill.

Gertrude Davenport died, aged 61, on 10 August 1962. Frank Davenport lived to the age of 92, spending his later years with Sybil in the original Norbet bungalow at the junction of Meadow Close with Main Street. He died on 16 June 1999, having proudly seen his daughter become the Rev. Davenport!

ROSE VILLAS: ANOTHER HIGHLY RESPECTED COUPLE

When John Gascoigne and his wife Annie moved in to the other half of Rose Villas, mild-mannered, devoutly religious Sybil Davenport greeted them by pulling up the flowers in their front garden. It happened pre-War, this unique moment of vandalism by the future Reverend Davenport... and it was all Mum's fault. "For some reason, she got me ready first for our weekly shopping trip to Newark", Sybil recalls. "I don't know why. She normally got herself ready first. Anyway, while she put her hat and coat on this time, I went trotting outside – and passed the time pulling up all the Gascoignes' plants. They were very understanding, but that didn't stop me getting a smack!"

Neither did the episode prevent the families becoming life-long friends. Mr. Gascoigne, who had moved from Pear Tree Cottage down Chapel Yard after his first wife (also Annie) died, spent his working life as a joiner at Waltons and his spare time was devoted to growing stuff: he was a prime motivator of the North Muskham Horticultural Society.

The Gascoigne family had moved to North Muskham from Buckinghamshire in 1897. Their father, Tom, born in Southwell in 1855, was lured back to his native county by Waltons, where he worked as a joiner and carpenter's labourer. Over half a century, he built a fine reputation by rearing prize-winning poultry – Bramas and Cochins – and also found time to serve the community as chairman of the Parish Council, a church warden and sidesman. Like many of his contemporaries, he fell victim to one of Muskham's harsh winters; he died from pneumonia in January of 1929. His wife Annie, who was a few months older, had her hands full looking after the home and the six kids: John had arrived first in 1883 followed two years later by Charles, who became a gardener. Billy was five years John's junior. Then came Elizabeth in 1890, Edward in 1892 and Kate in 1893.

One of John's most vivid early memories of the village came in January of 1901, by which time he was 14 and a choirboy at St. Wilfrid's. He recorded, doubtless in awe of the power of nature, that the Trent flooded to within 3 inches of the window sills of the Newcastle Arms.

His wife Annie was a member of North Muskham Mothers' Union for all the 48 years of her marriage and acted as its enrolment secretary for nigh on a decade. When it was obvious just before Christmas of 1953 that she was rather ill, her fellow members presented her with a reading lamp in recognition of her "devoted work". It was probably the first time an electrical gadget had been a formal gift to anyone in the village.

When lovely, gentle Annie died at the age of 69 less than two months later, on 24 February 1954, her support for the village's main women's organisations was vividly reflected at the funeral in the village church. Members of the Mothers' Union turned out in force, behind their standard bearer Mrs. March, who carried the banner of St. Wilfrid; and there were official representatives of the Women's Institute among her many friends.

Johnny was supported by the family they had reared: daughter Elsie, her husband Art Gray and their girls; son Bill, his wife Eva and their family; daughter Alice, her husband Harold Sly and their family; son Harry and his family; son Bernard, his wife Gladys and their boys.

And Johnny went on to serve the village, especially St. Wilfrids... In 1964 he wrote proudly of his service: "76 years a chorister, 72 years a bell ringer, 60 years a cross bearer, 16 years a church warden, and several years a hand bell ringer". The hand bell period began in 1920 when a survey of St. Wilfrid's revealed the church tower was so riddled with woodworm that bell ringing had to be curtailed. It was four years before the repairs were completed, by which time John was the bell ringers' captain, William Streeton was vice-captain and the rest of the team comprised Walter Brown from Cherry Cottage, Walter Jackson, Edgar Streeton and Arthur Worthington. On

7 March 1973 a BBC radio station mentioned Johnny's 90th birthday – and he was proud to point out: "I'm still singing in the choir!"

LITTLEDENE VILLAS: A CORONATION YEAR WEDDING
Alf Tandy and his wife Lucy saved their major 1953 celebration until December. It was then that their daughter Monica got married in St. Wilfrid's Church, North Muskham, to Pilot Officer Derek Riley, whose folks lived on Station Road, Sutton-on-Trent. The *Newark Advertiser* of 9 December contained a picture of the happy couple: the groom in his National Service uniform; the bride in a gown of ice brocade with a short veil held by a diamante tiara. Her bouquet was of red roses and trailing fern. The bridesmaids, her cousin June Bourne and sister-in-law Audrey Riley, wore gowns of kingfisher grosgrain and silver head-dresses. Their bouquets were anemones. The organist was Syd Thurman.

The Tandy family had inherited the house from Mrs. T's folks, Albert and Mrs. Neill. Indeed, Alf – who had a good job in management at Ransome & Marles – and Lucy moved in initially to look after the old folk, as was the custom of caring families in the age before the emergence of the philosophy that 'the State will provide'. Alfred Tandy died aged 60 after a short illness, on 8 November 1959.

LITTLEDENE VILLAS: SHOWING THE LIGHT(S)
Tom and Alice Baxter were valued so much by Muskham Methodists that a picture of them hung in the Sunday School Room beside the Chapel long after their deaths at ripe old ages.

They were not the first immensely conscientious generation of this family. Tom's parents had run the village Post Office from the cottage at the corner of Nelson Lane and Main Street (Costalot in the early 21st century). On the death of his father, his mother Sarah became sub-postmistress and his brother Edward the post-messenger as well as the devotee who played the harmonium at the Chapel. Alas, 1895 was a harsher winter than most. Horrible storms and intense frosts mingled with the usual smogs and floods. On 2 April, just when the village believed it was through the worst, 19-year-old Edward collapsed and died while delivering the morning's post.

Tom earned his crust as a signalman on the railways and never wavered in his religious beliefs. He earned the admiration of the village by spending his spare Sundays showing the light – excuse the pun – to countless children. Mrs. Baxter served on the North Muskham WI committee in the early 1950s. Their daughter, Dorothy Kathleen, found her beau from rather further afield than most local lasses. In August 1957, she wed Stanley Arthur Wheeler from Ryde in the Isle of Wight. The ceremony was conducted at North Muskham Chapel by the Reverend R. Rothwell.

Thomas Baxter died aged 80, on 20 June 1962. Alice Baxter was 88 when she died on 11 December 1973.

BATHLEY LANE
GRASMERE: SMALLHOLDER BAKES EXCEEDINGLY GOOD CAKES
Harold Kent brought his brood in 1944 to the bungalow opposite the Nelson pub, at the end of the railway sidings on the corner of the North Road and Bathley Lane. Mrs. Kent became an invaluable cog in the village's social wheel, which tended to revolve around the WI and its subsidiary activities. Sons Peter and Hugh contributed to village life in starkly different ways. Peter became the envy of every boy in the parish by piloting airliners around the world for the British Overseas Airways Corporation (BOAC), but always returned home between his flights to exotic places – first to Grasmere and, after his marriage to Ellen Kent, to The Lodge initially and for many years to The Warren. Hugh worked at North Road Farm, Lodge Farm, Old Hall Farm and Cordon Lodge before becoming a freelance gardener.

Both the boys were keen sportsmen. Indeed, Hugh had the dubious distinction of being the top scorer for North Muskham and Bathley CC in their match on Coronation Weekend at home to Flintham. Our heroes were all out for 17, of which Hugh contributed 6. Flintham's reply reached 40 for the loss of only one wicket before it was mutually agreed that the teams should retire to the Lord Nelson to celebrate the official start of the new regal era.

For Harold, the move to Muskham had represented a stark career change. He had been a baker – and continued to put his skills to good use by making wonderful wedding cakes, baking beautiful bread and cobs, and icing cakes for such celebrations as the WI birthday

Hugh Kent pictured during the Coronation celebrations.

136

parties. But his real mission at Muskham was to transform the triangle of land at Grasmere into a smallholding – a real predecessor of *The Good Life* as depicted by Richard Briers and Felicity Kendall on television. Harold reared pigs that were periodically transported to market by Garoods, and produced poultry whose eggs went off to the Newark Egg Packers beside The Wharf just over Newark Trent Bridge.

It ought to be added that Grasmere would never have seen the light of day if plans for North Muskham to have a railway station had come to fruition in the 1890s, some 40 years after the Great Northern Railway had linked London with the major cities of the North. The idea was mooted in 1893, when Nottinghamshire County Council announced it was considering where to build a new asylum. They seriously considered building in the fields on the Bathley side of the railway line. The Great Northern Railway Board was so supportive that it promised a railway station providing the asylum was built. Such was the enthusiasm generated that the Houses of Parliament approved a plan for a Newark to Ollerton railway line to branch-off towards Caunton from near the Bathley Lane crossing.

For a few heady years, North Muskham braced itself to become the centre of the county's attempts to house and treat the men and women who were routinely condemned to asylums in the Victorian era: not only the criminally insane but also unfortunates such as young women who became pregnant out of wedlock plus boys and girls who in the 21st century would be considered to be suffering from nothing more dangerous than learning difficulties. If the Ollerton line had gone through, then North Muskham would have become a main transport link between the North Nottinghamshire Coalfield and the rest of the country. It is history now that the asylum went to Rampton near Retford. North Muskham remained merely a village with three level crossings, of which Bathley Lane was the only one with a signal box.

CROSSING HOUSE: DEATH OF A KINDLY SIGNALMAN
Of all the crossings for boy trainspotters to choose – Norwell Lane, Bathley Lane, Mill Lane, South Muskham – Bathley Lane was best in the days when steam engines each had unique numbers painted large and white on their sides. There were three reasons.

There was a fence on the Bathley side of Bathley Lane where we could perch and have an unobstructed view of trains travelling both ways.
There were sidings between the crossing and the North Road Bridge where awesome steaming goods trains would have to park-up and wait for the sleeker passenger expresses to clickety-clack past on their way to London, Newcastle,

Edinburgh… huge places we could only dream of visiting.

The resident signalman, Charlie Lang, would frequently slide open the window of his signalbox and offer encouragement or a challenge… "Next one's never been down here before" or "Bet this one'll be going too fast for you" or the dreaded "Won't yer Mam wonder where yer've got to?" With his signalbox being so elevated – and containing the signals that controlled the whole of the section from Cromwell to the Tubular Bridge into Newark – his truly was the voice of high authority.

He was also as much a guardian angel as his mates at the other crossings when we little 'uns – or the adults, come to that – had to cross the line in the days when there were handgates for cycles and bigger gates for four-wheeled traffic. He'd see the cyclist coming, open the window and shout: "All clear if you hurry" or "He's not far off – just wait there, son" and then, if we were headed into Muskham, there'd be another call as we let ourselves through the second gate: "You mind the road now!" "Yes Mr. Lang. Thankyou Mr. Lang", we'd call as we pedalled off.

Jack Munks 'walking the length', a daily duty to check the railway line was completely safe.

We heeded his advice all right, but thought nothing of the fact he had volunteered it; and he accepted it as all part of his job in an era when folk instinctively looked out for one another. Charlie had looked after himself and his son Keith since the death of his wife, Margaret at the age of 58 on 3 September 1957. But he took his conscientious nature a bit too far on Saturday 14 December 1963. He said "Ta-ra" to Keith, who was about 20, as he went to work at 10 past one in the afternoon – and was dead 18 minutes later! **Fatal collapse of signalman** made front page news in the *Newark Advertiser* the following Wednesday, 18 December '63. Those were the days when rural road traffic was still so sparse, the big crossing gates were only opened when vehicles actually appeared, which was why the *Advertiser* report of the drama was written like this:

3. The Lanes to Bathley

"Crew of an express train travelling from Leeds to London on Saturday afternoon reported at Newark Northgate Station that they were held up at Bathley Lane crossing, North Muskham.

When railway officials investigated, they found the signalman collapsed. He was 67-year-old Charles John Lang. He was taken to Newark General Hospital but was dead on arrival".

Charlie had only worked on past the retirement age of 65 because British Railways had made such a mess of cost-cutting exercises that they had declared too many men redundant. Typical of the workers of the era, Charlie believed he owed them. He was there to serve the public. And he only let them down once – that Saturday afternoon just before Christmas 1963.

RAILWAY COTTAGES: DOWN BY THE BRIDGE...

Charlie Hall and his wife Sheila came to the tied cottage on the Moor Lane side of the railway bridge in the early 1950s primarily because Charlie was a signalman on the railway. Even more exciting to us boys, Charlie was also probably cricket's fastest bowler of his size until the West Indies and Hampshire unleashed the late Malcolm Marshall upon the rest of the world and the County Championship.

Charlie was, as his burly workmates put it, "no bigger than six pennuth o' coppers" – little more than 5ft 6in, slim but muscular and, to add to his friendly appearance, fair-complexioned face topped by a shock of light blond hair that fanned in the breeze as he accelerated towards the wicket. Then there would be a whirl of his right arm accompanied by an exaggerated dragging of his right boot toe along the ground, a momentary red blur and, like as not, a crash of timber as the ball, propelled from an unusually low trajectory for such swift speed, skidded off even the friendliest of pitches and seared past the batsman. Unlike most fast bowlers, Charlie was an exceptionally quiet and well-mannered young bloke.

His only fault was that he seemed to give up cricket at an early age. Maybe that was because of growing family commitments and all it entailed by way of growing enough vegetables in the garden at home. For Charlie and Sheila reared just about the village's last big family. There was Norma and Margaret and Stewart and Rosemary and Paula; and they remained a close-knit unit, even after the death of Charlie. Sheila Harriot Hall died on 11 January 2001.

Tom Worthington, the jolly giant of a railwayman who lived in the crossing house that nestled in a minuscule triangle between the upside of the railway line and the bridge over it, adopted a massive ready-made family when their father died... yet also found time to remain a regular in the village cricket team.

The railway crossing outside the house was rendered obsolete in the 1920s, when the bridge was built to carry the North Road over the line. Tom lived to the age of 77, passing away on 9 October 1968. His wife Edith outlived him by only 10 months and died aged 78 on 15 August 1969.

CORDON LODGE: FARMING AND AN OLD FORD POP

Len Wilson swapped life down the coalmines for the swampy fields beside Bathley Lane – bringing with him his wife, son Mick and in-laws, the Goodwins. They hailed from Wellow. Len seemed to work all light hours, as did most of his ilk.

Mrs. Wilson, small in stature, was always big in generosity when swamped by playmates of Mick, who was different from the rest of us in that he went to the Minster Grammar School at Southwell but was the same in that he played football and cricket with enthusiasm and vigour for the village teams. He was a bustling midfielder (to use a modern *cliche*) in some of North Muskham Juniors' best football winters.

Then, suddenly one summer, he had an advantage over the rest of us teenagers battling for places in the cricket team – a car in which to get to away matches. He got it, I think, on his 18th birthday; a Ford Popular (black, of course) that was somewhat more experienced than merely secondhand. Brian Needham in the front passenger seat, was surprised to look down and see the road flashing past beneath his feet. We in the back tried to persuade Mick to speed up on the gentle curve from South Muskham to the bridge over the river with the cry of: "Put yer foot down!" "OK, OK", he said. We all leaned forward, eyes fixed on the speedometer needle, which was pointing at 27mph. Mick's foot went down. The engine roared... or maybe groaned. The needle quivered – and settled at 26½mph. That car journey, from the Lord Nelson to the Sugar Factory Cricket Ground, was the first practical indication (to me) that we lads were growing up. Sort of, anyway.

John Thomas Goodwin died, aged 78, on 7 February 1959 – the dearly loved husband of Florence May and devoted father of Dorothy, Connie, Elsie and John; in-laws Les, Bert, Len and Shirley; and dear grandfather of Michael, Jane and Jonathan.

ASHURST: MINE HOST IN RETIREMENT

George Ranyard moved to the little bungalow that almost hid behind its high but neatly cut hedges beside Cordon Lodge after spending most of his working life as landlord first of the Crown Inn and then the Lord Nelson in North Muskham. His wife, Mary, had passed away in the Nelson, aged 65, on 9 October 1945.

Son John had married and moved away in the 1920s. Of their three daughters, Dorothy was married to Tom Guy and lived in the heart of the village; Elsie married a man called Arthur; and Nancy stayed home to look after ageing Dad. After her father's death, Nancy went to work in the offices of Hollingworth Dairies Ltd, one of a growing number of milk wholesalers.

Nancy was also a great supporter of village activities... a member of the WI, and such an avid supporter of the local branch of the Women's Conservative Association that she served as its treasurer for some time. Although this was a predominantly Conservative area, Nancy's post could not have been an easy one: the *Newark Advertiser* on 25 March 1953 reported that the Newark Division Conservative Association at its annual general meeting deemed that North Muskham and District Branch "must be regarded as lapsed". Yet the *Newark Herald* on 12 December 1953 reported a healthy turn-out when a whist drive was held at North Muskham as part of the campaign by the prospective Parliamentary candidate, Mr. Ronald Watson, to

North Muskham and Bathley CC in the Bathley Lane field (from left): back – Ron Newbold, Frank Swannack, Tom Worthington, Horace Kemm, not sure, Tim Gatley, Charlie Hall, Martin Briggs. Front – Fred Blore, Cyril Marriott, Billy Bourne.

visit his supporters in all parts of the district. By the start of 1958, the North Muskham & District Conservative Association had become the Muskham, Bathley and Cromwell Conservative Association… and was raising money by staging the occasional whist drive and, as a special treat, a whist drive and dance (which contributed £20 towards Party funds).

On 9 August 1958 Nancy popped down to South Muskham to attend the official opening of their nice new Village Hall. Sadly, it was the last time the public-spirited Miss Nancy Ranyard was seen in public. She passed away peacefully in her sleep four days later, aged only 56.

NORWELL LANE
FOXHOLES: LAST SQUIRE OF THE MANOR
It was entirely appropriate that Squire James Vivian Edge, the last of North Muskham and Bathley's dominant landlords, lived in a house that was really in neither village but was close enough for him to keep a stern eye on all developments within his domain. Aloof though he remained from the minions, his was an all-embracing, all-powerful presence. When he drove through either parish, men would doff their flat caps, women would dip a little curtsy, children would bow their heads (or else!). I always obeyed and so have no recollection of what he looked like… except that his car wheels were unusually shiny in such a muddy environment.

The family had pretty much controlled the lives of the villagers since 1836, when the Reverend J. Webb Edge of Strelley Rectory near Nottingham paid £21,000 for the North Muskham and Bathley estate. While the Edge family doubtless believed they ruled with benevolence, there are those who argue it was no coincidence that the appearance of street lights and, thus, the end of the village's dark age, only happened close to the end of the Edge reign.

They didn't call his ilk conservatives for nothing. Modernisation was a prolonged process. For example, the installation of street lights was first discussed by North Muskham Parish Council at its annual general meeting on 22 May 1950. The lights were finally working five-and-a-bit years later… a minor miracle considering that initially they had been totally rejected!

At that AGM in 1950, Councillors Syd Milnes (the owner of the North Road Garage, who was elected Chairman), Herbert and Cecil Clipsham (of the building family), Sid Thomas (from the bus family firm) and the omnipresent Squire Edge – he who must be obeyed – decided that the matter be left in abeyance "in view of the number of lights required and the eventual cost to the ratepayers".

3. The Lanes to Bathley

It was two years before anyone raised the subject officially again. The Parish Council discussed the issue at length on 27 May 1952 and decided that "further information be obtained as to procedures, and the matter be further discussed at a later meeting with a view to obtaining street lighting in the near future".

Five months later, there had obviously been dark rumblings from the populace: not quite a peasants' up-rising, but enough to make the guardians of the parochial purse believe they had a mandate to modernise. The official minutes of the Council meeting on 21 October 1952 state: "The Clerk reported the procedure to be adopted and method of obtaining street lights for the Parish, whether under the Lighting and Watching Act or the Public Health Act. After some discussion, in which it was agreed by all members that they were truly representative of the desire of the Parish to have street lighting and that no objections to any such scheme were known, it was proposed by Stan Cockerill and seconded by Reg Bell and unanimously agreed that immediate application be made to the Southwell RDC to obtain an Urban Powers Order as soon as possible with a view to street lighting being installed in the village". If the importance of a decision is reflected by the size of the sentence reporting it, this is probably the most momentous ever taken by representatives of North Muskham – not least because Squire Edge was neither the proposer nor seconder. There is no better indicator of what strong characters Stan Cockerill and Reg Bell were!

On 27 January 1953, the Parish Council decided where they wanted the lights: one on every telegraph pole along the Main Street, three in Crab Lane, two on Nelson Lane (to be strategically placed on the two sharpest S-bends), two on Waltons Lane, one on Bathley Lane (opposite Cordon Lodge, behind the cricket pavilion), two east of the level crossing and two west of the crossing on Vicarage Lane, one down Chapel Yard, one on Church Lane and one on Ferry Lane.

Impatience was the watchword on the third anniversary of the original 'No' to street lights. At the Parish Council meeting on 22 May 1953, it was agreed that "if no further information was received before 30 June, the Clerk should write to the Rural District Council to enquire when the scheme will commence".

While the June deadline came and went without remark, the Street Lighting Plan was finally approved on 6 August 1953 – and the Parish Council minutes promised that installation would be complete by Christmas 1954. In fact, it was the summer of 1955 before they were switched on.

Squire Edge died a few years later. His successor, a distant relative, sold the estate piecemeal – giving the sitting tenants first refusal on their properties at extremely reasonable rates. A few took advantage of the opportunity to become property owners. Many could not afford to and moved to other rented accommodation while their homes were sold to in-comers. Dad, for example, could not contemplate getting together £600 for our two-up, two-down in Bathley – even though Squire Edge's nephew was willing to throw in the unoccupied semi next door for free. And this in an age before 'buy one, get one free' had even been invented! By 2007, this dwelling had been extended to such an extent that it was on the market for more than £500,000.

Meanwhile, back in the stroll down Norwell Lane into North Muskham in the 1950s...

BUNGALOW: HOME FOR A BUILDER'S FAMILY
Bill Temporall, a builder's labourer with Clipsham's family firm, built a bungalow for himself, his wife and son Dennis next door to his bosses' homes. It was demolished in 2001, a modern house having been erected behind it during the previous two years in much the same manner as the way Bill put up the bungalow in his spare time.

Bill spent his working life as one of the team working for Clipsham and Sons. Son Dennis, who was at North Muskham School at the time of the 1953 Coronation, went on to become a successful motor mechanic, based at a garage in Sleaford Road, Newark.

CHERRY TREE COTTAGE: BUILDING A BETTER COMMUNITY
Evelyn Clipsham, one of the brothers who ran the family building firm of Clipsham and Sons, somewhat confusingly married Miss Evelyn Clark, a district nurse whose constructive contribution to the community was to oversee the births of many of the babies of the post-war boom. So that Mr. Evelyn and Mrs. Evelyn could be easily distinguished, Nurse Clipsham was happy to be known by her second Christian name, Nancy.

It was typical of their quiet, modest natures that they should call their sturdy house, with its splendid views over the countryside, a mere cottage. They had two sons, David, who grew up (and up and up) and became a hero of village football and cricket teams, and (hardly surprisingly) Evelyn, who brought up his own family in the family home and worked for many years as a lorry driver.

Nurse Clipsham used to cycle round the villages... Carlton-on-Trent, Cromwell, Norwell, Caunton as well as Little Carlton, South Muskham, Bathley and North Muskham... making sure mums-to-be were progressing as they should, and somehow contriving to be on the spot for actual deliveries (or arriving pretty soon afterwards) in spite of the absence of telephones in most homes.

Mr. Clipsham's estimates for building work always seemed to take account of the wealth (or, more likely, otherwise) of his clients – though, of course, he was far too nice a chap to be so condescending and let the factor show through his air of casual professionalism.

The Clipsham firm's trustworthiness was such that, for decades, they had contracts with Lords of the Manor such as the Dennisons at Ossington when it was a splendid estate complete with a Hall, servants' cottages and palatial walled gardens all perfectly maintained.

The only thing Mr. Clipsham was not so good at was collecting the monies owed to the firm. Indeed, employees say he was such a nice bloke that he simply didn't send out some bills to customers he considered to be particularly worthy of such extraordinary generosity.

BUNGALOW: OLDE WORLDE MANNERS MAKETH THE MAN

Cecil Clipsham, his wife Elsie (nee Sewards, from Bathley) and daughter Mary lived in the bungalow closest to North Muskham that completed the trio of properties in the middle of the moor on the north side of the heavily-hedged lane that led from Mousehall corner towards the Norwell Lane railway crossing.

'Sissell', as his Christian name was pronounced by all who knew and admired him, contributed much more than bricks and mortar to the village of his birth. He played cricket for North Muskham and Bathley in the 1930s in a paddock across the North Road from the Lord Nelson. He served on the Parish Council for years. He was well enough respected in agricultural circles to be accepted as a member of the Newark branch of the Notts Farmers' Union. Above all, he was a compassionate businessman; a throwback to the more genteel pre-War era in which his father had founded the firm.

Little wonder, then, that St. Wilfrid's Church was full for his funeral after he died, aged only 55, on 11 November 1956. He had been ill for 11 weeks and the mourners were led by Elsie, who was to go on to the grander age of 75 before passing away on 22 November 1977, and Mary, the dedicated daughter, who used to cycle to Newark to her work as a ladies' hairdresser at a salon at Beaumond Cross. As a mark of genuine respect rather than duty, Cecil's coffin was carried into church by four of the firm's workmen, Cyril Marriott, Bill Temporall, Jock Granger and George Seels.

Builders' tea-break for (from left): Bill Temporal, Evelyn Clipsham, Cyril Marriott, George Seels (from Sutton- or Carlton-on-Trent) and Harry Clipsham.

BRACKEN FARM: A TOUGH OLD-FASHIONED STRUGGLE

Pinky Dakin's set-up was typical of the majority of the 10 (and more) farms worked as separate entities in the village during and after the Second World War. Farm workers were exempt from fighting roles during the War because they were needed to win the battle to feed the home front. And for a decade (and longer) after peace was declared, the agricultural scene remained basically unchanged while food remained rationed by either Government decree or natural shortages.

Pinky had a few cows (hand-milked, for this was a traditional farm that never really modernised) that grazed in the meadow between Bracken Farm and the railway line. His fields were largely scrubland (in the days before fertilisers were invented to cope with any impediment) and frequently water-logged, making the annual chore of ditching absolutely vital.

It appeared to we children cycling past that just about the most productive crop for miles around was the blackberries that grew on the burgeoning brambles that dominated the broad swathe on the opposite side of Norwell Lane to his farm. They provided free puddings for countless families who could barely afford the nutritional necessities... until they disappeared as part of the scorched earth philosophy that led to the uprooting of miles of hedgerows.

Quite where the nickname Pinky came from is lost in the mists of time (he had been christened Frank), but it was well-established before the appearance of electricity pylons just down the Lane caused worries among the farming fraternity. The pylons carried the first section of a new 275,000-volt super-grid from Staythorpe Power Station to West Melton, near Rotherham. The line was inaugurated in mid-July 1953 by Sir John Hacking, who was deputy chairman (operations) of the British Electricity Authority. North Muskham was still two years away from its first street lamp, yet suddenly on its doorstep there arrived some of the first 42 miles of an overhead cable electricity supply for Britain that would eventually extend from Glasgow to London. It was costing £60 million and would be completed by 1960.

Not that the farmers were over-impressed. A story in the *Newark Herald* on 19 December 1953 revealed that drivers of farm tractors had complained of receiving electric shocks while driving their vehicles beneath the supergrid lines. Farmers were advised to hang a chain from their tractors to provide an earth for the current.

NORWELL LANE CROSSING: FAMILY TRAGEDY IN THE FOG
The resident crossing gatekeeper in the 1950s, Frederick Hague, was accustomed to living on a knife-edge. Visitors to the two-up, two-down railway house he shared with his wife frequently reported they had no problem knowing when a train was approaching: pottery would tremble on the table, ornaments would wobble across the mantelpiece and, as the train rattled past, the very foundations would shake.

But the most traumatic accident at this slightly isolated spot on the railway line happened on Monday 8 January 1962, a cold, grey morning when North Muskham School was re-opening after the Christmas holiday. Frank Speller and his 10-year-old son Keith from Bathley were killed as they pushed their cycles over the crossing. Their 9-year-old neighbour, David Handley, was saved only by the quick-thinking of Robert Bridge, the 65-year-old who was on duty as crossing gatekeeper at the time.

It sent a chill through the entire community because it was a tragedy that could have happened to any family using virtually any of the crossings into

North Muskham. For each crossing had two kinds of gates: wide ones that were closed to traffic except when a vehicle needed to cross; small ones that were never locked (except at Bathley Lane) and could be operated by pedestrians, cyclists and (with a squeeze) motor cyclists. The wide ones were opened to road traffic by the gatekeepers, who at Norwell Lane sat in a little wooden shed on the Muskham side of the line armed with a bank of keys that clicked up and down to tell them whether trains were approaching plus a telephone line that linked them with the manned signal boxes at Carlton-on-Trent and Bathley Lane. Under British Railways guidelines, the handgates were nothing to do with the gatekeepers – except every single man who ever sat in either the hut at Norwell Lane or the one at South Muskham crossing was always happy to pop outside and advise pedestrians whether it was safe.

And so to the foggy Monday morning when death arrived with an eerily silent swoosh on the 7.30am from Leeds to London King's Cross. Rather than a puffing and chugging steam engine that Frank and his flaxen-haired son would have doubtless heard, it was a new-fangled diesel, smoothing along at 80mph through the icily clinging fog on the swift straight from Sutton-on-Trent. With visibility down to between 80 and 90 yards, the diesel driver, a Yorkshireman called Herbert Hardisty, suddenly saw what he thought were three boys on the line and instinctively blared his hooter. It was 9.05am. In fact, little David was in front, Frank and Keith were side-by-side.

By the time of the inquest, someone had calculated that Driver Hardisty would have glimpsed them three seconds before the impact. What he saw in those three seconds were etched in agonised confusion in his mind forever: "One boy seemed to get ahead. The others hesitated – I think they slipped on the sleepers. Either they didn't hear the horn or they took no notice. They appeared to make a dash for it and slipped".

The boy who "got ahead", David Handley, the youngest of a large family whose Dad was a farm labourer for Squire Edge, owed his life to his speedy reaction. When Gatekeeper Bridge shouted: "Look out!" David instantly leapt towards him. Even as the gatekeeper threw him through the handgate, the train swept away Frank, a devoted father who was only able to do this 'school-run' because he was working nights at Cafferatas at Newark, and Keith, the oldest of his three children. Their bodies were found 80 yards away.

By a cruel coincidence, they lay beside a sign proclaiming that this was a "prize length" of line – a tribute to the workmanship of blokes like my Dad and Jack Blore, two of the Spellers' neighbours. Devoted father and innocent son died "absolutely instantaneously", said the doctor given the dreadful job of carrying out the post mortem examinations. Incredibly, David wandered

3. The Lanes to Bathley

on to School, over the North Road (which was as fog-bound and as dangerous as the railway), before someone noticed he was shaking with shock and he was taken back home to be consoled by his mum and older siblings John, Veronica, Pete and Mick.

At the inquest three weeks later, Gatekeeper Bridge was praised by the Coroner, Mr. Claude Mack, for "taking a chance with your own life" by reaching out to save David. The jury recorded verdicts of Misadventure on Frank, who was only 42, and Keith. They decided they could not call it Accidental death because the pair should not have been on the line.

The tragedy did more than stun the two villages, hardened though they were to North Road disasters by this time. It sparked British Railways to begin to rethink how country lane crossings should be operated. They were still re-thinking by the time the next winter's fogs began to roll in; and two or three community-conscious parents in Bathley – notably Ralph Waterfield, a devout Chapel-goer from the cottages on Carlton Lane, and Doug Smalley from the garage on the Green – made sure the 9 Bathley children always had a lift to and from school. They had to make themselves available because the Nottinghamshire Education Committee refused to provide a school bus on the grounds that the journey was too short. The Waterfield children, Jimmy (aged 9) and Peter (6), lived less than two miles from the school. And rules were rules, never mind that two humans had just died on that very journey.

Not that the bureaucrats who ran the Education Committee cornered the market in indifference. Their colleagues at British Railways were still putting their minds to the problem two years later – as proven when the same Norwell Lane Crossing became the scene on one Sunday night for what a barrister was to describe as "a Charles Chaplin-like farce". Chaplin had been the greatest comic of the silent films golden age in the 1930s, but a fair bit was said in The Case of the Norwell Lane Nincompoop before it reached a courtroom – the Nottinghamshire Quarter Sessions on 18 November 1964. There, a 32-year-old company director from Sheffield was fined all of £10 for obstructing the railway line.

What he had done was potentially catastrophic. He arrived at the closed crossing some time after 10pm, which was bedtime for the resident gatekeeper George Lawson and his wife (who had replaced the Hagues). The motorist reckoned he blew his hooter for six minutes before George appeared and ambled across the line to his little cabin. Having made sure no trains were approaching, he began to open the gate closest to the car. Big mistake! Tired of the length of time he'd been made to wait, the driver inched his car forward on to the line – and left it there. Which would have been funny, except that by now there was a train approaching. Fast. The car driver's wife was so frightened, she leapt out of the car and ran for her life. The gatekeeper's wife, awakened by the argument, became hysterical. The driver eventually reversed off the line. The gatekeeper closed the gate. The train roared past and disappeared into the night. "You behaved very stupidly", the company director was told by the judge, Arthur Ellis. "You could have caused considerable danger. As it was, you caused substantial inconvenience".

BR finally modernised the crossings in 1966, after producing census figures revealing that the Norwell Lane crossing was being used by 116 vehicles, 16 cycles or prams and 11 pedestrians (4 of them children) each day. Oh, and there were 72 trains in each direction each day. Not that the automatic, unmanned crossings were universally welcomed: when Southwell Rural District Council approved the new arrangement, our own representative, Councillor Charles Hallam (a poultry farmer at Little Carlton) made an intriguing contribution to the debate. He told his colleagues that BR already had 74 of the new crossings in use in East Anglia and Lincolnshire, and claimed that the accident rate was slightly less than on attended crossings. And he added: "They assure me it will be as safe as the other type. But how they come to that conclusion, I don't know".

SEMI-DETACHED COTTAGES: THE RED FLAG FLEW HIGH
With a name like his, Reginald Baden Bell simply had to be prepared to make an impact. After all, he shared his middle name with Baden Powell, who founded the Boy Scout Movement and coined the motto, 'Be Prepared'. And Reg was clearly ready and able to argue for his beliefs in an age when the vast majority of folk were still sufficiently inhibited to remember their place in society's class system.

Reg was a joiner by trade. The only ruling he was expected to do was to measure his pieces of wood. He was no young hot-head, either. He was well into his 50s. But he was probably the first man in politically 'true Blue' North Muskham to flaunt vivid red paraphernalia from his property, urging voters to elect Labour candidate George Deer to represent the Newark Division in Parliament in 1950 in place of the sitting MP, Sidney Shephard (Conservative). They did, too, though it must be added that it had more to do with the contributions of the coal miners living in the west of the Division than the agriculturists in our neck of the woods.

And Reg lost no time in making an impact on parish pump politics. He made his first appearance at a North Muskham Parish Council meeting on Tuesday 27 May 1952, and instantly got into a heated discussion over what should constitute a proper water supply for the Chapel Yard Cottages. Under 'any other business' at his first meeting, he laid down, in effect, challenges to two of his fellow councillors. First, he raised the question of a village playing field – doubtless to the surprise of Billy Bourne, who had already donated a field for the cricketers and footballers. The minute of the occasion records: "This was discussed and it was left that the matter should be borne in mind for the future". Billy himself raised the question at the Parish Council meeting on 27 January 1953, explaining that children playing on the streets were being chased off by the police owing to the dangers. He suggested that the Parish Council might pay some local person, to be approached by him, say £5 per annum for the right to use a field as a playing field for the village children. It was further agreed that a kissing gate would have to be erected to ensure stock would not be able to stray from the field owing to carelessness in not properly securing the ordinary gate. It was agreed that Southwell Rural District Council be approached to find if such action was permissible and, if so, Mr. Bourne and another member of the Council would try to negotiate the matter. The RDC wrote back but the Parish Council decided on 22 May 1953 to leave the matter to be discussed at a subsequent meeting. The topic was not re-visited… though there is no record of Mr. Bell muttering "told you so" after Billy ploughed up the cricket and football field slightly more than a decade later.

For his next contribution on his opening night on the Council, 'Red Reg' waded into a topic close to the interests of Squire Edge, who at this time was Chairman of the Council as well as landlord of most of the village. The official minute records: "Mr. Bell also raised the question of mains water supply for the cottages in Chapel Yard". One can imagine the Squire's reaction… the cottages had a perfectly good pump, didn't they? The official minute resumes: "As this was a landlord's matter and there was some doubt as to there already being a supply, the matter was not discussed further". In other words, it was none of Reg's business if the inhabitants of Chapel Yard had to queue outside in all weather to fill a bowl.

And Reg suffered a predictable setback in 1955 when he stood for the Norwell District (including North Muskham) on the County Council. He polled 349 votes to the 977 of the Conservative candidate, Mr. T. Bradley, who thus succeeded Mr. A. H. Galbraith with a majority of 628.

The General Election 6 weeks later enabled Mr. Bell to equalise, so to speak: George Deer retained the seat for Labour despite Mr. Watson's true blue efforts. The turn-out was 83½ per cent, the highest in the county, and way above the national average (but not quite as good as the 1951 figure of 85 per cent).

None of this prevented Reg becoming increasingly respected for his efforts to improve the lot of the villagers and he became chairman of the Parish Council in 1958 – the first overtly Socialist to hold the post in an era when most councillors at this level proclaimed themselves to be independents.

In the other half of these semi-detached cottages (which have been greatly expanded over the years) lived Archie Talbot and his wife, christened Flora MacDonald but known universally as 'Pru'. Compared with 'Red Reg', they kept themselves to themselves.

Archie spent most of his working life at Ransome & Marles. He and his missus had inherited the two-up, two-down from Pru's parents. Archie died aged 92 on 4 April 1994, poignantly only 17 days after the demise of Flora, who was 85.

THE JOHNSONS: BROTHERS IN SEMIS

Brothers Edgar and Charlie Johnson brought up their families in adjoining semi-detached houses built in the 1930s in the field that their father William – who arrived in the village to work as a railway signalman – formerly worked as a small-holding in his spare time.

Edgar Samuel Johnson and his wife, Edith Florence, lived in the Bathley-side house along with their daughter Eileen. Edgar spent his working life at Ransome & Marles after serving an apprenticeship at G. Brown and Sons, builders, in Newark.

It came as a huge shock when he died suddenly at home at the relatively early age of 56 on 13 June 1960. Many of his workmates attended the funeral service the following Thursday at North Muskham Methodist Chapel.

Eileen and her husband, Jim Walker, moved to live in Trent Farm Cottage and built for 'Florrie' a "grannie bungalow" where she lived until her death at the age of 81 on 19 December 1983. The bungalow then became the village newsagents, general store and, eventually, Post Office.

Charlie, the elder of the boys having been born in 1899, was widowed when his children were quite young. In the 1950s, he lived with daughter Betty and sons Alan and Peter. Charlie was a hard-working platelayer on the railway, and had a vital task on foggy or freezing nights when none of the workers had telephones at home. Having been alerted by the Norwell Lane signalman, he had to cycle round Bathley and North Muskham to "knock-up" workmates like my Dad, who would then spend the night strapping detonators to the line as emergency communications for train crews who could not see signals.

Betty married John Bland after they courted at First Aid classes run by John's father in the village. They moved to live in South Muskham. The older son, Alan continued to live in the family home for many more years. Peter, who was 11 at the time of the Coronation, delivered meat for Brewitt's Butchers for many years, and moved to live in Bathley on marriage.

SEMI-DETACHED COTTAGES: SWALLOWED BY THE HAULIERS

Bill Talbot and his sons Eric and John, occupied the Muskham-side cottage of the small semi-detached pair that eventually became swallowed-up (and dreadfully neglected) when a haulage business sprang up next door.

Eric, the older son, began the commercialisation of this neighbourhood by starting a motor repairs business virtually in the vegetable garden of the family cottage. It was a well-timed move, coinciding with an explosion in the ownership of private cars and a proliferation of crashes. The business succeeded to such an extent that Eric and his wife Shirley (nee Phillips-Moul) were able to follow the Witneys into the cottage opposite Church Lane.

In to the semi next-door during the '50s came the newly-wed Peels. Eric worked at the Sugar Factory – and continued to do so for 40 years. His bride Edith, one of the Marsh sisters from Trent Farm Cottage on Main Street, had worked at Larkins, the solicitors, in Newark since leaving the Lilley & Stone High School for Girls. They moved away from their little idyll when lorries began rumbling into the haulier's next door at all hours of the night as well as the day shattering what passed for peace and quiet between the railway and the main road.

EDGEFIELD HOUSE: MR. TRENT AND HIS POSH CARPETS

As befits a splendid former vicarage, Edgefield House was home in the 1950s to a country gentleman called Woodford Alan Muddell who became renowned nationally as 'Mr. Trent'. The surname was pronounced Mudd-ell as opposed to Muddle (decades before television's Hyacinth Bucket insisted she was Mrs. Bouquet) and, famous and controversial as our hero became, there was never any critical play on his name. Alan, as he was happy for his friends to call him, had retired early from farming at the end of the Second World War but was immensely important to every Trent Valley dweller who had been traumatised by the huge floods of 1947. When the Trent River Board was formed, Mr. Muddell became its chairman and was credited with playing an active part in flood prevention schemes notably at Nottingham and Gainsborough.

So determined was he to avoid a repeat of the tragedies that by 1954-55, his was the highest-spending river board in the country. Its out-goings totalled £456,806, a full £100,000 more than the next-highest spending authority. The Trent's income was also the highest at £396,775. And so was the year's deficit, £60,031. But that did nothing at all to dilute the esteem in which Mr. Muddell was held, either in the locality or in the industry.

He was also deputy chairman of the Nottinghamshire Agricultural Executive Committee and, in March 1954 (when he was aged 56), was appointed a magistrate on the Newark County Bench. None of which stopped him and his wife getting involved in village life. While he was the Vicar's Warden at the Church, Mrs. Muddell took an active part in several village groups.

For example, in July 1953, Mrs. Muddell hosted the annual general meeting of the North and South Muskham branch of the NSPCC at Edgefield House. They had subscribed £30 to the cause during the year. As if that wasn't enough, a few days earlier Mrs. Muddell had organised an afternoon of country dancing on her manicured lawns. Admission was 1 shilling (5p) and folk were asked to take their own tea (only fair with rationing still a post-war irritant). A *Newark Advertiser* report suggested a jolly time was had by all: "A fancy dress parade caused much laughter, and it was so difficult to choose between the entrants that they all received a prize". The occasion raised £10, which went to "the home for blind babies" (presumably in Newark or Nottingham, though the report does not state where this was).

There was general and genuine sadness in the village when the Muddells moved to The Avenue, just about Newark's poshest address, in 1955. There was also great intrigue when their "surplus furniture" was put up for auction by Edward Bailey & Son, chartered auctioneers and estate agents, on 20 May. Buyers from Sussex, London, Leicester, Lincolnshire and Nottinghamshire generated a brisk trade.

Some of the prices raised were...

£52 for a Turkish carpet
£100 for an Amritzar carpet
£55 for an inlaid Sheraton sideboard
£50 for a set of six Windsor chairs
£24 for a Welsh dresser
£25 for a Georgian wardrobe
£52 for a French bedroom suite
£17 for a mahogany chest of drawers
£40 for a 12-bore double-barrel shotgun

3. The Lanes to Bathley

The Muddells remained in the public eye – not least in 1959 when they went to Buckingham Palace for Alan to be made a Companion of the British Empire (CBE). He was also appointed as one of 10 members of the national Inland Waterways Redevelopment Committee. And they remained connected with North Muskham: Mr. Muddell, as Vicar's Warden at St. Wilfrid's, and was still reading the lesson on special occasions such as Harvest Festivals into the second half of the 1960s.

The Muddells were replaced in Edgefield House by Lanham Faulkner. Kind-hearted villagers remember him as the man who introduced artificial irrigation to the area's farmers and the family is probably best remembered for its little pony. It grazed in Clipsham's paddock beside the North Road, having presumably been bought for their daughter, Zilma, who was born at about the time of the Coronation. In an age when few parents could even afford a wooden rocking horse, never mind the real thing, for their children, it quickly became a popular toy for the local children but it could be rather skittish. For instance, it had a habit of biting Clipshams' cattle on their flanks and, for some unknown reason, treated Cyril Marriott to the same indignity when he ventured within range.

Mr. Faulkner transformed Edgefield House from a fine home into a business place. By the time the Newark Show of 1957 arrived, it was the office and main store of Wright & Faulkner Ltd, purveyors of spray chemicals, spraying and other machinery, and lime.

SMALL-HOLDING: A SECRET D. H. LAWRENCE MUSEUM!

One of the most intriguing book collections in Britain sat quietly in a slightly colonial-looking wooden bungalow from which Sam King and his wife Emily ran a little small-holding, almost hidden between Edgefield House and the increasingly busy North Road. All of the books were D. H. Lawrence first editions, for Emily was the sister of Nottinghamshire's most famous author. But the book that generated most interest remained hidden well past Coronation-time. Emily wasn't one for fuss.

She called her delicate little brother Bert. He called her Pam. Being three-and-a-half years older, she had the job of looking after him as they grew up in the mining village of Eastwood on the Notts-Derbyshire border. He used all of her attributes to create the character of the devoted sister Annie when he wrote *Sons and Lovers*.

Although Emily wed Sam in 1904, she remained close to Bert. While Lawrence the author pushed back the boundaries of morality, Bert the brother was fond of saying: "You know, Pam, blood is thicker than water, and the ties that bind brothers and sisters are as strong as any marriage vows". So it was no surprise that he visited the Kings regularly when he was in England and, even when he was abroad, if two weeks went by without Pam hearing from him, she knew something was seriously wrong. So one can imagine her trauma when, in 1928, she received a letter from Lawrence's wife Frieda. He was 43, and the message from Gstaad in Switzerland was dire: "Your brother's strength is failing. If you want to see him again, I think you had better come now".

Emily, born in Sutton-in-Ashfield and brought up a few miles down the road at Eastwood, was not so sure. She was a shy, quiet mother of two with no grasp of French or German, and no inclination to venture into Europe for the first time at the age of 46. As luck would have it, though, her older daughter Margaret was 19 and, as part of her grammar school education, was fluent in French. So off they went on a great adventure that clearly meant the world to Emily. It was the last time she saw Bert, though he lived for another 18 months... "He just wasted away", she said on one of the few occasions she broke her silence on the privacy of family life. "He weighed less than 6 stones when he died, though he was 6 foot 3 inches tall".

Not long afterwards, in 1932, the Kings moved to North Muskham, bringing with them the first editions of all his poems, short stories and novels. All were signed by the author. Some had the message: "To my dear sister Emily". His unique wedding gift to Sam and Emily also hung on a wall in their bungalow: a landscape that he had painted and framed especially for them.

Proud as she was of her young brother, Emily was self-effacing. To the average inhabitant of North Muskham, she was just another member of the village WI and Bright Hour. She and Sam loved taking part in the weekly whist drives in the winter months to boost the funds of one village organisation or another. After all, there was little else to do apart from sit at home, listen to the wireless and read books by the light of the paraffin lamp. She read all but two of Bert's books. The exceptions were *Psychoanalysis and the Unconscious* and *Fantasia of the Unconscious*. "They were a bit too deep for me", she said. " I only had an ordinary education".

She was speaking – exclusively to the *Newark Advertiser* – in November 1960 when the focus of the literary world was on the 'trial' of a book written by Lawrence decades earlier. *Lady Chatterley's Lover* contained such explicit passages that, when Penguin Books decided to publish the unexpurgated version, they were taken to court under the Obscene Publications Act. Emily, by now 78 years old, followed the sensational case from the comfort of her

3. The Lanes to Bathley

armchair in North Muskham, avidly reading reports of the evidence in newspapers brought home by her daughter, Joan. Emily revealed: "When I read that a bishop had given evidence for the defence, I thought to myself, 'Bert's going to win!'"

And when he did, she had only one regret. Though she had no financial interest in the book's publication, she felt Penguin should have sold it for its original price of 1 guinea (£1.05) rather than for 3s 6d (17½p) as a 'cheap edition'. "Then it would be bought by genuine students of literature", she reasoned. In the event, it was bought by some 200,000 within a matter of weeks… though Emily did not bring that particular first edition out of hiding (the guinea one) until the *Advertiser* called on her. Their report on 9 November 1960 read:

"A glance along the Kings' bookshelves revealed a copy of Lady Chatterley's Lover – but was it the full version as Lawrence wrote it? "I have the full text, of course", Mrs. King told me. "But I don't keep it there with the others. It has always had a special place of its own". And turning to her husband, she said: "Will you get it please, Sam?" Mr. King disappeared and came back after a few minutes with the famous book in his hand. It was a first edition, one of 1,000 copies printed in Florence on hand-made paper and signed by the author".

Accompanying the report was a picture of Emily, grey-haired, slightly chubby cheeked, eyes focussed on the camera, clearly not sure whether to smile. In her hand was her very own copy of *Lady Chatterley's Lover* – number 913 of the 1,000 printed. Wonder how that would have gone down as a prize at one of the whist drives in the Church Hall?

Emily Una King died in April 1962. She was 80 and had been in failing health for 10 years. Her funeral service took place at North Muskham Chapel and was followed by cremation at Mansfield. Despite marrying into such a celebrity family, Samuel King was content to make a living by breeding pigs and feeding fowls on about one acre of land – a common size for a small-holding either side of the Second World War.

Of their daughters, Margaret became Mrs. Needham and reared her family at Shipley in Derbyshire. Joan moved to South Muskham, to live in a bungalow in Church Lane and become a much-admired character in her own right. Her love of gardening was such that she frequently succeeded at Muskham and District Horticultural Society shows.

And for decades, she continued to visit North Muskham regularly in all weathers… walking to services at the Chapel, cycling to the Post Office and generally defying her advancing years in a manner that would have made Mum, Dad and Uncle Bert quietly proud.

4. THE OLD NORTH ROAD

LORD NELSON: DEATH OF 'LITTLE PRINCESS'

After the Coronation of Queen Elizabeth II, the next time the village gathered together in great numbers they were mourning the death of North Muskham's own "little princess". Susan Elizabeth Cockerill was but two-and-a-half years old when she died on 19 July 1953, the tiny victim of leukemia in an age when cancer of any kind was so feared that few dared mention its name.

The Lord Nelson pictured by John Harris glistening in the Coronation Day rain. John was on the opposite side of the North Road. Note how close the road northbound was to the Nelson!

4. The Old North Road

She had only been poorly for six weeks; but what made it all the more touching was the fact that her fatal illness happened in a kind of public glare because she was the youngest child of the landlord of the Lord Nelson pub, Stan Cockerill, and his wife, Flo; and because it was literally only a vehicle's width from the North Road, it thrived on passing trade as well as loyal customers from North Muskham, Bathley and several other villages.

The Cockerills were an ideal pub pair. Always had a smile to welcome every customer. Instinctively seemed to know whether a quip or a condolence would be most appropriate. Encouraged the village cricket club to base itself there. Welcomed into their paddock folk who wanted to set up home in caravans. Even dressed-up the first storey of an old barn as a social club for groups of villagers desperate for somewhere to stage a dance or whist drive.

Stan Cockerill, the popular landlord.

Stan and Flo were effortlessly making the transition from Wartime austerity and forced optimism to 50s' bravado bordering on invincibility. Indeed, Stan was so respected by the village elders that he was co-opted on to the Parish Council at the annual general meeting in May 1951. The family had everything going for them, as well as a bustling business: son Brian passed 9 GCE O-levels that summer at the Magnus Grammar School; older daughter Jacqueline was on her way to passing her 11-plus at North Muskham County Primary School; and, after Susan arrived, Flo's widowed mum Mrs. Twells had moved in to help. So they were yet another perfect example of an extended family instinctively pulling together.

The result: the Nelson was a home-from-home for a growing number of regulars. All of which made the fatal illness of the little one so much harder to bear. Jean Baggaley from North Road Farm next door was 9 at the time and Jacky's best playmate yet she was so cocooned from the tragedy that the first hint came one Sunday morning when her Mum said quietly to her: "Go to Sunday School on your own today, darling". "Why can't I call for Jacky?" asked Jean. "Because little Susan has died", said her Mum quietly.

The incomprehension was not limited to young Jean. It was accidentally illustrated by the *Newark Advertiser* of 22 July. One brief story reported: "The annual general meeting of the North and South Muskham branch of the

National Society for the Prevention of Cruelty to Children was held at Edgefield House last week, Mrs. Muddell presiding. Mrs. Marsh Rapson gave an account of the work of the Society and spoke of the great need of financial help. A vote of thanks was moved by Mrs. Dent. £30 was subscribed by the branch during the year".

Three columns away, the cruelty of nature was simply too evident in the death announcements:

COCKERILL. On July 19th 1953 at the Lord Nelson Inn, North Muskham, Susan Elizabeth, dearly loved daughter of Stan and Florence, and sister of Brian and Jacky. Aged two-and-a-half years.
Funeral today (3pm).
Peacefully sleeping in God's tender care.

The little one's death touched so many hearts, virtually the whole village not only went to the funeral but sent flowers. The *Newark Herald* of 25 July painstakingly listed those who had sent wreaths:

There was the extended family: "heartbroken Mummy and Daddy"; Brian and Jacky "to our little sister"; Nana Twells; Grandma Cockerill and Aunty Betty; Auntie Maudie, Uncle Eric and John; Auntie Phyllis, Uncle Reg and Sooty; Auntie Doris and Uncle Frank; Auntie Olive and Uncle Ron; Aunt Lizzie and Uncle Billie; Pat and Ron (Scotland), Auntie Emily and Auntie Alice; Auntie Lily, Auntie Annie, Auntie Mary; Auntie Gert, Uncle Arthur and Violet, Sylvia and boys; Auntie Nellie; Uncle Sid and family (London); Cousin Jane (London); Uncle Bernard, Auntie Edna, Hazel and Val; 'Auntie' Maisie, Uncle Jim and Clement; Auntie Renee, Uncle Stan, Susan and John; Auntie Minnie, Uncle Laurie, Enid and Trevor.

And the friends included villagers and folk who had simply used the field for a caravan park yet had warmed to the instinctive hand of friendship offered by the Cockerills. They were, in no particular order, because they all felt equally desolate: Mrs. Hazard, Gwen and Harold (from the house just over the Trent Bridge towards the Sugar Factory); Mr. and Mrs. Franklin and Jack (Little Carlton); Peter, Ellen and little friends Jane and Pat (the Kents who we'll meet shortly); Pat, Mabel and the Lambert family (Little Carlton); the Clipsham family; Janet, Pearl and Marion; Mr. and Mrs. G. Harker; Mr. and Mrs. Lang and family; Mr. and Mrs. Scarborough and family; Mr. and Mrs. Wells and family; Mrs. Lewis, Mrs. Henneberry, Mrs. Gatiss and Mrs. Milnes; Allen and Tony Faisey; Mr. and Mrs. W. A. Muddell; Mr. and Mrs. F. Davenport and Sybil; Mr. and Mrs. S. Thomas and Susan; Mrs. John

4. The Old North Road

Gascoigne; Dr. and Mrs. Lees; Robert Marston; Mr. and Mrs. J. Hibbs; John Cotton's drivers; Sybil, Martin and Gillian [the Briggs family who went on to become the village's chief suppliers of milk and deliverers of papers]; Mr. and Mrs. Purdy and Elaine; Margaret and Mrs. Dye; Mr. and Mrs. Judson and family; Mr. and Mrs. Flint senior; Mr. and Mrs. Scott (Farndon); Mr. and Mrs. R. Bell; Mr. and Mrs. Baggaley and Graham; Jean [the Baggaleys' daughter]; Mr. and Mrs. Charles Potter; Mary and Elsie; Mr. and Mrs. Staniforth; Mr. and Mrs. Price, Philip, Barbara and George Allison; Mrs. E. Rick; Phyl, George and family; 'Auntie' Maisie and Mrs. Brewin; Mr. and Mrs. Calladine and playmate Johnny; Renee, Bill and Faye Bridgewater; Mr. and Mrs. White (Lincoln Street); Mrs. Peel (Newark); Florence M. E. King [deputy head at the village school]; Edie Reynolds; Frank and Alice Coyne; Mr. and Mrs. Kent and Hugh; Mr. and Mrs. E. Johnson and Mr. C. H. Johnson [from Vicarage Lane]; Mr. E. C. Godfrey and family.

And the village organisations sent their floral tributes though little Susan had not even lived long enough to be aware of their existence: North Muskham Church Sunday School, North Muskham and Bathley Cricket Club, the Lord Nelson darts team, North Muskham County School; North Muskham Women's Institute.

In the formal announcements column of the same newspaper, the family's despair and dignity was there for all to see:

Mr. and Mrs. Stan Cockerill of the Lord Nelson Inn, North Muskham, wish to express their heartfelt thanks to Dr. R. Lees, Sister Young and Nurse Walker for their devoted attention to their daughter Susan, for which they are extremely grateful. They also wish to thank the many friends and customers of the Lord Nelson for their kind enquiries which were a great help to them in their trouble, and thanks are also extended to the great many friends for their letters of sympathy and for the beautiful floral tributes. Mrs. Twells (grandmother) wishes to be associated with this expression of thanks.

And, to their enormous credit, the Cockerills picked up their lives and set about ensuring that as many other people as possible reaped the benefits.

Not that everything always ran smoothly. In the wee small hours of a Friday early in December of 1958, they became the village's first victims of a thief who literally walked in off the North Road and went on his way slightly the richer. The family daschund heard the window smash and kicked up a fuss, but as Stan told the *Newark Advertiser*: "I turned over and went back to sleep because the dog barks every time anyone goes down the road past the house". This particular passer-by went down the road with £15 out of the bar till and £30 in cigars and cigarettes, but left all the alcohol. So the police were pretty sure they were seeking a hitch-hiker, but there were almost more of them to the mile than there were vehicles in the dead of night in that era, when (for example) young men on National Service tended to hitch lifts between their home and wherever they were stationed.

And Stan did not let the setback deter him. He rose to be vice-chairman of the Newark and District Licensed Victuallers' Association and made local newspaper headlines with his views on the new-fangled breathalyser being used by police in an attempt to curb excessive drinking by drivers. "I am not here to defend drunken drivers", said the landlord who perhaps benefited from 'passing trade' more than most others in the area. "He is a social menace and must be made to realise this. But let's keep this cause of accidents in its true perspective". The crux of his argument, paraphrased in the front page lead of the *Newark Herald* on 30 January 1960, seemed to be that private parties and clubs were as much to blame for drunken drivers as public houses. Villagers who knew him refused to accept that that was his argument – in essence, that three wrongs made a right. Stan was always a much more caring bloke than that.

Busy though he remained behind the bar of the Nelson, he continued to find time to serve on the Parish Council and to become Chairman of the Governors of Muskham County Primary School, resigning only in 1968 because he and Flo had decided it was time to retire. Sadly from the village's point of view, they also decided it was time to leave the district.

Thomas Stanley Cockerill died aged 75, on 10 May 1988. Florence Edna Cockerill followed, aged 80, on 7 December 1992.

NORTH ROAD FARM: LITTLE BO PEEP ESPIES TRAMPS

Bubbly Jean Baggaley will never forget the village's curtailed Coronation celebrations. "I was in the three-legged race with Jane Chadd and we fell over", says the farmer's daughter who went to the fancy dress parade as Bo-Peep. The fall was a minor calamity compared with the one that befell big brother Graham when he went to work for Frank Swannack, the village-based agricultural engineer. Graham had the ends of his fingers chopped off in an accident.

But he persevered in businesses connected with the improvement and modernisation of the farmer's lot, finally settling in Southport on the Lancashire coast with his wife and their four boys.

As Graham developed via North Muskham School and, after passing his 11-plus, the Magnus Grammar School, he grew up to play in the village's

4. The Old North Road

junior football team – and Jean well remembers her dad, Jim, allowing the boys to play in the paddock next to their farm. Her Mum was sports-minded, too, and had a table tennis set-up in the barn... though there were occasions when they had to make sure they had no surprise spectators when they popped in for a game. "It was amazing how many tramps used to stop for the night in the barn", Jean recalls. "We used to find quite well-to-do people in there on some mornings!"

Probably the most memorable intruder, however, was found by Mrs. Baggaley in the farmhouse kitchen one day... The resident bull had wandered in there. But there was no China Shop scenario. Calm as you like, Mrs. Baggaley ushered the ambling and amiable beast back out into the yard where Dad always preferred to be tinkering with motor engines rather than battling the livestock.

The Baggaleys had taken over North Road Farm when Mrs. Annie Doncaster called it a day. In truth, she'd had to surrender the reins to her farm manager, Arthur Geeson, quite a few years before she actually dragged herself away from the battle she and her late husband John (who died aged 52 in 1922) had had with the poor-quality land; the early morning sessions hand-milking the cows; the endless rounds of trimming the hedges and digging the ditches so that the land was irrigated as well as it could be, given how close it was to the level of the Trent.

It was far from the jolly 'good life'; but, like the Doncasters before them, the Baggaleys made the most of it.

Mrs. Baggaley was the arch-typical farmer's wife of the era: hard-working, unflappable, tireless in her attempts to keep the children occupied... and with a heart of gold. "She used to hand on the clothes I'd grown out of to poorer families in the village", says Jean. "We used to take them up to the School, and I think Miss King quietly handed them on". Which is probably why Jean can add of the controversial teachers: "As far as I'm concerned, the Kings were super people".

Jean seemed to this outsider to be the arch-typical farmer's tomboy daughter – and she proved it one day by taking Graham's air rifle to the squeaking sparrows on the telephone wires above the caravans in the Nelson field immediately to the south of the farm. "I remember pinging one of the caravans and being terrified that I'd get into trouble", she says.

Her dad, James A. Baggaley, died at the relatively young age of 64 in 1965; and by a cruel twist of fate, Graham was the same age when he succumbed to cancer. Mrs. Baggaley lived out the rest of her life in a bungalow at South Muskham. Jean was married in 1966, to Dennis Carr, and they reared their daughter and two sons at Westborough, just over the Notts-Lincolnshire border towards Grantham.

GARAGE: KEEPING UP WITH THE TIMES

No family in North Muskham moved more successfully with the rapidly modernizing post-war times than the Milnes, Syd and his wife Nancy, who was sister of Jack Needham, the railway signalman who lived in Ferry Lane Cottages.

The Milnes took over the Garage at the junction of Waltons Lane with the North Road from Mr. Fineral: a line of petrol pumps, hardly a lorry width off the southbound lane of the main road between Scotland and London, in front of a tin shed in which Syd Milnes carried on his trade as a motor mechanic.

Milnes Garage, pictured from the junction of Walton's Lane with the North Road. The white house is the Old Vicarage (also known in the 2000s as Muskham Castle). The car on the extreme left is travelling south past the Lodge (known locally as the Concertina House).

4. The Old North Road

He employed at one time or another Herbert Mitcherson from Bathley, Ron Lowe from South Muskham and Jack Duncan, who eventually merged his skills as a mechanic with his love of two-wheeled machinery by running a motor-cycle shop in Northgate, Newark.

By the mid-1950s, Milnes' garage had also become the area agency for farm machinery manufactured by Allis-Chalmers; and in addition to offering full sales and service facilities Syd was exhibiting the machinery at the Newark Agricultural Show. A few years later, he was a dealer for New Holland farm machinery – and took over the Lord Nelson one night to put on a film show for local farmers. Thirty-five of them turned up to watch *Hay In A Day*, demonstrating USA machinery "not yet known in this country". The star of the film was "a mower-crusher-dryer" which, Anglicised, became better known as a combine harvester. The *Newark Advertiser* farming correspondent, C. David Edgar, reported: "It was a long evening – 6.30 to very much later for some – but not so long as English haymaking sometimes seems".

In a two-storey brick built house beside the garage, Mrs. Milnes reared their two sons, Ronnie and Roger. Ronnie was named after Mr. Milnes' brother, who lost his life when HMS Royal Oak was sunk at Scapa Flow at the outset of the Second World War. Sybil Davenport was not even old enough to be going to school at the time, but she clearly remembers: "Syd's mother came to tell my Grandma that her Ronnie had gone down with his ship. I asked, 'Why is Mrs. Milnes crying?' I wasn't used to the grown-ups showing emotion like that".

The body of Boy 1st Class Ronald William Milnes, P/JX 158116. H.M.S. Royal Oak. Royal Marines. the son of Grace Milnes of North Muskham, who died aged 16 on 14 October 1939, lies at plot P, row 1, grave 23 in the Lyness Royal Naval Cemetery, Orkney.

Nancy Milnes had good reasons to be proud of her family as the years rolled on.

Syd was so respected in the village that he became Chairman and Treasurer of the Parish Council in the early 1950s. His business grew as motoring became more popular and prospered enormously when the North Road was dualled. The bad news was that the homely old garage and its smarter-looking house had to be demolished to make way for the wider road. The Milnes took over the modern filling station at the north end of the village and moved into a bungalow built beside the Old North Road a short distance from their old home.

Showing a great awareness of what the motoring public required, Syd sought permission to build a motel in 1966. The Planning Department of

Southwell Rural Council turned down the application on the grounds it would be "outside the confines of any existing community". Blandly ignoring the fact that it was them who had planted the new garage outside the confines of the main North Muskham community, they condemned the idea as an "undesirable intrusion into the rural scene". More than two decades elapsed before a Travel Lodge was constructed beside the garage. Another two decades on, it remains difficult for many motorists to find. If only they had been heading for a hotel with the fairy castle façade of the old Grange!

Meanwhile, the Milnes suffered heartbreak when their younger son, Roger, lost his life in a motoring accident on the old North Road at Carlton-on-Trent, aged only 28, on 24 August 1978. Sydney Vernon Milnes died, aged 77, on 3 June 1993. His widow, Nancy Lennox Milnes, remained a familiar and friendly sight, driving around the village, until her death on 5 June 1996 aged 79. Ronnie continued to live with his family in a house built close to the newly-sited Garage – and was good enough to keep his private lane open so that the villagers could reach the new garage to fill up with fuel.

TRANSPORT CAFE: FRESH FRUIT, FRY-UPS AND FROLICS

Between the Milnes' modest empire and the Old Vicarage, as the North Road curved towards the Grange grounds, was a lovely orchard containing an incongruous railway carriage in which lived Mrs. Goldson, a widowed market gardener.

The carriage had door handles of polished brass. Her muslin polka dot curtains were a genteel world away from the muck and grime of the steam engines that had towed her home in its first life. The goods she sold seemed to belong to a more casual era than the one she could see out of her windows: an increasing number of lorries grinding up and down the North Road in competition with the beleaguered trains. Her soft fruit was an economic treat for many a family enjoying a walk around the village.

And, in the unlikely event of them feeling even more peckish, beside the orchard was a Transport Cafe that also doubled as a dance hall. This predecessor of the Muskham Little Chef was run by the Gatiss family, Thomas and his wife, who lived in a wooden bungalow next door. The Cafe was largely for the pioneering lorry drivers who were slowly (because they were restricted to a top speed of 30mph) but surely wresting the heavy haulage market from British Railways and for the growing numbers of travelling salesmen who smoothed their way from town to town selling wares, and thrived in the era, pre-supermarket, when Britain was a nation of shopkeepers.

4. The Old North Road

Come certain evenings, when the roads were virtually deserted and all hope of hungry customers had ground to a halt, the Cafe took on an entirely different, much more vibrant, life. The tables and chairs were swept to one side and it became a dance hall, usually in an attempt to raise money for good causes. The Red Cross was one deserving beneficiary. One regular dancer was Lucy Marriott – obviously a liberated lady long before the term was even thought of. Her daughter, Jill, remembers: "On a dance night, Mum would go off to the Cafe. Dad would stay at home, looking at the clock with increasing frequency as the night drew on. As soon as Mum came in, Dad would leap off and nip off to the Nelson 'for a quick pint' before closing time".

There were two Gatiss children, Bill and Eva. Bill was so impressed by the passing trade that dropped in to be refreshed by Mum and Dad, he went into transport – as a Wright's bus driver, plying the routes from Newark through villages not covered by Lincolnshire Road Car. The death of the Bungalow Cafe – along with that of the old Garage – was heralded by a compulsory purchase order issued early in 1962 under the Highways Act of 1959.

OLD VICARAGE: 'CLUCK' THE KING OF THE CASTLE

Almost half a century before the property became known as Muskham Castle, the double-fronted house on the crown of one of the North Road curves was the home of a king for a day. Mark Lewis won the Coronation Day fancy dress parade dressed as a monarch on stilts. The outfit was titled "Lord of all I survey" – probably by his father, Alex, an English master at the Magnus Grammar School, Newark, where the pupils nicknamed him 'Cluck' in recognition of his clipped accent. I must admit to bias here. He was my English teacher, and English was my best subject by quite a distance. I didn't realise what an impression I was making on him until, midway through my third year, I referred in an essay to a 'pastime'. His glee was expressed in red ink in the margin of my schoolbook: "Gotcha! There's no such word". In an age when many masters tended to rule by fear (which was probably why they insisted on being called masters rather than teachers), Cluck earned respect without raising either voice or hand.

Born in Birmingham, where he was educated at the King Edward VII Grammar School and the city's University, he arrived at the Magnus in 1926 and became a popular and effective Senior English Master. He became secretary of Newark Lawn Tennis Club and a busy member of the local Literary Society and Newark Amateur Operatic Society. During the War, he was an officer of 1260 Squadron of the Air Training Corps, attached to the Magnus.

For years, he travelled between Muskham and school on the same buses as we children; and his mere presence was enough to ensure that we behaved impeccably – to the point of keeping our caps on, giving up seats to our elders and even arguing quietly over which High School girls we would most like to sit beside (though, as the girls got on the bus last, the choices were theirs). While much of this obedience was in honour of Cluck's presence, there was a practical reason why we hesitated to run the risk of a detention for denting the reputation of the school (sorry, The School). If we were kept in for an extra hour, there was always a chance we'd have to pay a bus fare, rather than get away with a flash of our free passes, on one of the crowded 'works specials' at 5.20pm or 5.45pm.

No doubt who made 13-year-old Mark's suit for the Coronation fancy dress. His mum, Elsie, was one of those practical ladies capable of transforming sow's ears into silk purses. She was as handy as her husband when it came to composition, too: at the September 1953 meeting of North Muskham WI, the competition, a poem entitled 'Our WI', was won by Mrs. Lewis. A few months later, she was elected onto the WI committee and was put in charge of its Sunshine Fund, which handled donations to charities.

Mark handled his studies better than most sons of the village. When he left the Magnus in the summer of 1958, he earned a scholarship to the University of London to study modern Japanese – a move that was to earn him a role travelling the world as a buyer with Selfridges, the respected London store.

Meantime, one can imagine the shock in the Lewis household over Christmas of 1958 when 'Cluck' fell ill. He was only 55. By mid-January, he was in Newark General Hospital; and I'm sure I wasn't the only pupil wondering if he was watching the school buses trundling back and forth along London Road. Neither was I the only one stunned when Alex Edward Lewis died on 1 February 1959 without leaving the hospital. Mrs. Lewis was ultra-practical in the moment of the devastating loss. In the death notice in the local papers, she insisted: "No flowers by request and please no letters but donations to North Muskham Parish Church".

There wasn't a spare seat to be had in the Church for the funeral on the following Friday (followed by cremation at Wilford Hill near Nottingham). Among the mourners were most of the sixth-formers he was preparing for GCE A-level exams, many of his teaching colleagues, officers and cadets from the ATC, as well as huge numbers of the local community. And the admiration was pretty well summed-up by the Vicar, the Rev. H. A. Dunn, who said: "We all saw what his calling meant to him by the way he went back to his school at the beginning of this term although he was not a fit man. It was an act of courage and determination, and if it cost him his life, I'm sure he would not have minded. I think he would like to feel he had given himself in the end wholly to his calling as a school master".

When the A1 dual carriageway came along, the Old Vicarage survived. But 144 square yards of its front garden were the subject of a compulsory purchase order so that the 'old North Road' and extension of Waltons Lane could be linked up (hence the strange angles of the boundary walls). Mr. Lewis would definitely have clucked.

LODGE HOUSE: UPWARDLY MOBILE NEWLY WEDS

Peter Kent and his bride, Ellen Bourne, began married life in the 'Concertina house' more formally known as the Lodge House, which stood at the start of the drive in to the Grange grounds from the North Road. They were a couple who more than epitomised the upwardly mobile mood of the era. The quietly spoken Peter traversed the world as an airline pilot, returning frequently to modestly take his place in the village cricket team. Ellen, the oldest of Billy's girls from up the North Road at Lodge Farm, was the joint owner of a shop in Middlegate, Newark, that seemed (to the casual gaze of the passing schoolboy) to specialise in a racier-than-Mum-would-wear line in lingerie. There was general celebrating when she became a Mum herself: in November 1953, North Muskham Women's Institute minuted its congratulations to Mrs. Kent Jnr on the arrival of a daughter. The first of three, as it happened: Jane, Pat and Diana.

When the young Kents moved out of earshot of the North Road in the mid-50s, they introduced civilisation to the cart track known as Mackleys Lane, a muddy route through the flood plain opposite Waltons Lane to the river. Peter and Ellen commissioned Clipshams to build them a house in which to rear their girls. The builders' labourers named it The Warren in tribute to the rabbits that nightly undermined the foundations they were digging out.

The new occupiers of The Lodge were the Barbour family. Stanley Archibald Barbour, who had helped build the Ossington aerodrome at the onset of the Second World War, further enlarged what had been an extremely sharply-angled property – hence its nickname – for his wife, Jessie Mundell Barbour, and their son, Billy, who had attended the Magnus in the 1940s. While Jessie died at the age of 58 on 30 January 1978, having witnessed the removal of the North Road a few more yards away from their back windows, Stanley reached the age of 82, and saw the Grange and Park developments completed, before his death on 25 January 1994.

THE GROVE: NICE HOUSE, PATRIOTIC MAN

Arguably North Muskham's greatest royalist of them all lived in The Grove, a substantial house on the junction of the A1 and the south side of Norwell/Vicarage Lane. Jack Fineral – "a military man through and through" in the memory of his great-nephew, Ronnie Milnes – decided to spread bunting across the North Road. Clambering up a ladder, he tethered it tightly enough to the top of a telegraph pole on the village side of the road and, unable to find a similar staging post on his side of the road, fed the festive line through his bedroom window and tied it to his bed head. Alas, when the rain began to fall during the early hours of the morning, the bunting stretched and sagged… and when a tall furniture van happened along, Mr. Fineral awoke with a start as his bed accelerated across the room at speed before crashing into the wall. The above story comes courtesy of Colin Granger, who remembers Mr. Fineral as a kindly man whose business acumen was probably some way ahead of his time.

For what makes the accident between the furniture van and his bed all the more surprising is the fact that Mr. Fineral was the mechanically-minded man who started the garage business taken over by his nephew, Syd Milnes.

He was an unconventional man and lived an unconventional life. As a soldier in the Boer War, he took part in the Siege of Ladysmith; and The Grove contained quite a few mementoes of bloody battles in South Africa. Jack made sure that it also contained a little treasure: he took in as his ward a little girl called Lucy Jarvis, who became the wife of Cyril Marriott. And genial Jack ensured that Syd Milnes was taught how to succeed him as the resident motor mechanic. Syd bought the Garage from Jack around 1939. This doubtless delighted the growing numbers of car owners, who tended to become impatient by the laborious way in which old Jack served the petrol. "He was too slow to carry coffins out of church", said one old driver with a wince. But Jack is still not lacking in defenders, who point out the petrol pumps of the time had to be literally pumped to raise the fuel out of the storage tanks, and did so in spurts rather than with a continuous flow.

This extended family was succeeded in The Grove by a typical post-war family: John A. Gatley (known to all as Tim for some unknown reason), a quietly spoken ex-airman who played cricket for the village team, with his wife Betty and their children Jill and Robert.

Mrs. Gatley, one of the sisters of Jack Needham, the Methodist signalman from Ferry Lane, had become sufficiently integrated in North Muskham WI to be taking her turn at providing the refreshments by early 1957. And Tim became utterly unique on the evening of 17 August 1960 – the only man ever

4. The Old North Road

to hit the winning run for North Muskham and Bathley Cricket Club in a Cup Final.

If Mr. Fineral had still been around, he'd surely have put the bunting back up!

Alas, the Gatleys departed the community when the property had to be demolished to make way for the A1 dual carriageway – though it remains possible to envisage where it stood. All one has to do is walk up Vicarage Lane towards the Norwell Lane level crossing, and look back towards the old School House (the right-hand edge of the Woolhouse Hall row). This gives you the old line that Vicarage Lane took to the old North Road. The Grove stood pretty much where a cluster of trees has been allowed to grow in the crook of the sliproad that curves off the north-bound A1 to halfway up the Vicarage Lane bridge.

COTTAGES ON THE GREEN: LIFE IN A GRASSY TRIANGLE

Two families lived in a pair of semi-detached cottages that stood on The Green. The houses faced the North Road at the widest point of the triangular green formed by its junctions with Main Street and Vicarage Lane. Beside the cottages were vegetable gardens. Behind them were a boggy area (where the village pond had been inadequately filled-in three decades earlier) on which stood a gas chamber during the Second World War, and a grassy area just about level enough for schoolchildren to play football, cricket, tag and whatever else fell into fashion. The chamber was there in case the dastardly German Luftwaffe began to fight dirty. More effective gas warfare came at regular intervals in the shape of the mobile 'shop' carrying the school dentist from victim to… sorry… from patient to patient. Like lambs to the slaughter, the children would be led across the road to be inspected.

One family that lived on The Green, fittingly, was called Green – Mr., Mrs. and their daughter Helen. He was the school attendance officer – an imposing man obviously dedicated to his task of ensuring the little ones did not skive. There were children who seriously believed the man was psychic. One recalls: "You only had to miss half a day at school and he'd be round, knocking on the door, asking what was wrong, why you weren't at school, when you could be expected back".

The other family on the Green was Mr. and Mrs. Cox, who suffered more than most. They were early victims of the rapid growth in passing traffic in that their young daughter, Rita, died in an accident as she crossed the North Road near their home. As if that wasn't grief enough, her mother, Amy, was confined to a wheelchair after falling down the stairs at home. In spite of – or maybe partly because of – all this, she remained an immensely compassionate lady, helping to look after infirm neighbours. It was the kind of behaviour that had been instilled in her during her childhood in the close confines of the cottages in Chapel Yard.

One can only imagine the rigours of her life, though. Every morning before Bill Cox went to work for British Waterways, he would carry Amy down the stairs that had crippled her and place her in her wheelchair. While he spent the day operating the Newark locks that were immensely busy with commercial barge traffic, she would do what housework was possible from her wheelchair and make sure the older neighbours lacked for nothing. To this end, her shy spinster sister Doris would shuffle along from Chapel Yard to push her round the village and doubtless pass on the gossip about what was happening at the heart of the community.

And just when they thought life couldn't get worse, the long heralded plans to expand the North Road came along. The men from the Ministry, having procrastinated until the south-bound queues stretched from Newark beyond Carlton-on-Trent on most summer weekends, decided the nice houses on The Green would simply have to go. At about the same time, the slum shifters from the District Council decided Chapel Yard must meet the same fate. It didn't occur to them that seven tiny homes could be modernised as three, two or one. Slum clearance meant clearance. And as road widening operations were similarly unsubtle, there was no way a fresh route could be found for the A1 across the soggy moorland to the west of the railway line. Those houses would have to go. And as for the descendant of the ancient Toll Bar House across the North Road...

TOLL BAR HOUSE: KINDLY AUNTIES AND GENEROUS BUILDERS

It is typical of the era that Toll Bar House is best remembered by children of the '50s not as the headquarters of Clipsham & Sons' building firm (which it was), nor as a thriving little farm (which it was), but as the home of two kindly spinster sisters, Edith and Alice Clipsham. Their hospitality was one of the major bonuses of being a playmate of their oldest nephew, David Clipsham. Their paddock, which stretched from the south end of the house some 200 metres to Vicarage Lane, became a Sunday morning football or cricket pitch depending on the season, and the young players were always lavishly rewarded for their efforts with pop served by the kindly sisters. Quite why there were never any concerns about the danger of a ball escaping on to the adjacent North Road is a mystery 50 years on... maybe

4. The Old North Road

the ball control of the participants was as exemplary as some of their idols, Stanley Matthews and Tom Finney... or maybe the lack of nannying was all part of growing up.

Either way, the only time Edith and Alice would attempt to impose themselves was when they deemed the games were running too long and that parents would be tiring of keeping Sunday dinners warm. There would then be a gentle shoo-ing in much the same tone that they tried to dissuade their chickens from gathering under the back porch on wet days.

But it must have been a lovely place to work because Edith and Alice's brothers were equally as considerate. The out-buildings that were not packed with building materials – the basics of bricks, sand, cement, wood and glass in these days before pre-stressed concrete dominated the industry – were full of animals.

There was one cowshed with room for nine milkers, two more down the drive with room for six each, a few pigs and a lot of fowls, recalls Colin Granger, who was taught to milk as a 12-year-old by his older brother, Jock. The milk was instantly in demand: villagers were welcome to take their little cans and buy it direct from the churn.

Edith and Alice had spent many years looking after their Mum (as well as their four brothers, sundry builder's labourers, farm-hands and children). Their Dad, Henry Clipsham, had died on 5 April 1929 aged 65. His widow, Sarah, survived to the age of 83, and finally passed away at the family home on 28 March 1950. She had lived all of her life in the village and was a founder member of its Mothers' Union branch. Judging by the gentle demeanour of her children, she was an excellent mother of her era.

When the modern-day highwaymen decided Toll Bar House would have to go, they graciously allowed a modern dwelling to be erected in a corner of the paddock furthest away from the widened A1. It was considered by many to be a modern, characterless monument to the qualities (in thoughts and deeds) that the Clipshams had brought to the village.

It did not even occur to the modernizers of the 1960s to do what their predecessors had done when the arrival of the railways in the 1850s forced the demise of toll bars: once they finally demolished the old Toll House and its offices in 1872, they sold 20,000 of its "good old bricks", 2,000 pantiles, doors, windows, etc. Clipsham's builders would have appreciated such recycling!

As it was, the loss of the old house pretty much coincided with the firm being run down and eventually closed. Truly the end of an era.

HOMESTEAD: WIDOW AND TWO CHILDREN = 90p A WEEK

The Grangers moved in from Ossington as soon as Clipshams (the builders, not the spinsters) had completed the construction of the Homestead in 1947 – the village's first brick-built bungalow. It cost £900: a bathroom (rather than a tub that appeared once a week in front of the fire), large kitchen with coal-fired cooking range, pantry, three bedrooms, scullery and coal house. All it lacked was glass in the top of the windows. Post-war shortages of materials were such that roofing felt had to be tacked into the gaps.

So throughout the harsh winter of early 1947, the Grangers had the literally chilling experience of huddling in their beds watching the felt billowing and failing to prevent the icy winds blasting into their rooms. It was a small inconvenience when compared with their experiences.

The Grangers, widowed mother and three offspring, were suitably dignified, hard-working inhabitants who had experienced more heartbreak than most. Mr. Stephen Granger never fully recovered from being badly gassed in the First World War and died, aged only 47, in 1938. A year earlier, the family had suffered the loss of 9-month-old baby Arthur.

When they moved to Muskham, at a time when coal cost 10s 6d (52½p) a ton, Mrs. Granger was expected to raise her family on 18s (90p) a week: 10s (50p) for herself, 5s for 15-year-old Peggy and 3s (15p) for 9-year-old Colin. Her elder son Stephen (known to all as Jock) was old enough to look after himself – and, in fact, took on the responsibility of helping care for his siblings, too.

By the early 1950s, Jock was tending the Clipshams' herd of 20-25 milking cows; daughter Peggy was at college in Didsbury, Manchester, preparing for a career in teaching that was to stretch for 38 years; and Colin, five years younger than Peggy and fresh out of Muskham School, was helping brother Jock and the builders. They remained at the Homestead until 14 November 1957, when they moved into the first new bungalow to be built on the south side of Waltons Lane.

One of Colin's most vivid memories of the Clipshams is their generosity. He recalls: "I'd often be working in the yard when a gentleman would drive in and ask if Mr. Clipsham was about. Invariably I'd have to explain that all the Mr. Clipshams were at work. Then the visitor would ask me to give them a message – he'd say, 'Ask him to send me my bill. The work was done last year but I still haven't been asked to pay'."

Colin, who went on to work as a gardener in Newark for 25 years before ill health forced his early retirement, continued for decades to keep an eye on the parish on daily cycle rides from the home he shared in Newark with

4. The Old North Road

Peggy. The Homestead also survived into the 21st century while most of the buildings around it, apart from some of the old farm sheds, were demolished

NORTH ROAD COTTAGES: GIVE US A LIFT, CYRIL
On the north-bound side of the North Road stood a row of four cottages (which were demolished in the 1960s when the A1 was dualled). In the early '50s, they were occupied by the Rowlands (who were replaced by the Marriotts), old Joe Swaby, the Temporalls and the Rushbys – every one a character.

Frank Rowland worked for Billy Bourne at Lodge Farm across the North Road. Mrs. Rowland was a district nurse who helped countless local mothers not just to give birth but to get used to motherhood. And she never lost a chance to help those less fortunate.

For example, she was the ace cake-maker whenever the National Society for the Prevention of Cruelty to Children staged a money-raiser in the village. She was also sufficiently house-proud to frequently relegate Mr. Rowland to the garden, where he had a little greenhouse in which he could shelter from

North Road Cottages, which were demolished – to make way for the wider North Road.

175

Cyril Marriott – Wartime hero in Africa.

4. The Old North Road

the elements. Being busy all hours tending for others, Mrs. Rowland had little inclination to encourage Frank to add to her housework!

After she died, Mr. Rowland went to live with their son, Don, who worked as a herdsman for "Sonny" Brown, a farmer and butcher at Norwell who travelled around the neighbouring villages selling his meat out of a van. Frank was 95 when he passed away, on 4 August 1962.

The Rowlands were followed into the row by Mr. and Mrs. Marriott, cheerful Cyril and quiet little Lucy, nee Jarvis. They moved in from The Grange with their daughter, Jill, and had a son, Dennis. Cyril, back from spending the Second World War fighting in much hotter conditions (as you'll gather from the picture on the left), was a labourer for Clipsham's builders and a character who was always prepared to play a part in village life, particularly as an inspirational captain, wicketkeeper and slogging batsman of the village cricket team.

Another of Cyril's 'life and soul of the party' contributions was as the master of ceremonies at whist drives held in aid of various causes close to local hearts – from the cricket club to the Conservative Party. It was North Muskham's loss of a little of its communal heart when the cottages were demolished to make way for the dualling of the A1 and the Marriotts had to move to the new council houses at South Muskham.

Joseph Swaby happily took the road from 'gottle of geer' to 'God is great', transforming himself from hard-drinking engineer to Methodist lay-preacher as he approached middle age. He was a long-time widower, his wife having died while they were living at Sycamore Cottage in the village during the 1930s. Such were the insensitive ways of the world at that time, his daughter, Edie, never forgot the sight of a post mortem being performed on her mother as she lay dead on the table in their kitchen.

Maybe the loss of his wife at a relatively young age persuaded Joseph to become a born-again Christian. Until he was in his 30s, he enjoyed a pint or three with the lads after his shifts at Ransome & Marles where he was a belt man. This meant it was his duty to ensure the conveyors continued to flow efficiently with the world's biggest (best!) supply of ball bearings.

He then spent more than half his life singing the praises of the Lord. Being a lay-preacher involved giving one's time to a group of chapels; and Mr. Swaby's devotion was such that he overcame huge problems with his false teeth to continue taking Sunday services. Such was the approximate nature of dentistry during the era, his false teeth seemed to be too big for him and threatened to fall out every time he opened his mouth. But he avoided such an embarrassment by perfecting a technique of keeping his mouth shut like a ventriloquist yet still managing to speak clearly enough to get his message over from sundry Chapel pulpits. And there was no slumbering when he was in the congregation, either. Many's the time he would punctuate the monologue of even the most mundane of preachers with wholehearted cries of 'Bless the Lord!' or 'Hallelujah!'

When Joseph died, at the age of 86, on 3 November 1958, there were no grand eulogies. The death notice in the *Newark Advertiser* merely referred to him as "Joe the beltman". His penchant for good deeds lived on, though: he was the paternal great grandfather of John Pollard, who coincidentally spent much of his working life at the Milnes Garage on the opposite side of the A1 dual carriageway to where the cottages used to stand, and then moved on to ply his trade from Smalley's Garage at Bathley while living with his own family on North Muskham Main Street. Old Joe surely smiles down approvingly on John's considerate treatment of his customers.

Joe's next door neighbours on the North Road were Mr. and Mrs. George Temporall, parents of Bill whose family lived in the '50s in Norwell Lane and great uncle of Ted whose family resided at Costalot (earlier known as Holly Cottage) at the junction of Main Street and Nelson Lane into the early years of the 21st century.

George, a nippy little bloke with a moustache (one of the fashionable accessories for the modern man at the time), worked as a platelayer on the railway. He became "quite eccentric" – in the considerate words of his neighbours – in his old age, and would set off as late as 10pm to walk down the dark and dangerous North Road into Newark. Quite what he did when he got there is not known; but he always found his way home in time to hurl insults at the neighbours the next morning.

Ginny Rushby, a widow, was devoted to her disabled son Harold to such an extent that she spent hours each day wheeling him around in a bathchair. Poor Harold, who always answered to the nickname 'Sonny', had suffered from tuberculosis when he was young, was never able to walk, always had a pasty-white face no matter how much time he spent in the fresh air, and grew (and grew) to weigh 19 stones despite, one imagines, years of help and advice from kindly Nurse Rowlands.

Obviously Harold became too much of a handful for his old Mum, who nevertheless never failed to try and move him from his bathchair into an easy chair at night. Inevitably, he would finish up in a helpless heap on the floor of the living room and Ginny would pop to the Marriotts to ask Cyril to give her a hand. Cyril always did.

One day, there was a little more edge than usual to her voice. "I can't wake Sonny up, Cyril", she called. "Can you come?"

Sensing the urgency, Cyril ran into his neighbour's and crouched over the stricken lad. "I shan't be able to get him up today, Ginny", he said quietly. "You'll have to call the doctor".

They called Harold's death natural causes; and they might as well have added that it was a death sentence for his Mum. She had devoted the final years of her life to her lad.

LODGE FARM: BILLY AND HIS HIGH-FLYING BROOD

Billy Bourne, arguably the highest profile farmer in the parish, was based at Lodge Farm, on the south-bound side of the A1 as the river Trent winds towards Cromwell Weir. His confidence in his importance stemmed from the fact that generations of Bournes had farmed in Bathley and North Muskham as well as Collingham – most of them much more successfully than Daniel Bourne, who was found hanged in his bedroom in June 1864, 18 months after he won a law suit against his father. Once the coroner had recorded a verdict of suicide at the inquest, held in the Newcastle Arms, Daniel was buried after nightfall without religious ceremony.

The drama left no lasting scar on the family. John Bourne was elected North Muskham's way warden on 1 April 1875, replacing one Richard Mackley, who gave up the job because his 33-year-old wife Elizabeth was terminally ill. She passed away on 29 July 1875 and Richard himself died a year later at the age of 44. The village responded by giving the name Mackley to the cart-track closest to the heart (as in centre) of the village.

Back to the Bournes and the 1950s... Billy was an assertive bloke, too. Born in North Muskham, he left the village school at the age of 12 and made his reputation on the land – in business as a hard-working farmer, in sport as a fanatical cricketer, in life as a man who always said what he thought.

He was highly regarded in the farming world as chairman of both the Nottinghamshire Farmers' Union and the Sugar Beet and Potato Committee, acting as supervisor of the liaison between the growers and the sugar factories. This, remember, was an era when crops were moved on relatively small carts towed by slow-moving tractors (and, in a few cases, pairs of shire horses). So it was just as well there were more sugar factories: one at Colwick served south Nottinghamshire while the one on the North Road into Newark was our local generator of fugs to supplement the late autumn smogs (but not so many foul odours as became the case when the south winds wafted in the 21st century).

Billy also became a member of the Newark Agricultural Show Council to reinforce the message that the village boy had risen among the cream of the county. Indeed, his practical approach saved the show jumping competitions – world No.1 Pat Smythe and all – at the 1958 Show. When the top riders threatened to withdraw because the surface was too hard, Billy nipped home and fetched his portable irrigation plant. Linking it to a stream that ran between the Winthorpe Airfield and where the A1 Great North Road bypass was to be built, Billy poured 600 tons of Trent Valley water on the parched earth. The Show Council's annual report some months later said: "On the days of the show many expressions of appreciation of the good going were made and this aspect is very important because of the valuable animals galloped around the ring". The following year, the Newark Show had County status for the first time. Who knows how big a part Billy and his water pipes played in this elevation!

Not that Billy ever forgot his roots: he welcomed fishermen to his stretch of the Trent bank and he allowed the village cricket and football teams to play in one of his fields just over the Bathley Lane level crossing.

In an era when every step of the Trent towpath was open to the general public and relentless efforts were made to ensure it remained accessible, Billy rented his fishing rights to the New Inn Public House at Newark, and their bailiff, Joe Fletcher, became a regular on the village scene. Reflecting the innocent absence of *double entendres*, an edition of the *Newark Advertiser* in October 1953 quaintly referred to fishing "in Mr. J. Fletcher's water at Muskham".

Tragically, genial Joe's love affair with the village and its riverside led to his death on Thursday 22 May 1958, four days after his 47th birthday. As often happened at the end of one of his shifts as an engineer's under-foreman, he biked over to Muskham to meet his mates at 'the Ferry'. Then they went for a walk along the river bank to look at the rebuilding work going on at Cromwell Lock – an expedition that refreshed their thirst. Back at 'the Ferry', they had three more pints, then Joe set off to bike home to his wife, a plump and pleasant dark-haired lady, in Wood Street, Newark. He never arrived. Down the Sugar Factory straight, at around 11.10pm, his bike came into collision with a car driven by another Newarker, who'd had four half-pints of mild – "nothing to drink worth talking about" – with relatives at Bathley Crown. At the inquest, Joe's best mate Titch Faisey swore the back light of the bike had been shining brightly as he pedalled off from 'the Ferry'. The car driver and his front seat passenger were equally certain they had seen no back light before they felt a bump as three cars sped past in the other direction. The coroner's verdict was: Accidental death. The Trent bank humour was never quite the same again.

4. The Old North Road

Back in Billy Bourne's domain, the football and cricket field was a source of pleasure, pride, dreams and the occasional nightmare until an unholy row broke out over who should be allowed to play in the cricket team. Billy, whose skill and enthusiasm for cricket had led him to lay out a practice wicket beside Lodge Farm, always insisted on a rule that membership was open only to inhabitants of North Muskham and Bathley.

As post-war ambitions encouraged village boys to think further than careers on the land or in shiftwork at Ransome & Marles, Worthington-Simpsons or Nicholson's, it became increasingly difficult to raise an XI from live-at-homes. Billy, who still liked to play in the odd match in his late middle-age, remained intransigent that the rule would not be rescinded. Alas the dilemma was resolved one night when a message appeared on the sightscreen. In red paint, it did not flatter Mr. Bourne. "It said something about him being a rotten sod", Hugh Kent recalls. Billy ordered the cricket field be ploughed up. Legend has it that he ordered Hugh, the team vice-captain and one of his farm labourers, to do it. "I can't remember that", says the unusually diplomatic Hugh, whose brother Peter was already married to Billy's oldest daughter Ellen. "But, yes, it was ploughed up". With it went North Muskham and Bathley Cricket Club.

The shock was matched only by the suddenness of Billy's death, on Thursday 11 March 1965. He had gone with his wife to the annual dinner of the Newark branch of the Nottinghamshire Farmers' Union at the Robin Hood Hotel, Newark, but collapsed as the guests assembled. While the meal was being served to Billy's friends and associates, frantic efforts were made to save him in the privacy of an upstairs room. They were in vain. Nearly 250 people attended his funeral at St. Wilfrid's on Tuesday 16 March: the village folk with whom he'd grown up, the landed classes who had learnt to respect him and, most important of all, the five women in his life – his widow and their four daughters.

Mrs. Bourne, one of the Cameron daughters from the School House, always played almost as big a part in village life as Billy – some achievement in an era when a married woman's place was considered to be in the home. OK, it sounds mumsy to report that she baked the cake for the North Muskham WI birthday parties and, at the 'do' in 1952, looked on proudly as her eldest, Ellen won the paper hat competition for a pink bonnet she had created.

But she also became president of the village WI at the end of 1953 at a time when attitudes were a-changing; and one can almost hear her hushing the men of the Parish Council and putting the case for housewives to have a bench on which to rest after they'd lugged their shopping off the bus from Newark. Her practical outlook was probably best illustrated by the kind of competition she encouraged at the WI on the night she became President. She invited every member to fill a Christmas stocking for a children's home, won the competition herself (with Mrs. Barker from Cromwell Lock and Mrs. Eley from South Muskham in second and third places) and then made sure all the stockings got to – you've guessed – a children's home.

And when the village cricketers won the Ransome Subsidiary Cup in 1960, it was the instinctively practical Mrs. Bourne who organised a celebratory dinner at the Lord Nelson. The bowler who'd taken 6 wickets in the semi-final and 5 in the final (me) was banned because a 15-year-old couldn't darken the lounge-step of licensed premises but, by all accounts, the party went with the kind of swing you'd expect of a club in possession of its first (and last) silverware. *(Mrs. Bourne is pictured here with our Cup.)*

After Billy died, Mrs. Bourne moved from Lodge Farm in to the Trentside bungalow, between Mackleys Lane and Ferry Lane, to which they had intended to retire close to Ellen and Peter.

Of the other daughters, June, a sister at Newark General Hospital, married a Cotswolds-based school teacher, Michael Watson, on Saturday 19 March 1955 and moved to live near Cirencester; Anne, who was acting as Press correspondent of North Muskham WI in 1953, became Mrs. Emmanuel and settled in Australia; and young Janet poignantly returned to St. Wilfrid's less than a month after her father's death, on Saturday 3 April 1965 to wed Peter Chapple, who took her to live in Bristol.

Ellen maintained the family presence, even after she and Peter moved to live in Newark, as a member of the village WI and attendee at many social events. But neither the cricket nor football clubs survived for long.

4. The Old North Road

THE NESS: HEAD OF THE COUNTY'S FARMERS

Percy Jackson farmed The Ness, the somewhat isolated northern outpost of North Muskham between the North Road and the River Trent towards Cromwell; and must have made a pretty good job of it, because early in 1950 he was elected Chairman of the Nottinghamshire branch of the National Farmers' Union, which at the time boasted in excess of 2,500 members. As if to prove they had elected a capable man, the *Newark Advertiser* of 25 January produced a photograph of a giant piece of kale grown amid "a useful crop" on the land at The Ness. Harry Edlin was pictured, somewhat self-consciously, holding it… or maybe wrestling with it, for it was stubbornly L-shaped and looked as if, straightened out, it would have been at least 8-foot tall. It must have been a true champion, for during the weeks that followed the *Advertiser* did not carry a single follow-up story claiming that a challenger had been unearthed for Percy's kale.

The Jacksons did not allow the professional duties or the distance of their house from the village to debar them from playing a full part in North Muskham's life. When the village WI was founded in 1947, Mrs. P. J. Jackson was enlisted as its first member. Percy and his wife were obviously a warm-hearted couple, too. They donated a pig – not just any animal but a pure-bred in-pig gilt – to a national appeal for the victims of floods that devastated the Lincolnshire coast in early 1953. The pig was auctioned at Newark Cattle Market for £60 to Mr. J. Speir of Westborough. In total, farmers in the Newark area contributed £1,785 towards the appeal.

The Jacksons' animals were also in the news in 1957. Two of their cattle died, struck by lightning while grazing in a field beside the Trent on the evening of Saturday 6 July. It was described in the following Wednesday's *Advertiser* as "one of the severest storms in living memory" and cut-off the electricity supplies to much of the district.

The Jacksons were as caring about humans, too. They were quite happy for one of their labourers, William Cary, to live with them at The Ness long after his retirement until his death, aged 72, on 13 October 1959.

And the link with the Jackson family remained strong into the 21st century: The Ness remained in the hands of Sheila Davenport, who had arrived from her home in Sheffield in 1953 as a 15-year-old servant and made such a loving impression on the Jacksons that she inherited the place. Such was Sheila's vibrancy that, even after spending long days working as the legs of the elderly housekeeper, she had the energy to star at the dances held in the new village halls that made Norwell and South Muskham so appealing to the teenagers of the '50s and '60s.

BY-PASS BEATEN BY DOG IN SPACE

The deceptively short straight stretch of the North Road between the Vicarage Lane crossroads and the curve towards Cromwell was the scene of an horrific accident on 29 December 1954 – one of several that had villagers clamouring for a better trunk road. A 24-year-old airman was killed and his pillion passenger, a 19-year-old guardsman hitch-hiking back to camp, seriously injured when his motor cycle collided head on with a lorry. Both vehicles caught fire.

A by-pass had initially been mooted in October of 1947, with the official warning that there was no prospect of it being built "for some time". Not even parish councillors who had dithered over the supply of electricity and the introduction of street lighting could have imagined (a) that two decades would pass before the promise was kept and (b) there would be so many deaths in the meantime.

Within two months of the airman's death, there was another compelling reason for the North Road to be dramatically improved. A long-distance bus driver was hurtled to his death onto the railway line in the early hours of 25 February 1955 when his express coach smashed into the parapet of the bridge. It could have been much worse: 14 passengers escaped uninjured and completed their journey from Glasgow to London later in the day by train. Although the road was icy at the time, it remained a mystery why the 32-seater coach had drifted over to the offside at such a speed that its front was ripped off by the impact. One thing was crystal clear to the villagers, however, as the mist lifted from the scene of devastation: the sooner the North Road was replaced, the better.

The Ministry of Transport in December 1953 announced plans for a Newark By-pass costing £500,000. Work would take between one and two years. What the report did not mention was how many years would elapse before the work actually started.

So when the Ministry of Transport announced in the autumn of 1957, without a hint of apology for the delay, that a £1.7million Newark By-pass (note the rapidly rising cost!) would be started in three years' time, the *Newark Advertiser* was quite cynical in its *Under The Castle Wall* column: "That will be in 1960, well into the space age and satellite era, with a fly-over at North Muskham. It is anticipated that a dog will be sent through with the first lorry". (This was a satirical reference to the first occupant of a Soviet sputnik shot into space being a little dog.)

Villages were not amused; by now, many winter weekends were marred by awful accidents. Arguably the worst happened just before Christmas 1956. Three people died in a head-on collision between two cars on the railway

4. The Old North Road

bridge. For goodness sake! The bridge had been built in 1927-28 as an improvement. "Muskham's robots are worth watching", reported the *Newark Advertiser* on 24 August 1927. It explained that a huge mechanical tractor was taking voracious bites from a field and piling the banks for the 680-yard bridge that was to replace the adjacent level crossing.

Yet on 21 December 1956, just as the fog was clearing and locals felt immediate danger was over for another day, an accident claimed the lives of a woman and her six-year-old daughter in one car and an expectant mother, aged 24, in the other vehicle. Worse, the expectant father became the first person in the Newark police area to face a charge of causing death(s) by dangerous driving. Four months later, on 17 April 1957, the driver, a 25-year-old commercial traveller from Harrogate in Yorkshire, was wheeled out of Mansfield's Harlow Wood Hospital, where he was still being treated for his own horrific injuries, to face the charges. Newark Magistrates heard all the evidence and committed him for trial to the Nottinghamshire Assizes. The case was heard by a judge and jury at Nottingham Shire Hall on Wednesday 26 June 1956, and the driver was found not guilty.

Alas, it was 1962 before the contract to construct the by-pass was signed; six years in which the only people to profit were the garage staff who had the traumatic tasks of clearing away the debris from the frequent pile-ups. The cost of the new road had risen to £2,083,010. The contractors, a Manchester-based company called Robert McGregor & Sons, said the work would be completed by "late autumn of 1964". Worse still, it brought the thundering traffic closer to the village, rather than taking it to the western side of the railway line as many villagers felt would be logical.

The way in which it turned a rather introvert village into more of a suburb of cities for miles around is another story…

BY THE SAME AUTHOR

The Road to Athens with Bill Adcocks,
published in July 2004 by Amrec 69, £9.95.